CONTAGION

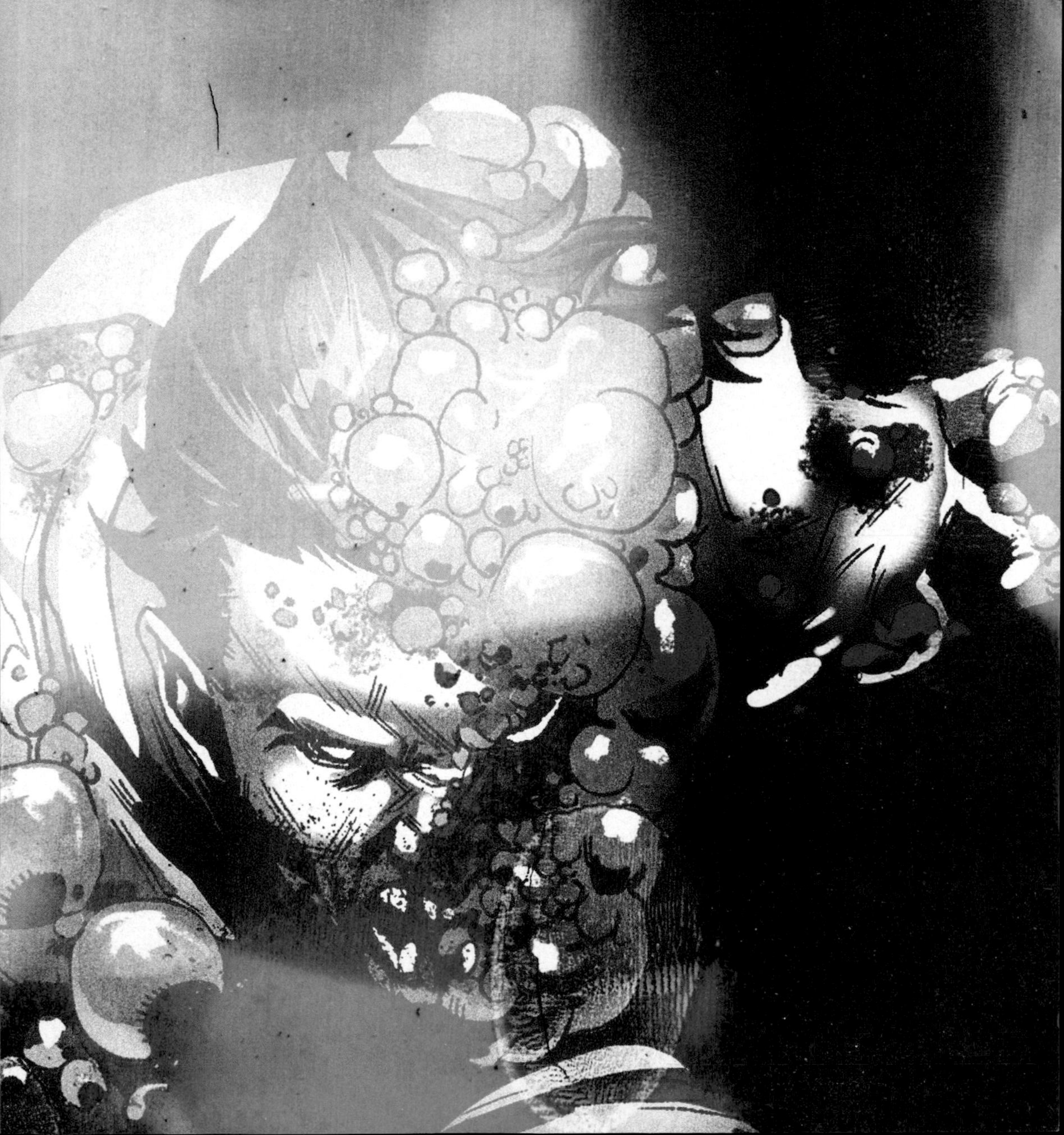

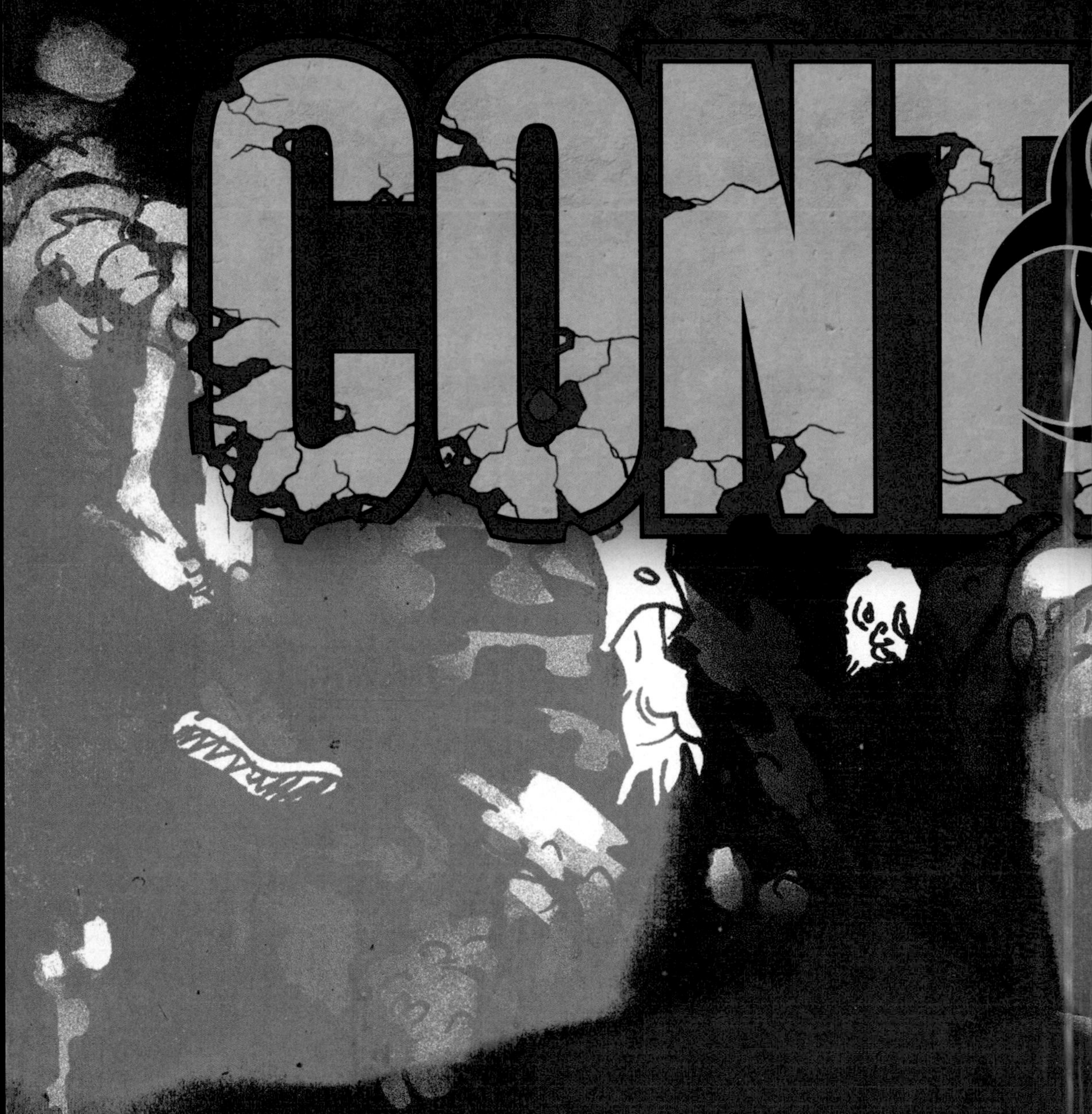
CONT

COLLECTION EDITOR **JENNIFER GRÜNWALD** ASSISTANT EDITOR **CAITLIN O'CONNELL**
ASSOCIATE MANAGING EDITOR **KATERI WOODY** EDITOR, SPECIAL PROJECTS **MARK D. BEAZLEY**
VP PRODUCTION & SPECIAL PROJECTS **JEFF YOUNGQUIST** BOOK DESIGNER **JAY BOWEN**

SVP PRINT, SALES & MARKETING **DAVID GABRIEL** DIRECTOR, LICENSED PUBLISHING **SVEN LARSEN**
EDITOR IN CHIEF **C.B. CEBULSKI** CHIEF CREATIVE OFFICER **JOE QUESADA**
PRESIDENT **DAN BUCKLEY** EXECUTIVE PRODUCER **ALAN FINE**

CONTAGION. Contains material originally published in magazine form as CONTAGION (2019) #1-5. First printing 2019. ISBN 978-1-302-92189-7. Published by MARVEL WORLDWIDE, INC., a subsidiary of MARVEL ENTERTAINMENT, LLC. OFFICE OF PUBLICATION: 135 West 50th Street, New York, NY 10020. © 2019 MARVEL No similarity between any of the names, characters, persons, and/or institutions in this magazine with those of any living or dead person or institution is intended, and any such similarity which may exist is purely coincidental. **Printed in Canada.** DAN BUCKLEY, President, Marvel Entertainment; JOHN NEE, Publisher; JOE QUESADA, Chief Creative Officer; TOM BREVOORT, SVP of Publishing; DAVID BOGART, Associate Publisher & SVP of Talent Affairs; DAVID GABRIEL, VP of Print & Digital Publishing; JEFF YOUNGQUIST, VP of Production & Special Projects; DAN CARR, Executive Director of Publishing Technology; ALEX MORALES, Director of Publishing Operations; DAN EDINGTON, Managing Editor; SUSAN CRESPI, Production Manager; STAN LEE, Chairman Emeritus. For information regarding advertising in Marvel Comics or on Marvel.com, please contact Vit DeBellis, Custom Solutions & Integrated Advertising Manager, at vdebellis@marvel.com. For Marvel subscription inquiries, please call 888-511-5480. **Manufactured between 11/22/2019 and 12/24/2019 by SOLISCO PRINTERS, SCOTT, QC, CANADA.**

10 9 8 7 6 5 4 3 2 1

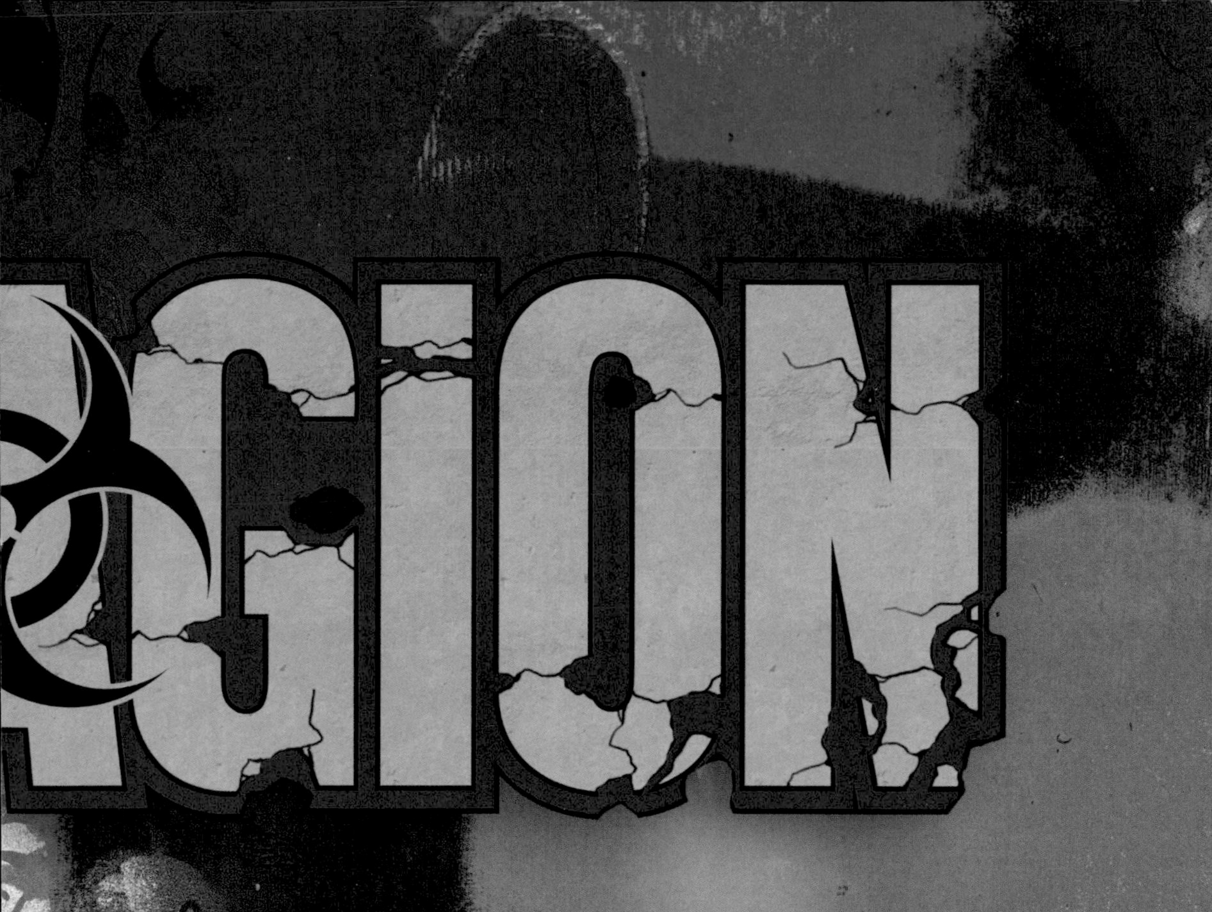
AGION

WRITER **ED BRISSON**

ARTISTS **ROGÊ ANTÔNIO** (#1),
STEPHEN SEGOVIA (#2-3),
MACK CHATER (#3),
DAMIAN COUCEIRO (#4)
& **ADAM GORHAM** (#5)

COLOR ARTISTS **VERONICA GANDINI**
WITH **ANDREW CROSSLEY** (#3)

LETTERER **VC's CORY PETIT**

COVER ART **JUAN JOSÉ RYP** & **JESUS ABURTOV**

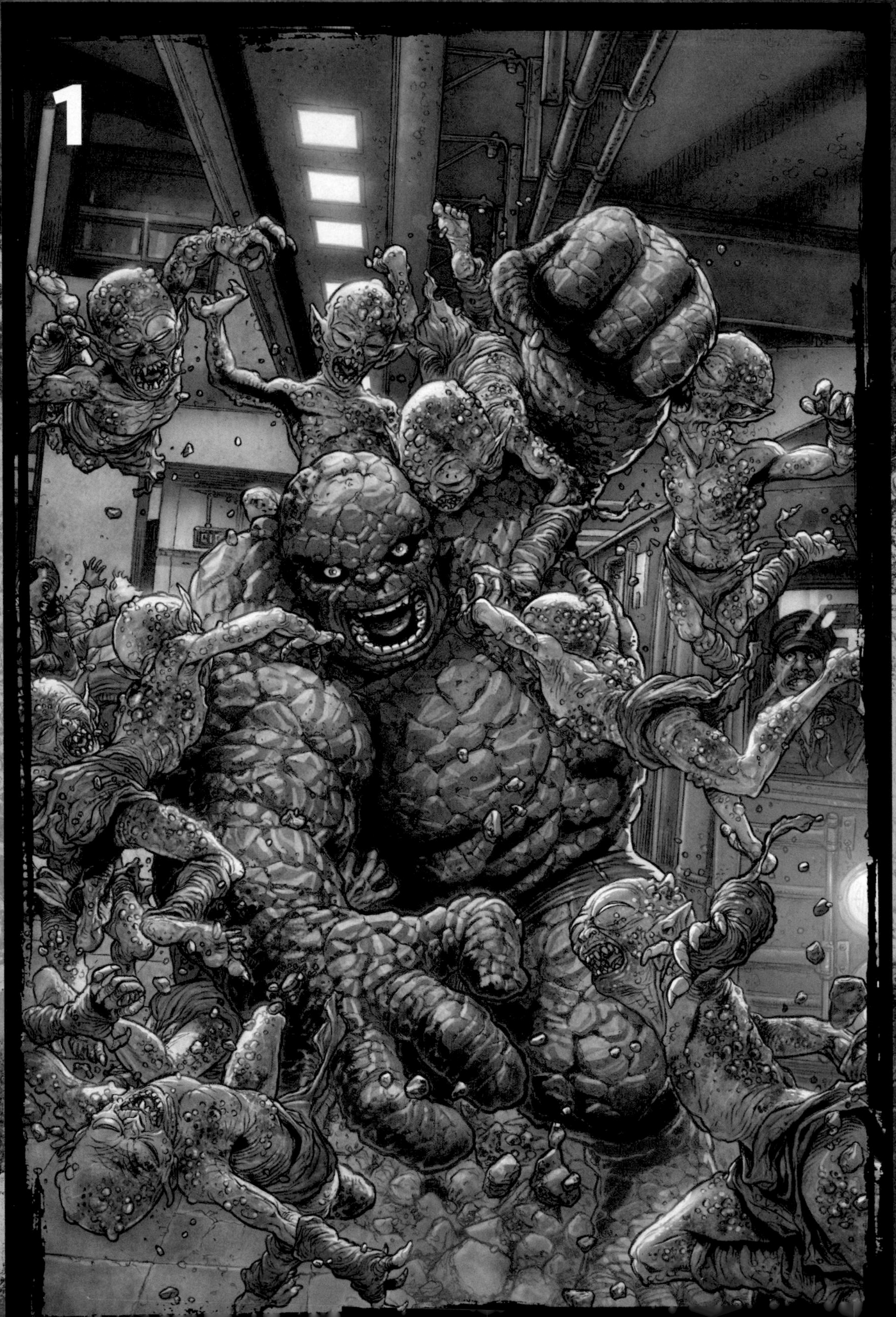
1

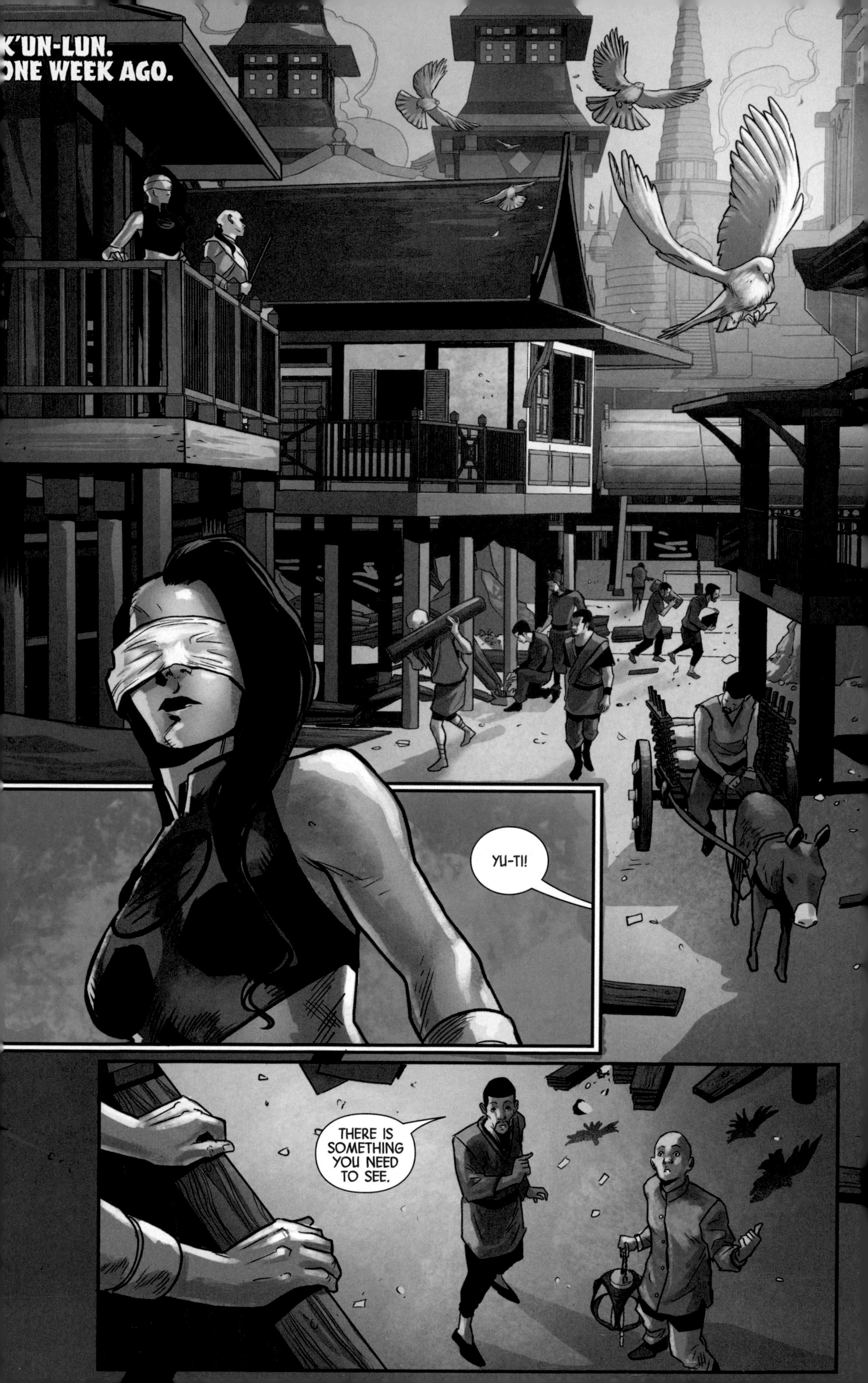
K'UN-LUN.
ONE WEEK AGO.
YU-TI!
THERE IS SOMETHING YOU NEED TO SEE.

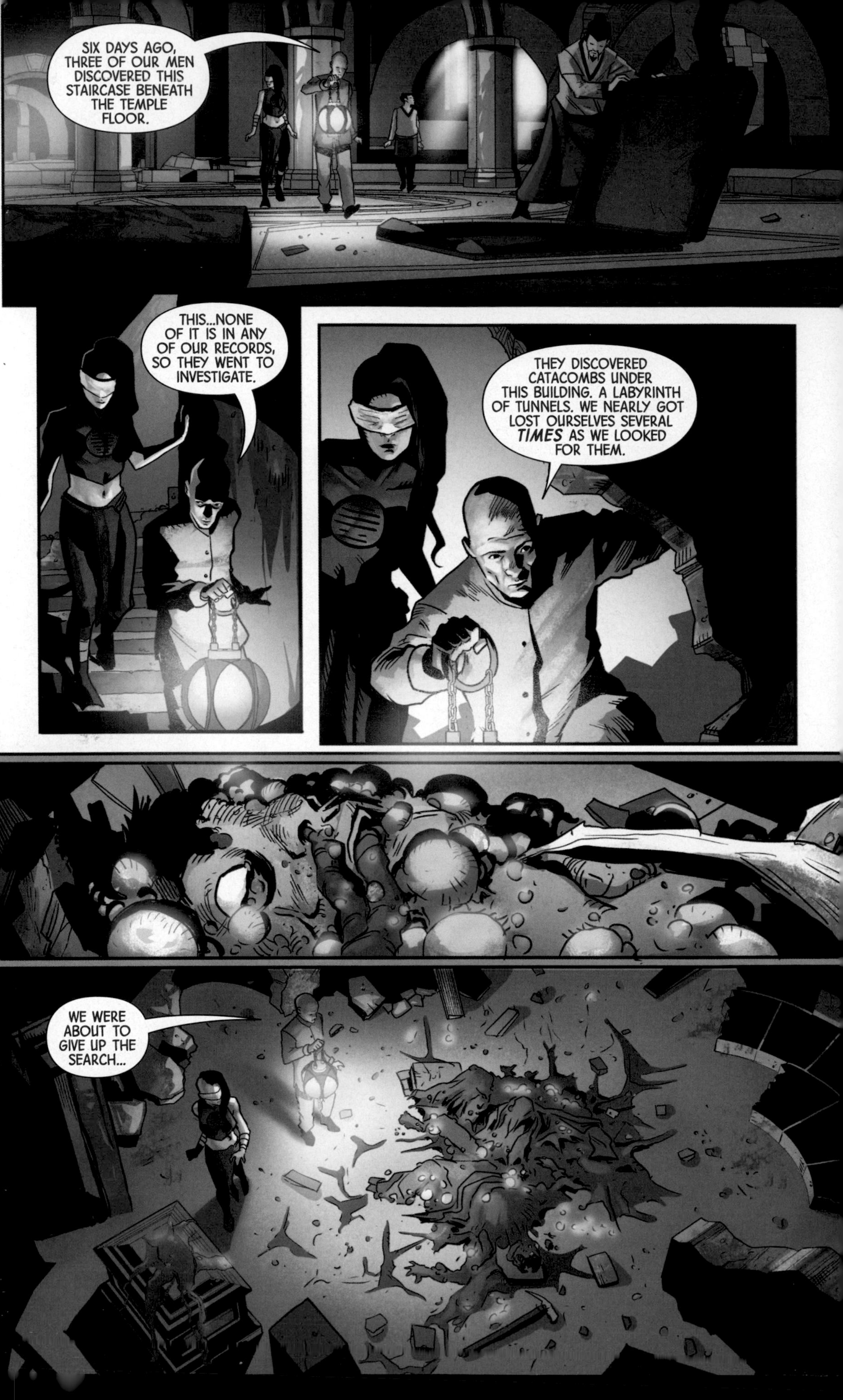
SIX DAYS AGO, THREE OF OUR MEN DISCOVERED THIS STAIRCASE BENEATH THE TEMPLE FLOOR.
THIS...NONE OF IT IS IN ANY OF OUR RECORDS, SO THEY WENT TO INVESTIGATE.
THEY DISCOVERED CATACOMBS UNDER THIS BUILDING. A LABYRINTH OF TUNNELS. WE NEARLY GOT LOST OURSELVES SEVERAL *TIMES* AS WE LOOKED FOR THEM.
WE WERE ABOUT TO GIVE UP THE SEARCH...

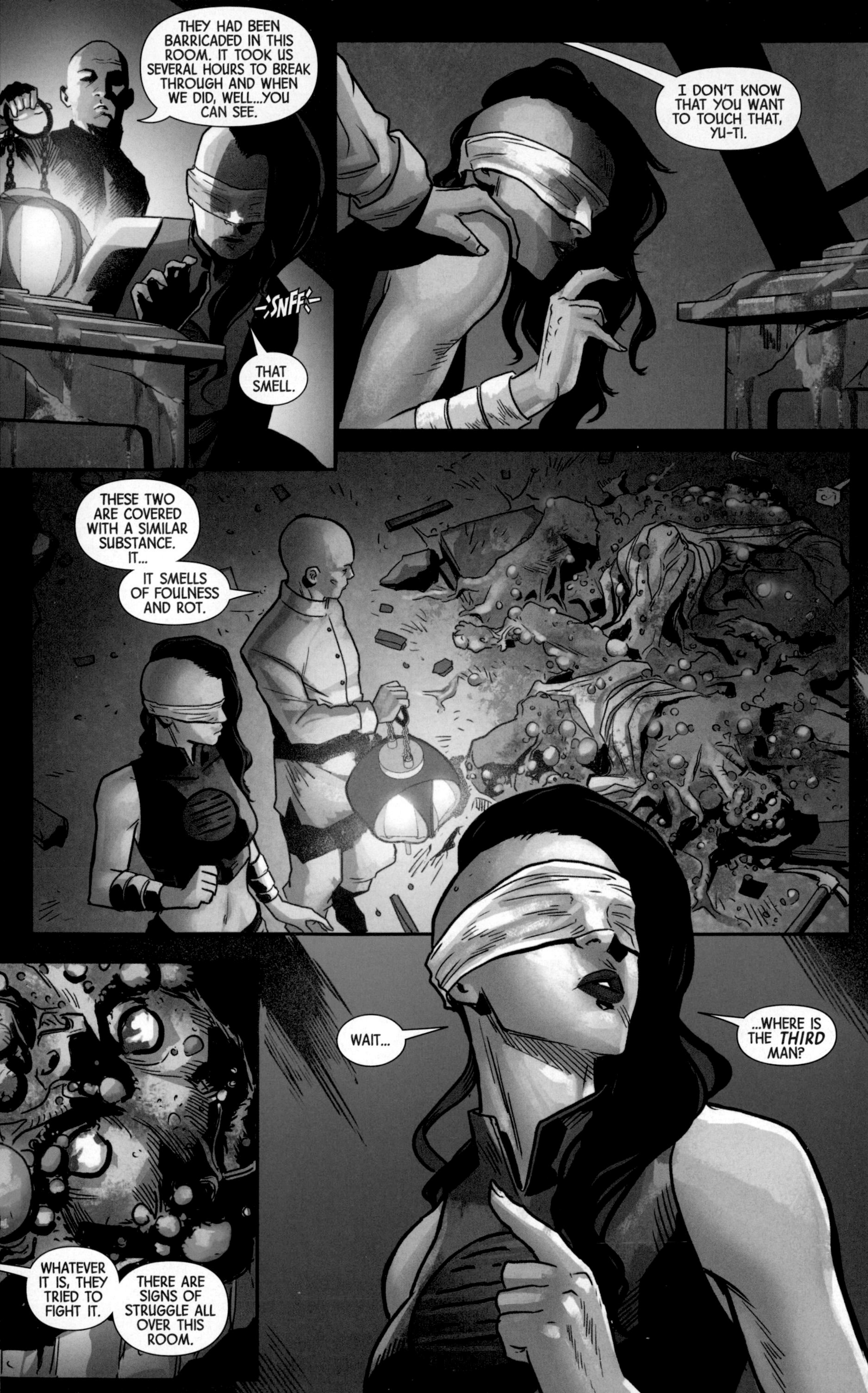
THEY HAD BEEN BARRICADED IN THIS ROOM. IT TOOK US SEVERAL HOURS TO BREAK THROUGH AND WHEN WE DID, WELL...YOU CAN SEE.
SNFF
THAT SMELL.
I DON'T KNOW THAT YOU WANT TO TOUCH THAT, YU-TI.
THESE TWO ARE COVERED WITH A SIMILAR SUBSTANCE. IT...
IT SMELLS OF FOULNESS AND ROT.
WHATEVER IT IS, THEY TRIED TO FIGHT IT.
THERE ARE SIGNS OF STRUGGLE ALL OVER THIS ROOM.
WAIT...
...WHERE IS THE *THIRD* MAN?

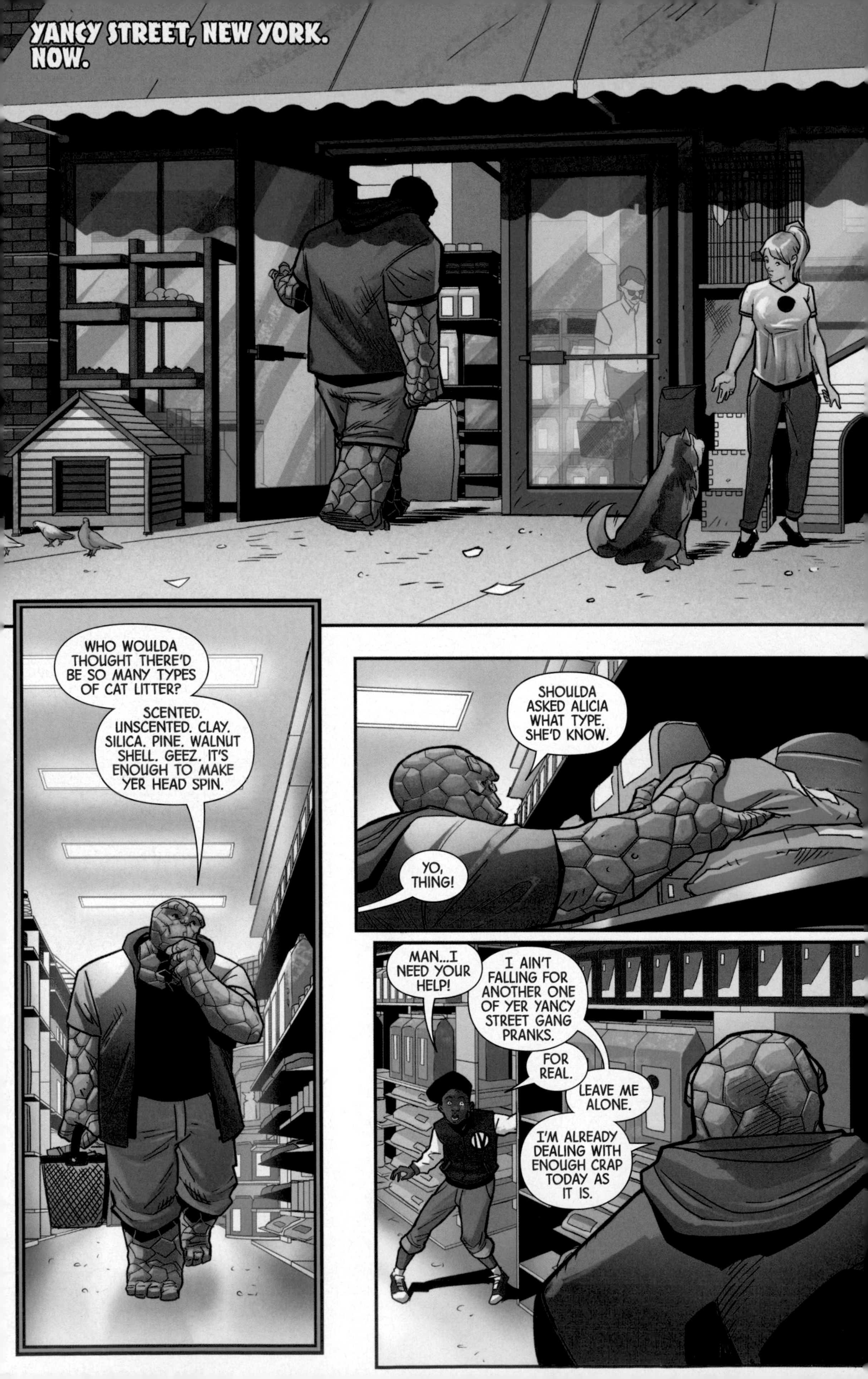
YANCY STREET, NEW YORK. NOW.
WHO WOULDA THOUGHT THERE'D BE SO MANY TYPES OF CAT LITTER?
SCENTED. UNSCENTED. CLAY. SILICA. PINE. WALNUT SHELL. GEEZ. IT'S ENOUGH TO MAKE YER HEAD SPIN.
SHOULDA ASKED ALICIA WHAT TYPE. SHE'D KNOW.
YO, THING!
MAN...I NEED YOUR HELP!
I AIN'T FALLING FOR ANOTHER ONE OF YER YANCY STREET GANG PRANKS.
FOR REAL.
LEAVE ME ALONE.
I'M ALREADY DEALING WITH ENOUGH CRAP TODAY AS IT IS.

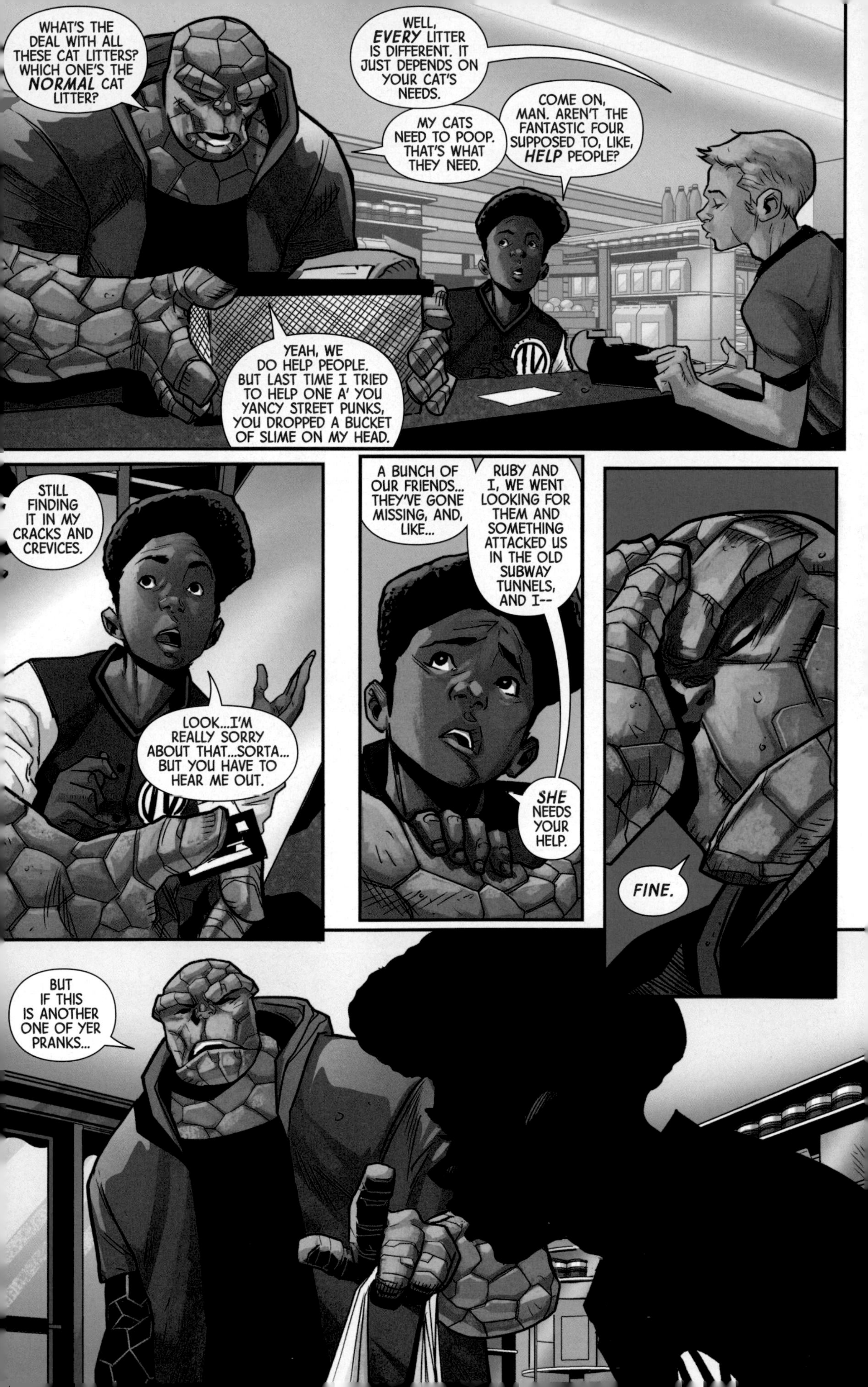
WHAT'S THE DEAL WITH ALL THESE CAT LITTERS? WHICH ONE'S THE NORMAL CAT LITTER?
WELL, EVERY LITTER IS DIFFERENT. IT JUST DEPENDS ON YOUR CAT'S NEEDS.
MY CATS NEED TO POOP. THAT'S WHAT THEY NEED.
COME ON, MAN. AREN'T THE FANTASTIC FOUR SUPPOSED TO, LIKE, HELP PEOPLE?
YEAH, WE DO HELP PEOPLE. BUT LAST TIME I TRIED TO HELP ONE A' YOU YANCY STREET PUNKS, YOU DROPPED A BUCKET OF SLIME ON MY HEAD.
STILL FINDING IT IN MY CRACKS AND CREVICES.
LOOK...I'M REALLY SORRY ABOUT THAT...SORTA... BUT YOU HAVE TO HEAR ME OUT.
A BUNCH OF OUR FRIENDS... THEY'VE GONE MISSING, AND, LIKE...
RUBY AND I, WE WENT LOOKING FOR THEM AND SOMETHING ATTACKED US IN THE OLD SUBWAY TUNNELS, AND I--
SHE NEEDS YOUR HELP.
FINE.
BUT IF THIS IS ANOTHER ONE OF YER PRANKS...

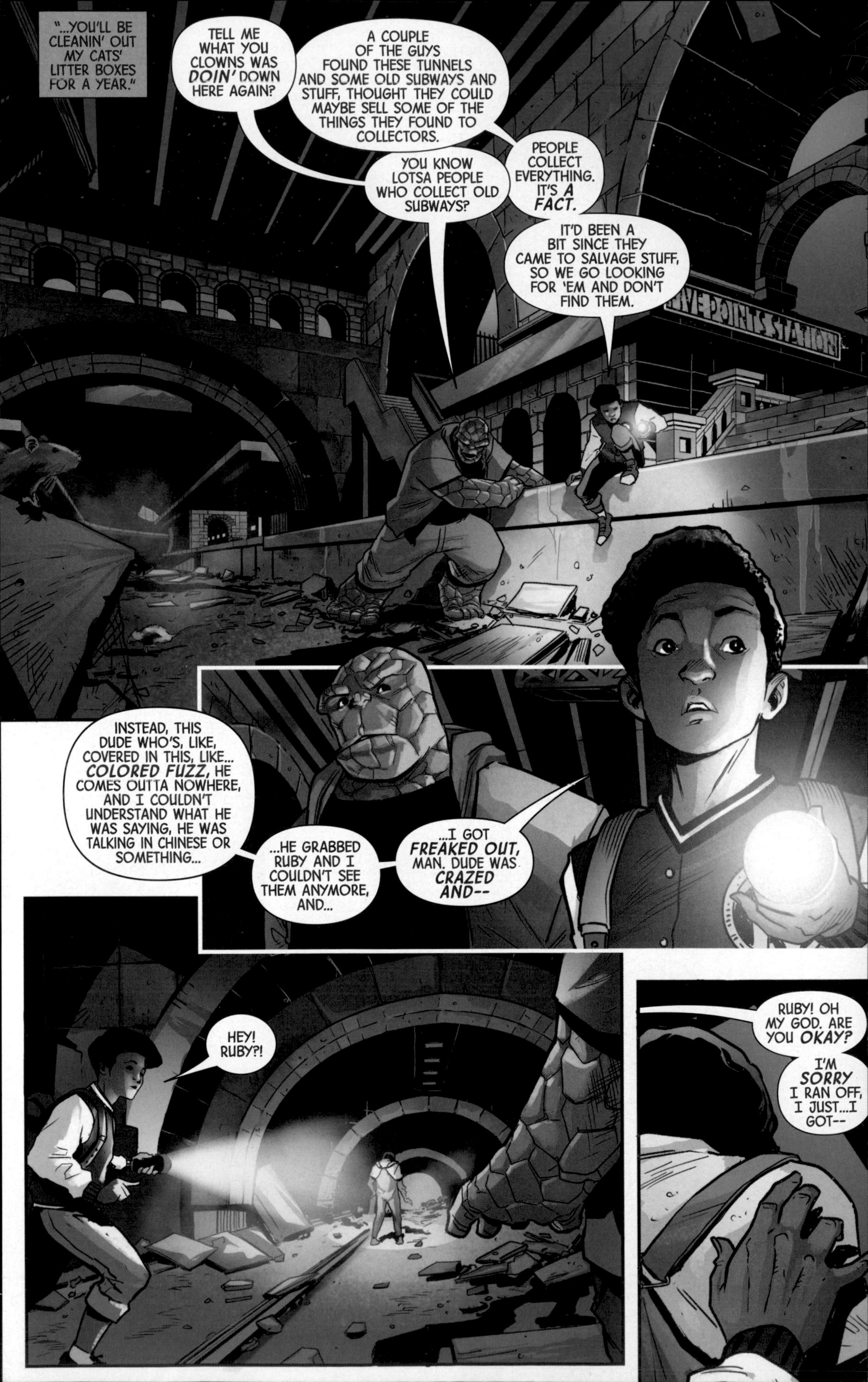
"...YOU'LL BE CLEANIN' OUT MY CATS' LITTER BOXES FOR A YEAR."
TELL ME WHAT YOU CLOWNS WAS DOIN' DOWN HERE AGAIN?
A COUPLE OF THE GUYS FOUND THESE TUNNELS AND SOME OLD SUBWAYS AND STUFF, THOUGHT THEY COULD MAYBE SELL SOME OF THE THINGS THEY FOUND TO COLLECTORS.
PEOPLE COLLECT EVERYTHING. IT'S A FACT.
YOU KNOW LOTSA PEOPLE WHO COLLECT OLD SUBWAYS?
IT'D BEEN A BIT SINCE THEY CAME TO SALVAGE STUFF, SO WE GO LOOKING FOR 'EM AND DON'T FIND THEM.
INSTEAD, THIS DUDE WHO'S, LIKE, COVERED IN THIS, LIKE... COLORED FUZZ, HE COMES OUTTA NOWHERE, AND I COULDN'T UNDERSTAND WHAT HE WAS SAYING, HE WAS TALKING IN CHINESE OR SOMETHING...
...HE GRABBED RUBY AND I COULDN'T SEE THEM ANYMORE, AND...
...I GOT FREAKED OUT, MAN. DUDE WAS CRAZED AND--
HEY! RUBY?!
RUBY! OH MY GOD. ARE YOU OKAY?
I'M SORRY I RAN OFF, I JUST...I GOT--

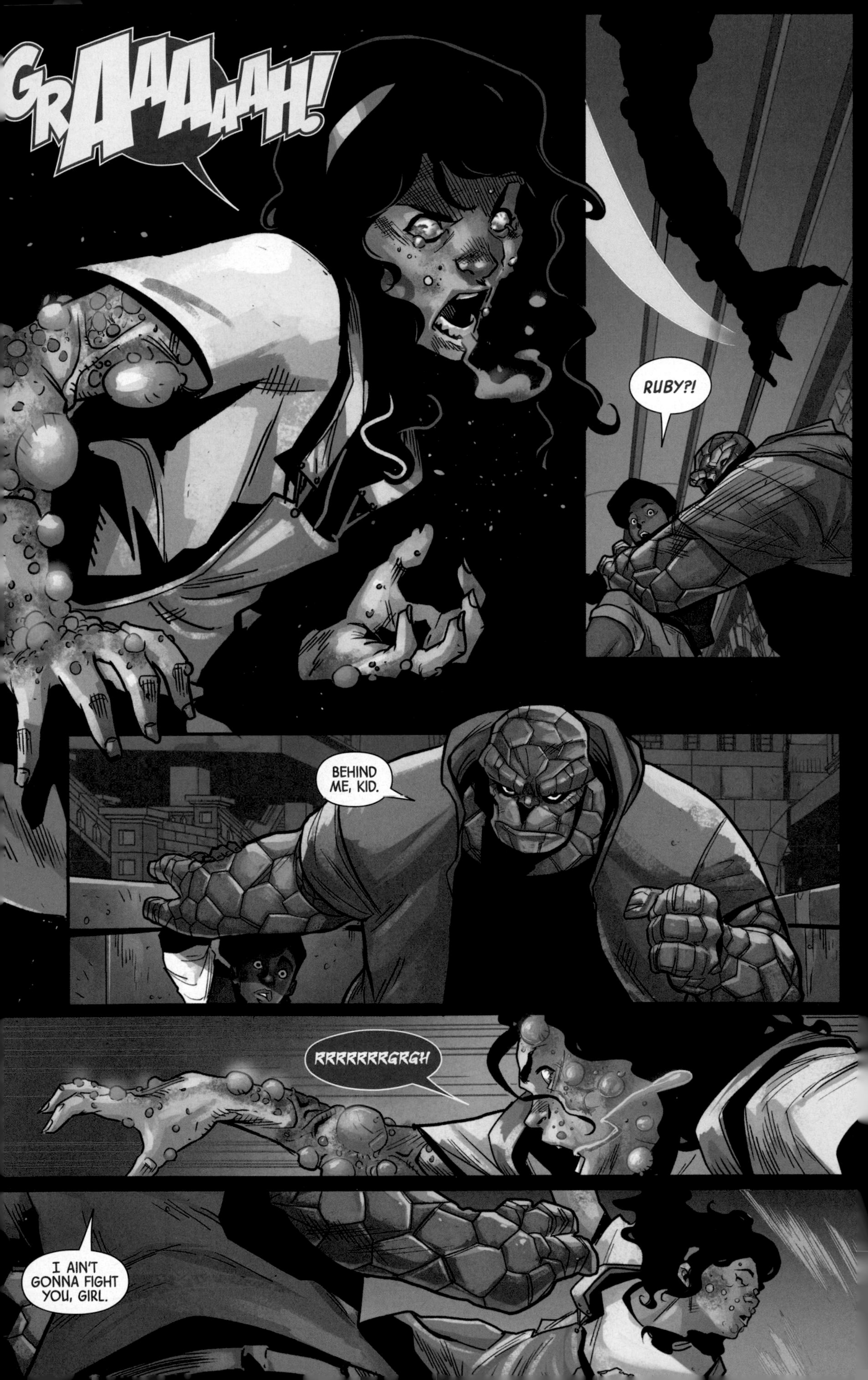
GRAAAAAH!
RUBY?!
BEHIND ME, KID.
RRRRRRRGRGH
I AIN'T GONNA FIGHT YOU, GIRL.

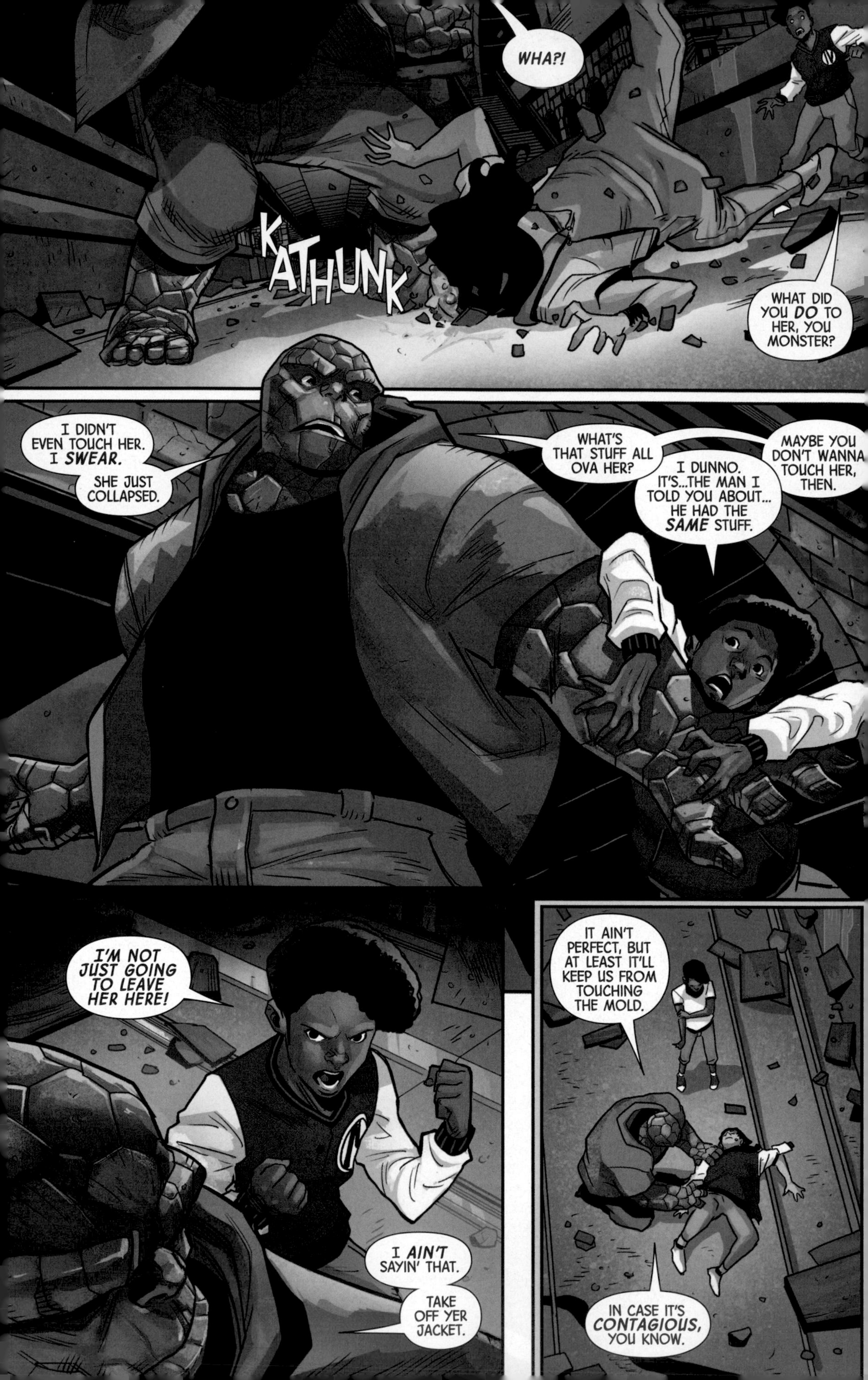
WHA?!
KATHUNK
WHAT DID YOU DO TO HER, YOU MONSTER?
I DIDN'T EVEN TOUCH HER. I SWEAR.
SHE JUST COLLAPSED.
WHAT'S THAT STUFF ALL OVA HER?
I DUNNO. IT'S...THE MAN I TOLD YOU ABOUT... HE HAD THE SAME STUFF.
MAYBE YOU DON'T WANNA TOUCH HER, THEN.
I'M NOT JUST GOING TO LEAVE HER HERE!
I AIN'T SAYIN' THAT.
TAKE OFF YER JACKET.
IT AIN'T PERFECT, BUT AT LEAST IT'LL KEEP US FROM TOUCHING THE MOLD.
IN CASE IT'S CONTAGIOUS, YOU KNOW.

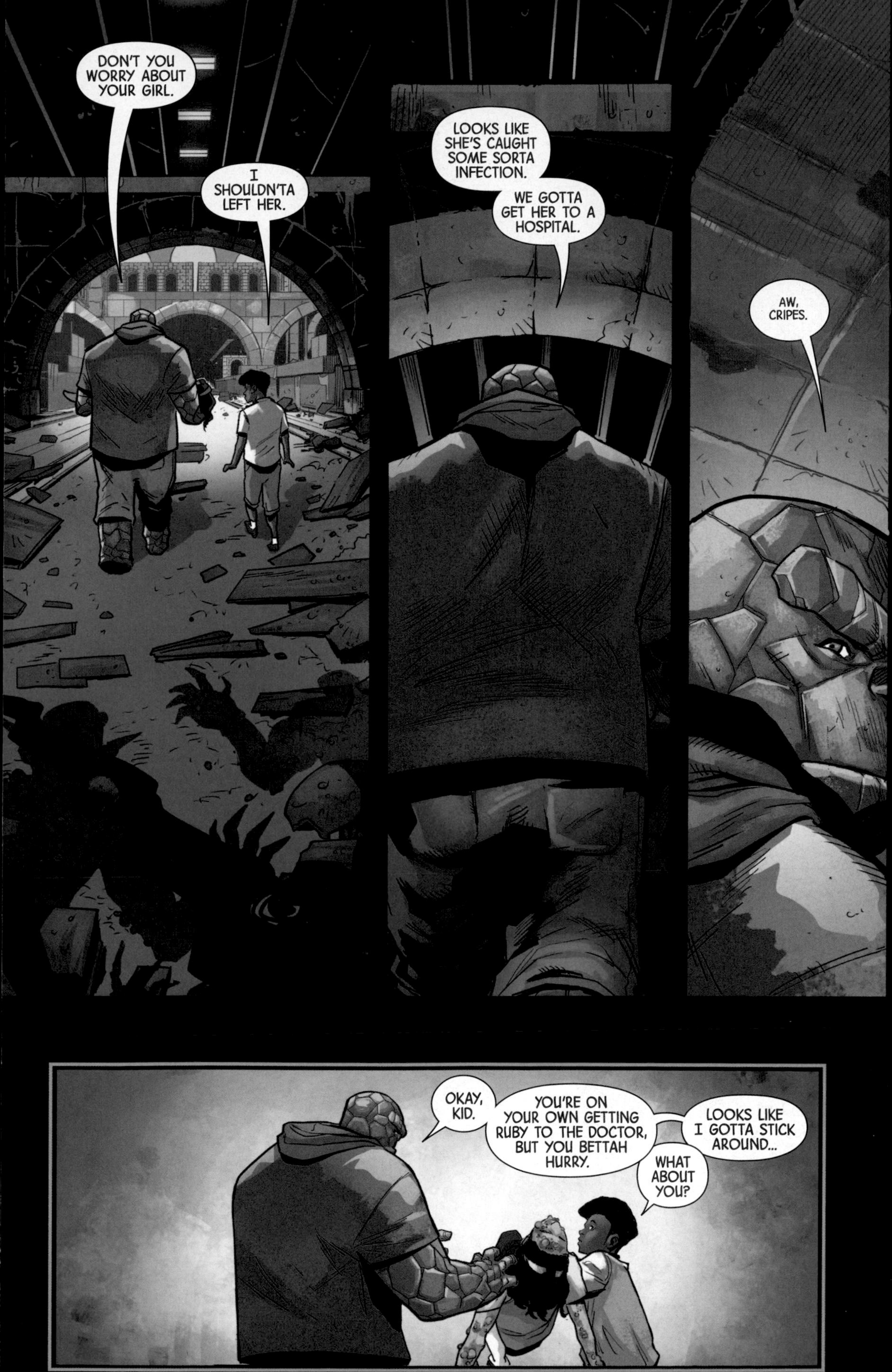
DON'T YOU WORRY ABOUT YOUR GIRL.
I SHOULDN'TA LEFT HER.
LOOKS LIKE SHE'S CAUGHT SOME SORTA INFECTION.
WE GOTTA GET HER TO A HOSPITAL.
AW, CRIPES.
OKAY, KID.
YOU'RE ON YOUR OWN GETTING RUBY TO THE DOCTOR, BUT YOU BETTAH HURRY.
WHAT ABOUT YOU?
LOOKS LIKE I GOTTA STICK AROUND...

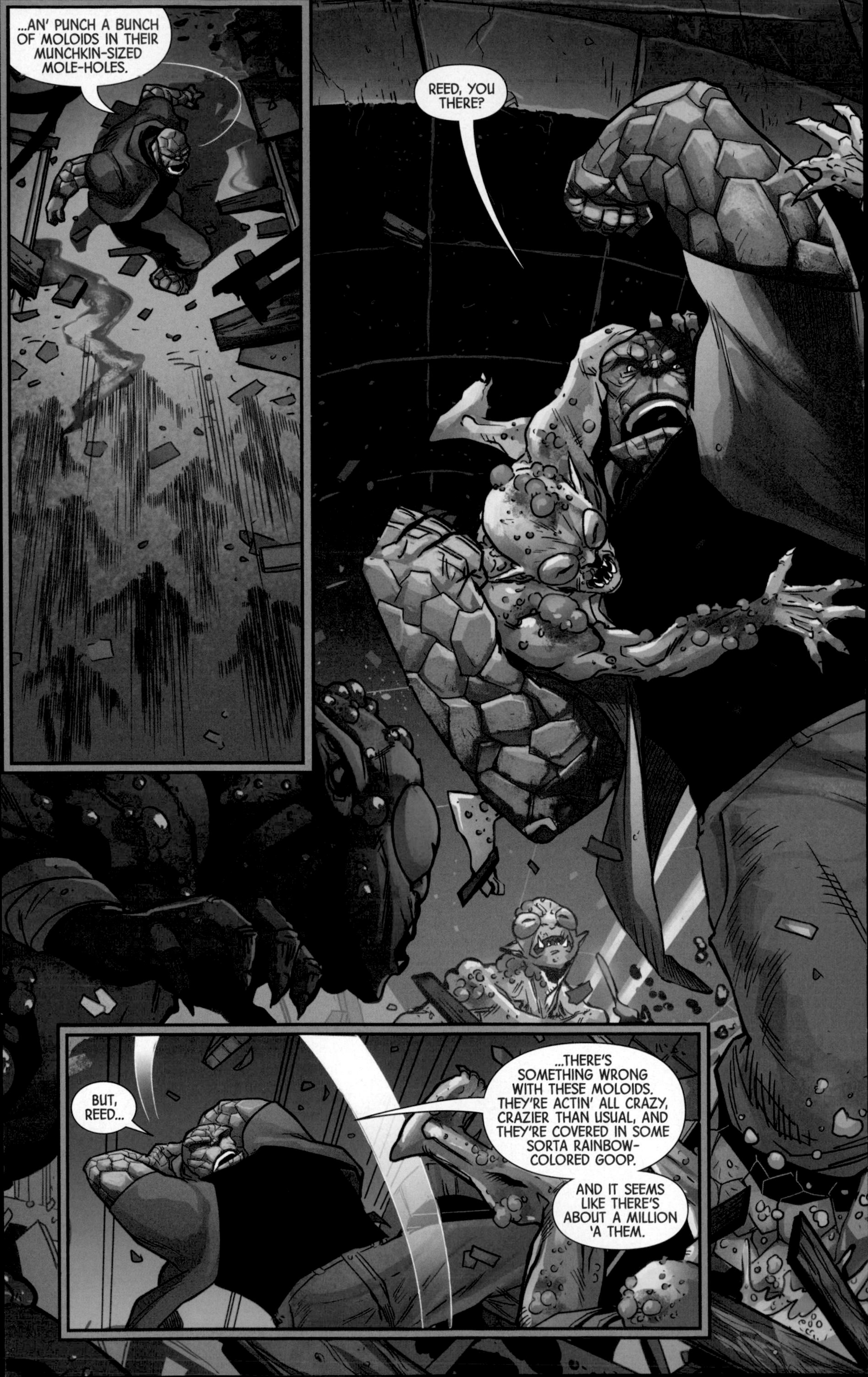
...AN' PUNCH A BUNCH OF MOLOIDS IN THEIR MUNCHKIN-SIZED MOLE-HOLES.
REED, YOU THERE?
BUT, REED...
...THERE'S SOMETHING WRONG WITH THESE MOLOIDS. THEY'RE ACTIN' ALL CRAZY, CRAZIER THAN USUAL, AND THEY'RE COVERED IN SOME SORTA RAINBOW-COLORED GOOP.
AND IT SEEMS LIKE THERE'S ABOUT A MILLION 'A THEM.

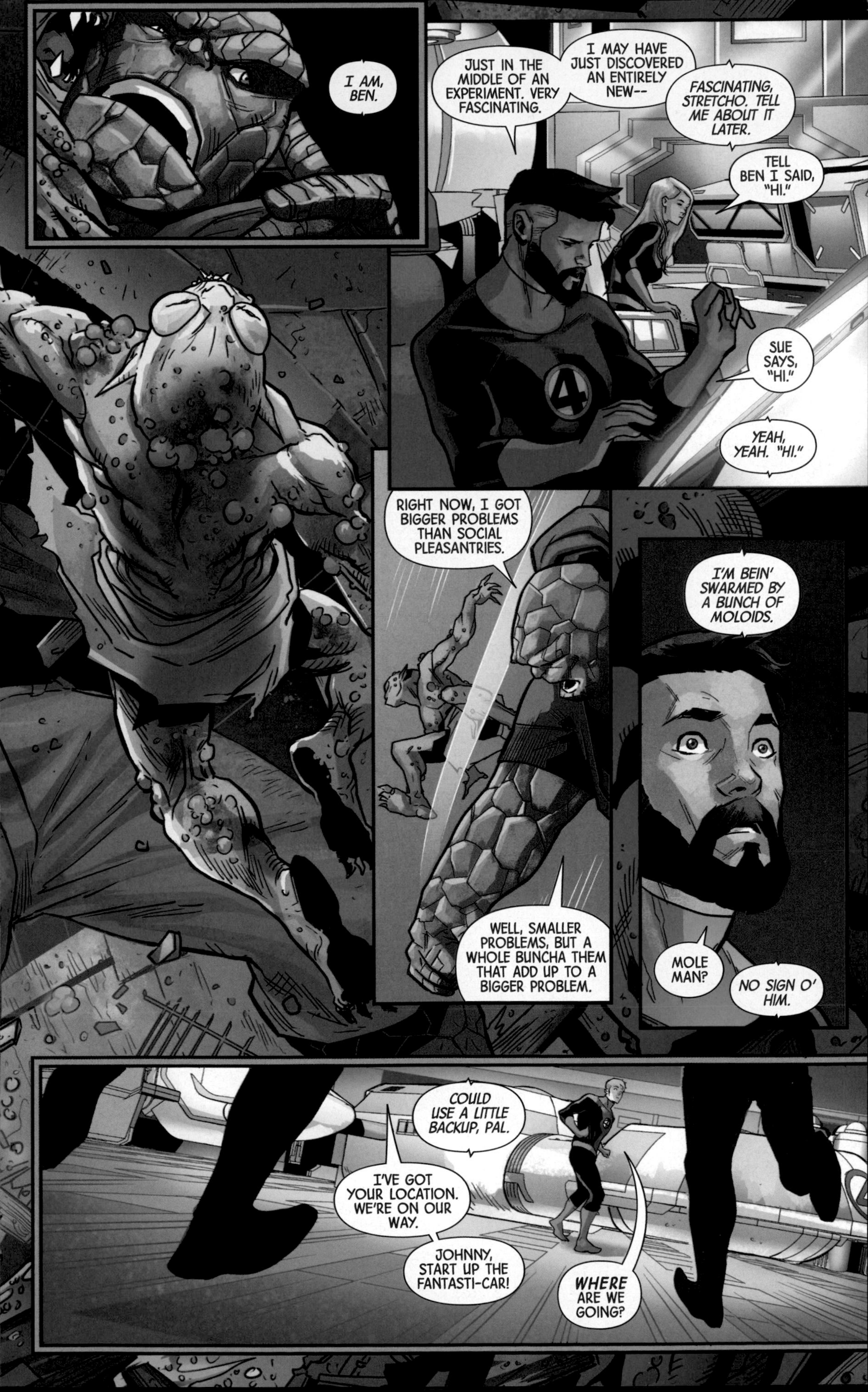
I AM, BEN.
JUST IN THE MIDDLE OF AN EXPERIMENT. VERY FASCINATING.
I MAY HAVE JUST DISCOVERED AN ENTIRELY NEW--
FASCINATING, STRETCHO. TELL ME ABOUT IT LATER.
TELL BEN I SAID, "HI."
SUE SAYS, "HI."
YEAH, YEAH. "HI."
RIGHT NOW, I GOT BIGGER PROBLEMS THAN SOCIAL PLEASANTRIES.
I'M BEIN' SWARMED BY A BUNCH OF MOLOIDS.
WELL, SMALLER PROBLEMS, BUT A WHOLE BUNCHA THEM THAT ADD UP TO A BIGGER PROBLEM.
MOLE MAN?
NO SIGN O' HIM.
COULD USE A LITTLE BACKUP, PAL.
I'VE GOT YOUR LOCATION. WE'RE ON OUR WAY.
JOHNNY, START UP THE FANTASTI-CAR!
WHERE ARE WE GOING?

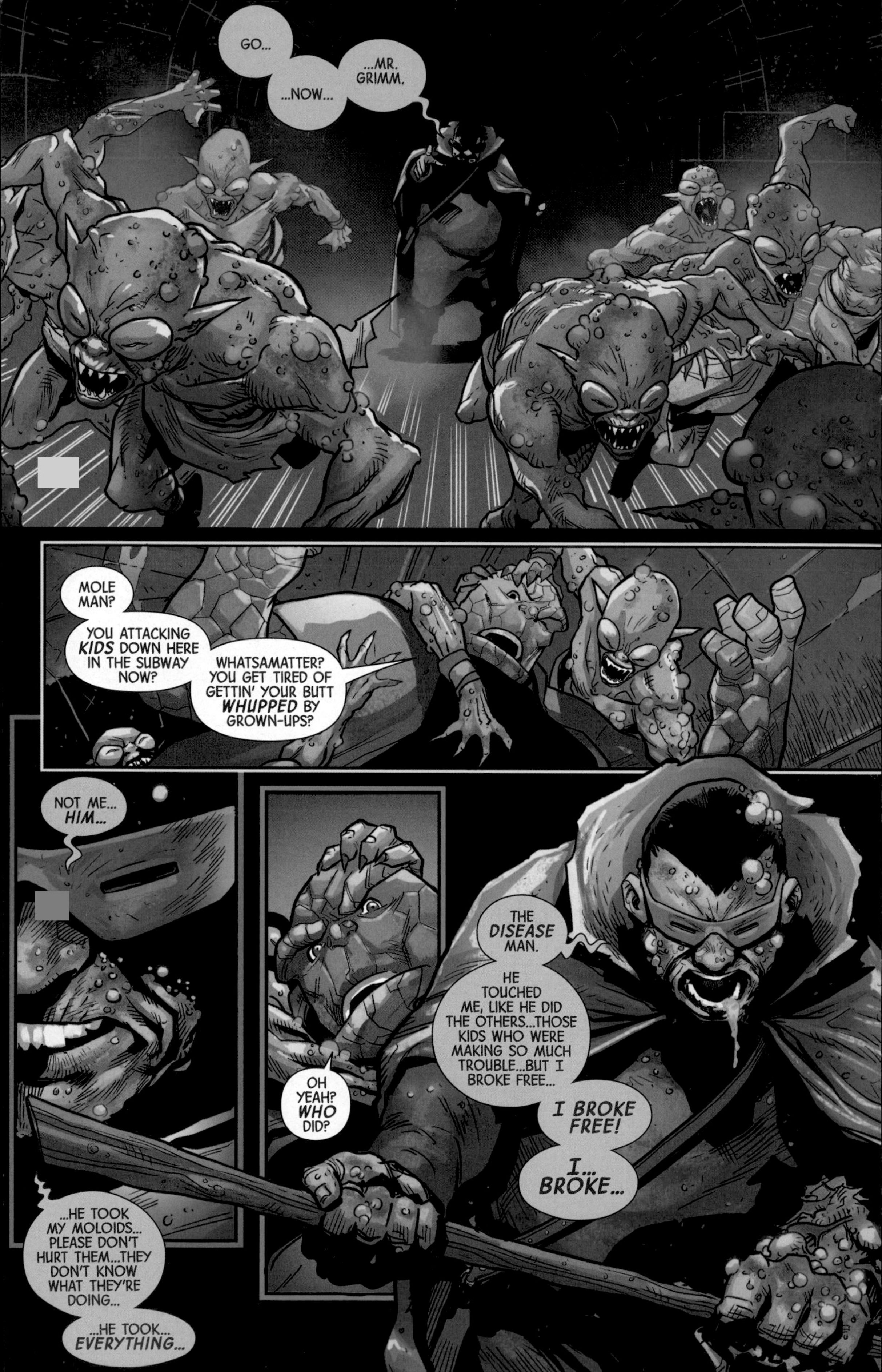
GO...
...NOW...
...MR. GRIMM.
MOLE MAN?
YOU ATTACKING KIDS DOWN HERE IN THE SUBWAY NOW?
WHATSAMATTER? YOU GET TIRED OF GETTIN' YOUR BUTT WHUPPED BY GROWN-UPS?
NOT ME... HIM...
...HE TOOK MY MOLOIDS... PLEASE DON'T HURT THEM...THEY DON'T KNOW WHAT THEY'RE DOING...
...HE TOOK... EVERYTHING...
OH YEAH? WHO DID?
THE DISEASE MAN.
HE TOUCHED ME, LIKE HE DID THE OTHERS...THOSE KIDS WHO WERE MAKING SO MUCH TROUBLE...BUT I BROKE FREE...
I BROKE FREE!
I... BROKE...

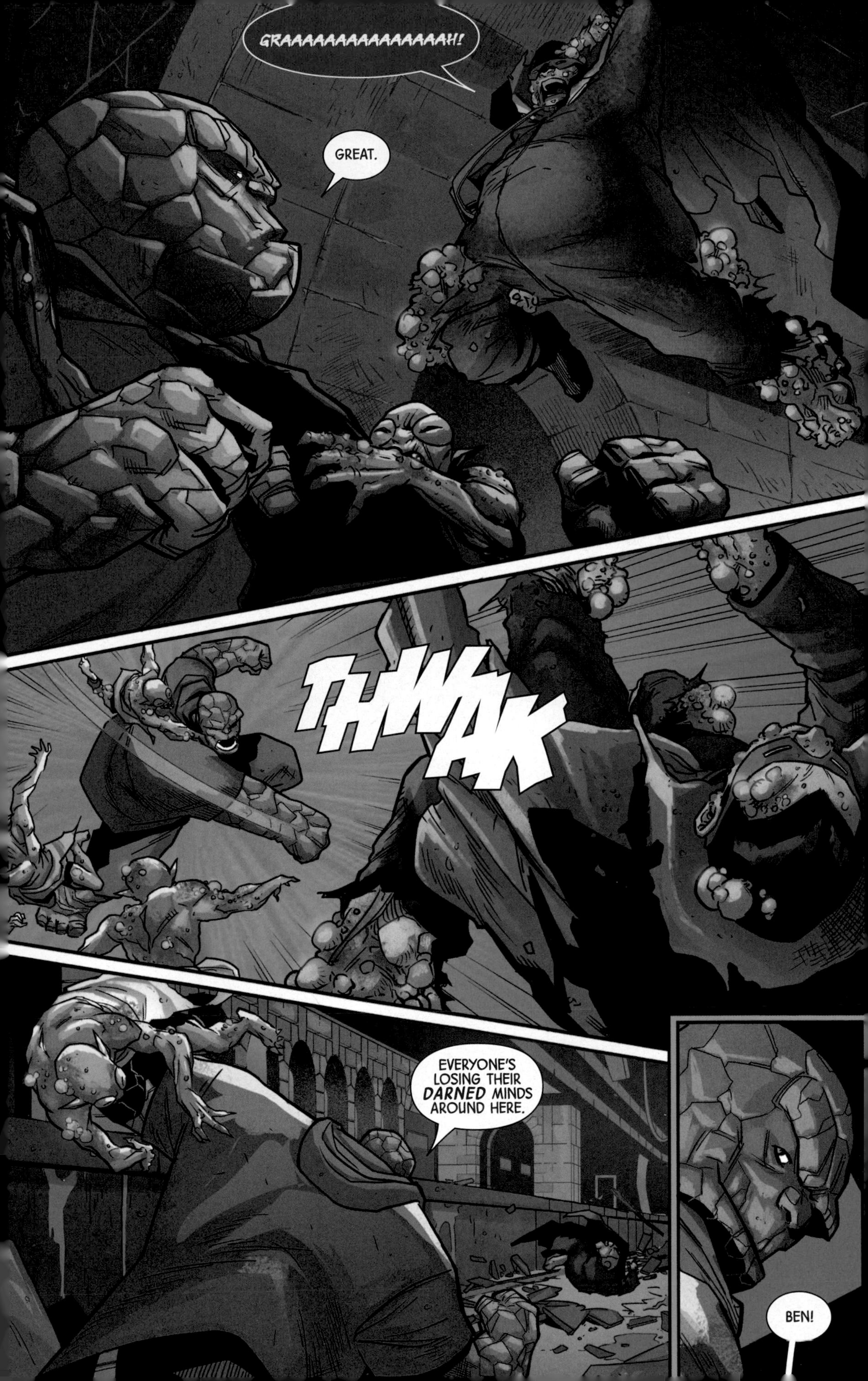
GRAAAAAAAAAAAAAAAH!
GREAT.
THWAK
EVERYONE'S LOSING THEIR DARNED MINDS AROUND HERE.
BEN!

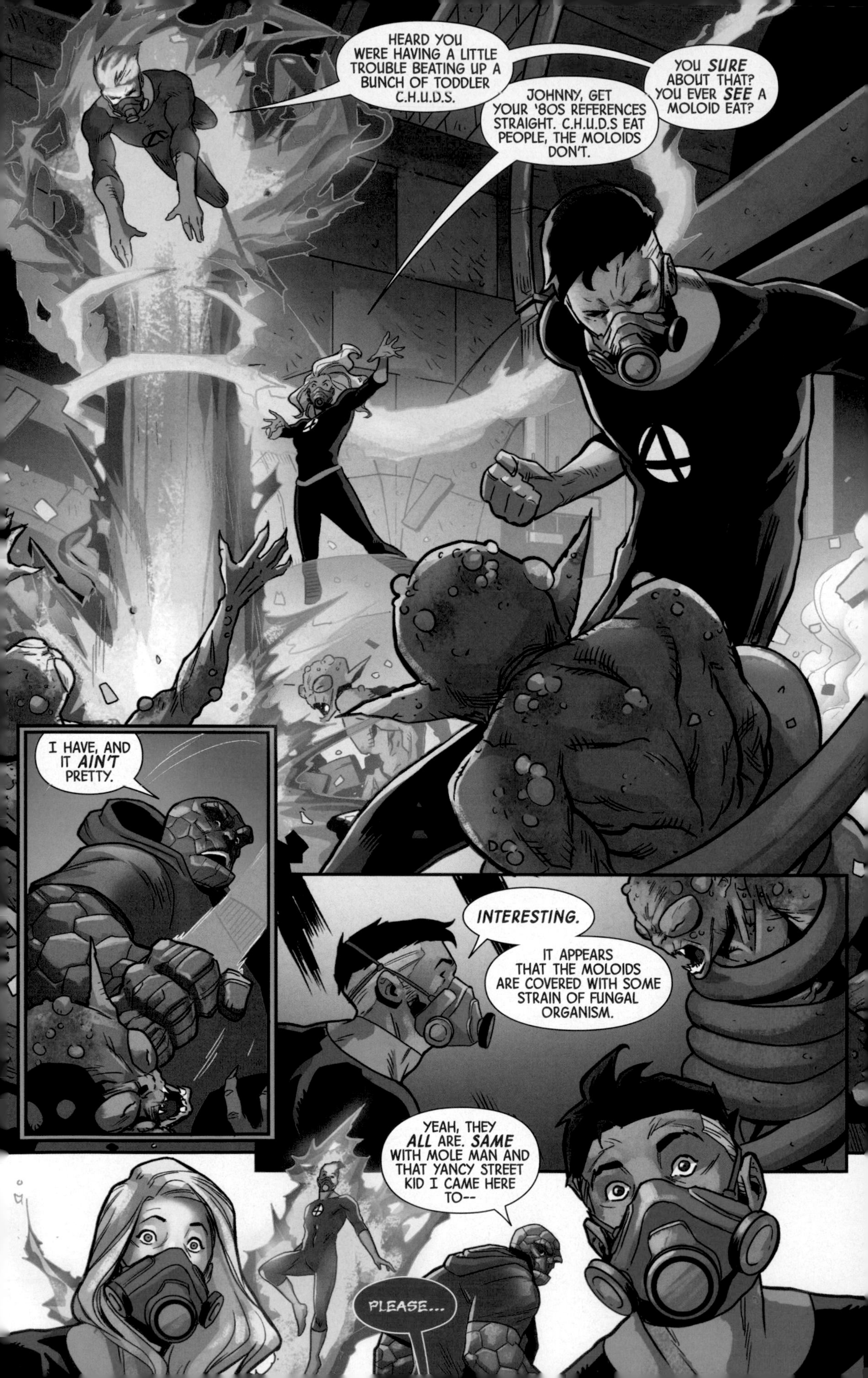
HEARD YOU WERE HAVING A LITTLE TROUBLE BEATING UP A BUNCH OF TODDLER C.H.U.D.S.
JOHNNY, GET YOUR '80S REFERENCES STRAIGHT. C.H.U.D.S EAT PEOPLE, THE MOLOIDS DON'T.
YOU SURE ABOUT THAT? YOU EVER SEE A MOLOID EAT?
I HAVE, AND IT AIN'T PRETTY.
INTERESTING.
IT APPEARS THAT THE MOLOIDS ARE COVERED WITH SOME STRAIN OF FUNGAL ORGANISM.
YEAH, THEY ALL ARE. SAME WITH MOLE MAN AND THAT YANCY STREET KID I CAME HERE TO--
PLEASE...

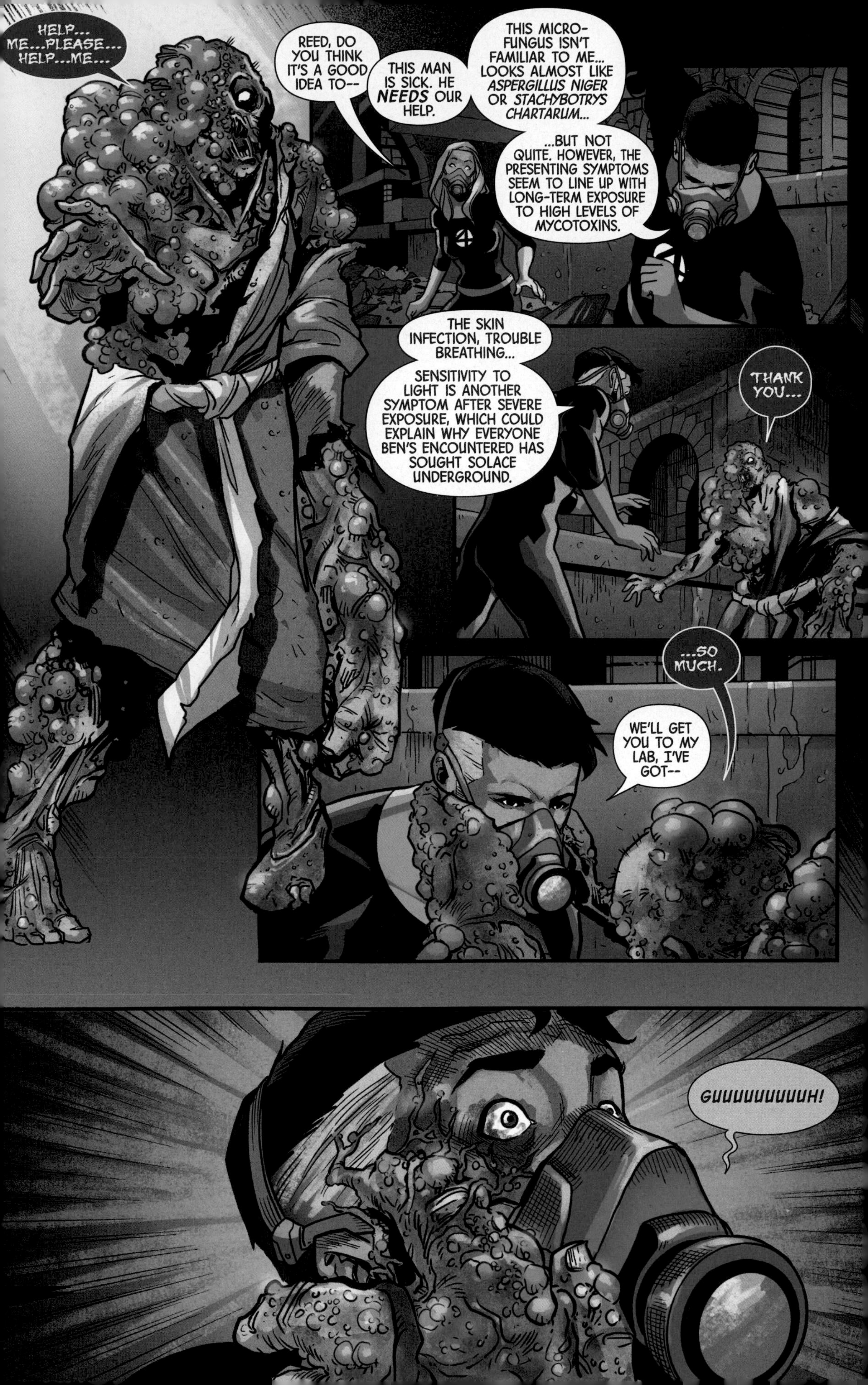
HELP... ME...PLEASE... HELP...ME...
REED, DO YOU THINK IT'S A GOOD IDEA TO--
THIS MAN IS SICK. HE *NEEDS* OUR HELP.
THIS MICRO-FUNGUS ISN'T FAMILIAR TO ME... LOOKS ALMOST LIKE *ASPERGILLUS NIGER* OR *STACHYBOTRYS CHARTARUM*...
...BUT NOT QUITE. HOWEVER, THE PRESENTING SYMPTOMS SEEM TO LINE UP WITH LONG-TERM EXPOSURE TO HIGH LEVELS OF MYCOTOXINS.
THE SKIN INFECTION, TROUBLE BREATHING...
SENSITIVITY TO LIGHT IS ANOTHER SYMPTOM AFTER SEVERE EXPOSURE, WHICH COULD EXPLAIN WHY EVERYONE BEN'S ENCOUNTERED HAS SOUGHT SOLACE UNDERGROUND.
THANK YOU...
...SO MUCH.
WE'LL GET YOU TO MY LAB, I'VE GOT--
GUUUUUUUUUH!

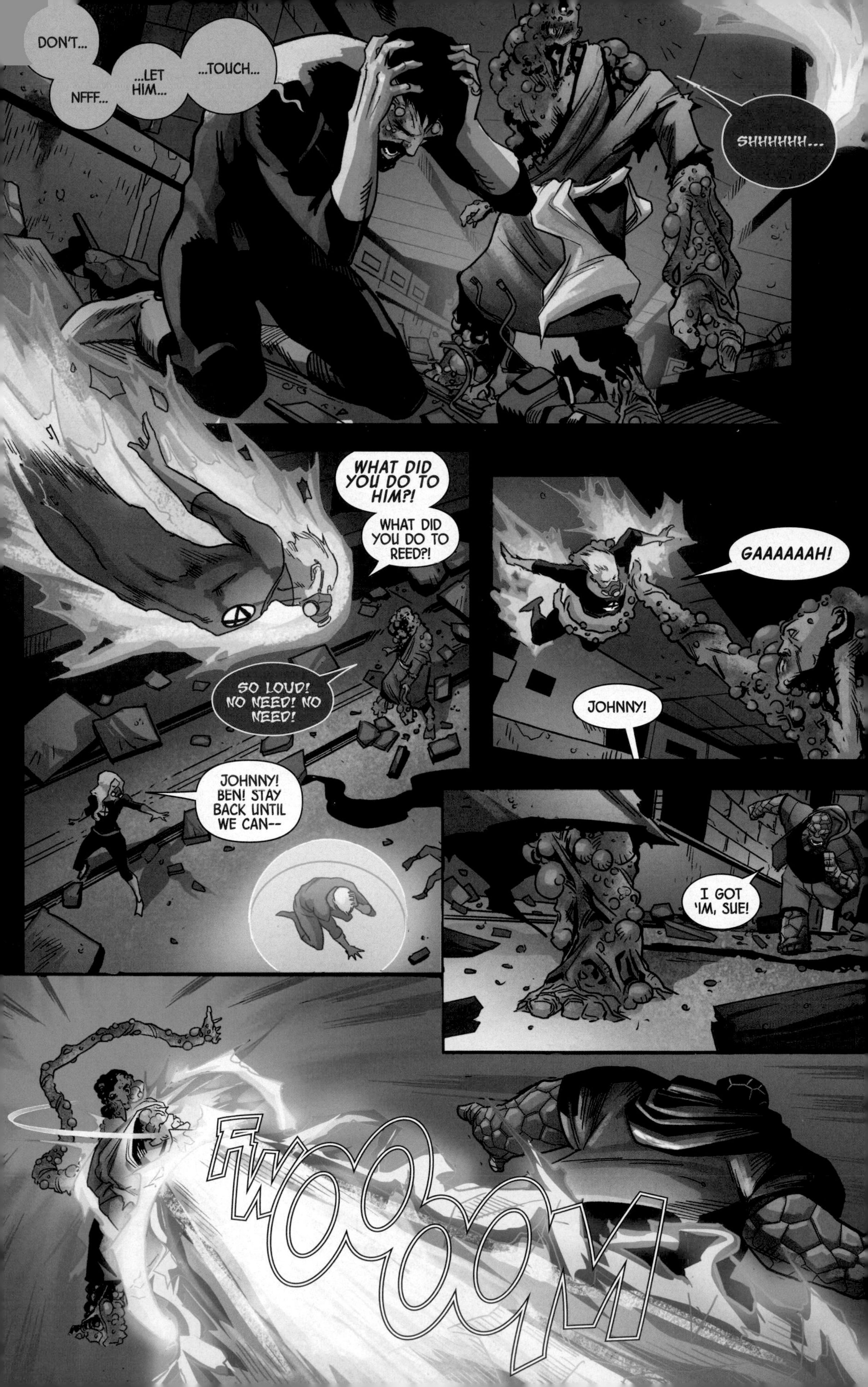
DON'T...
NFFF...
...LET HIM...
...TOUCH...
SHHHHHH...
WHAT DID YOU DO TO HIM?!
WHAT DID YOU DO TO REED?!
SO LOUD! NO NEED! NO NEED!
GAAAAAAH!
JOHNNY!
JOHNNY! BEN! STAY BACK UNTIL WE CAN--
I GOT 'IM, SUE!
FWOOOOOM

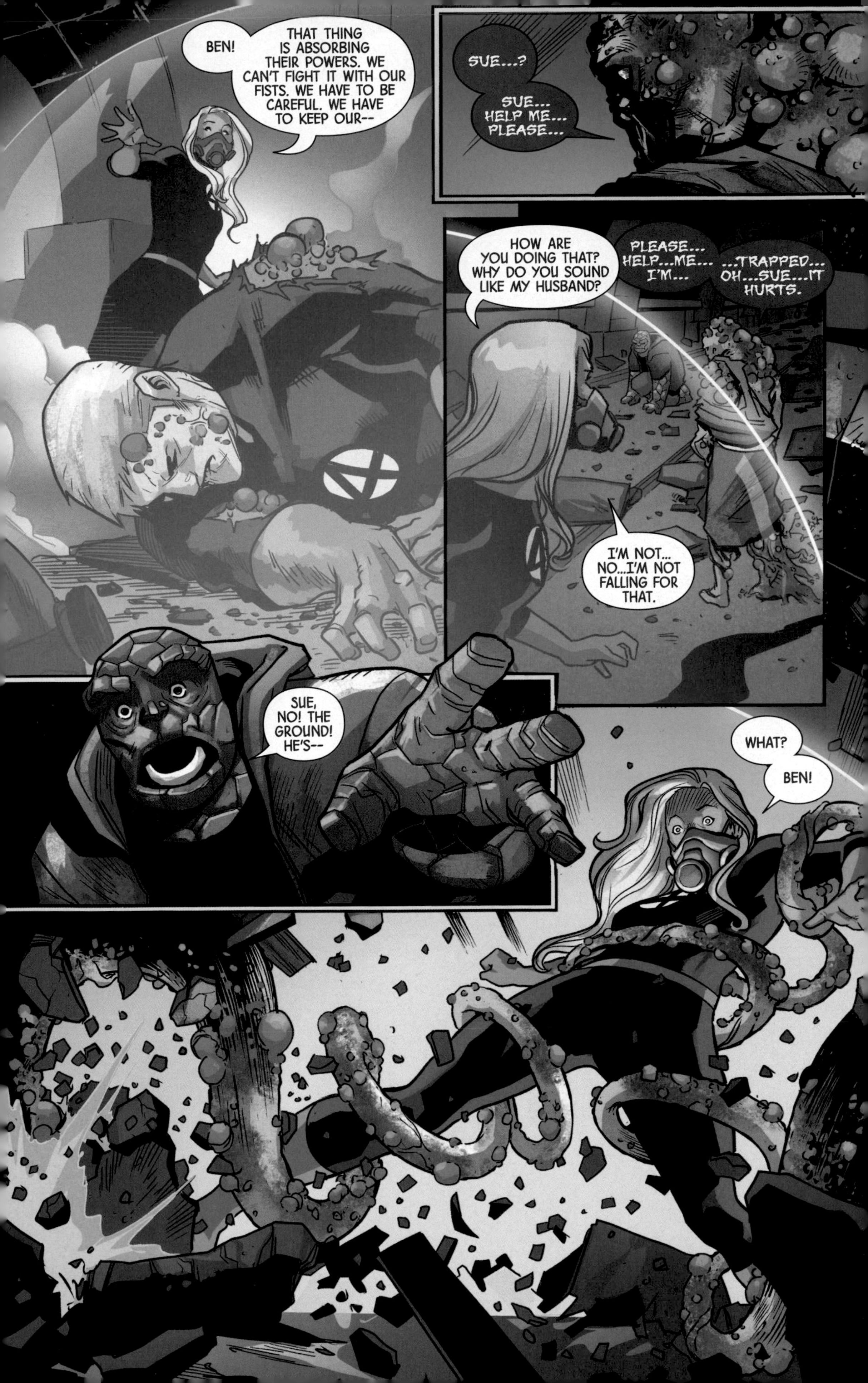
BEN!
THAT THING IS ABSORBING THEIR POWERS. WE CAN'T FIGHT IT WITH OUR FISTS. WE HAVE TO BE CAREFUL. WE HAVE TO KEEP OUR--
SUE...?
SUE... HELP ME... PLEASE...
HOW ARE YOU DOING THAT? WHY DO YOU SOUND LIKE MY HUSBAND?
PLEASE... HELP...ME... I'M...
...TRAPPED... OH...SUE...IT HURTS.
I'M NOT... NO...I'M NOT FALLING FOR THAT.
SUE, NO! THE GROUND! HE'S--
WHAT?
BEN!

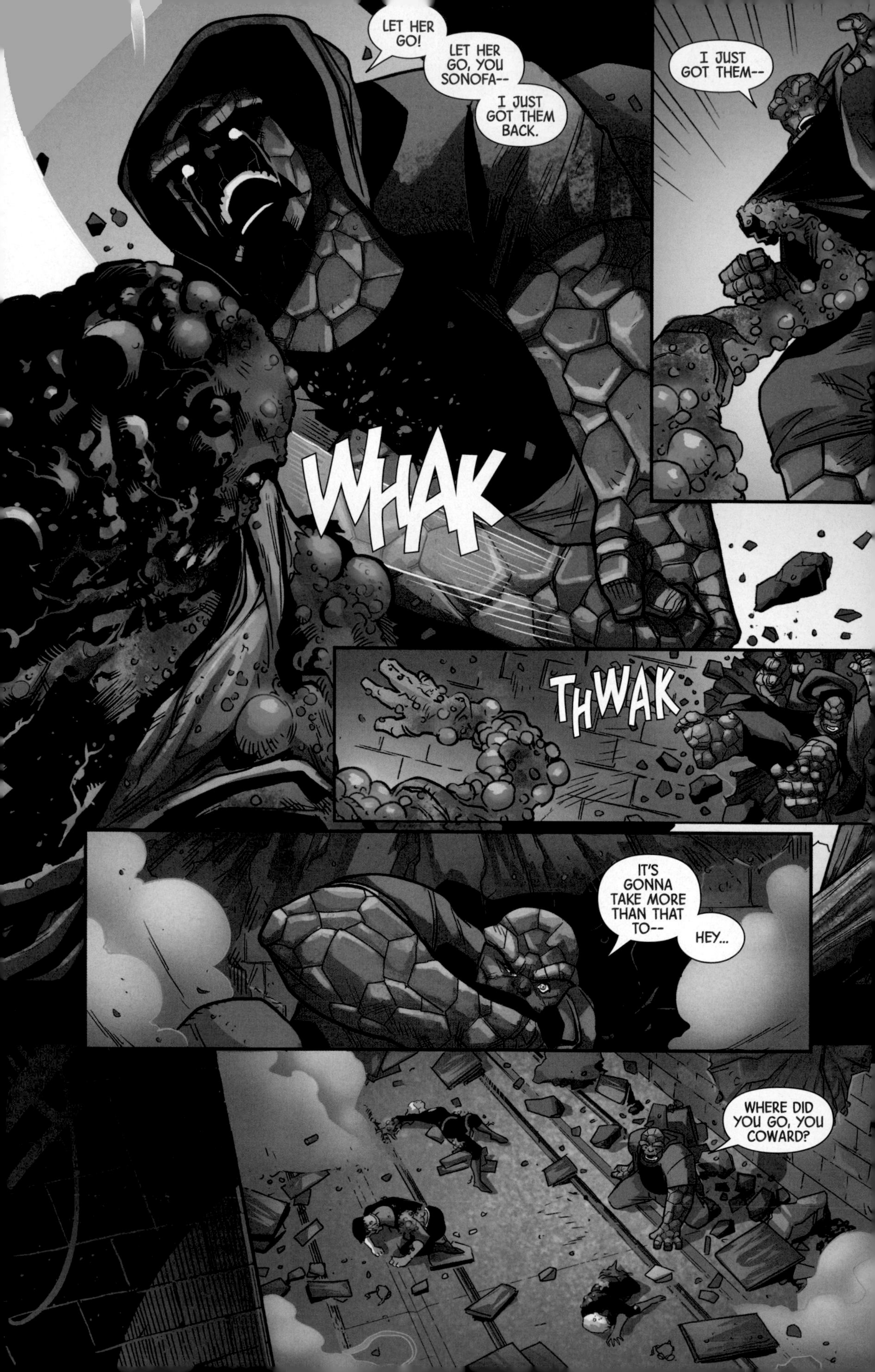
LET HER GO!
LET HER GO, YOU SONOFA--
I JUST GOT THEM BACK.
I JUST GOT THEM--
WHAK
THWAK
IT'S GONNA TAKE MORE THAN THAT TO--
HEY...
WHERE DID YOU GO, YOU COWARD?

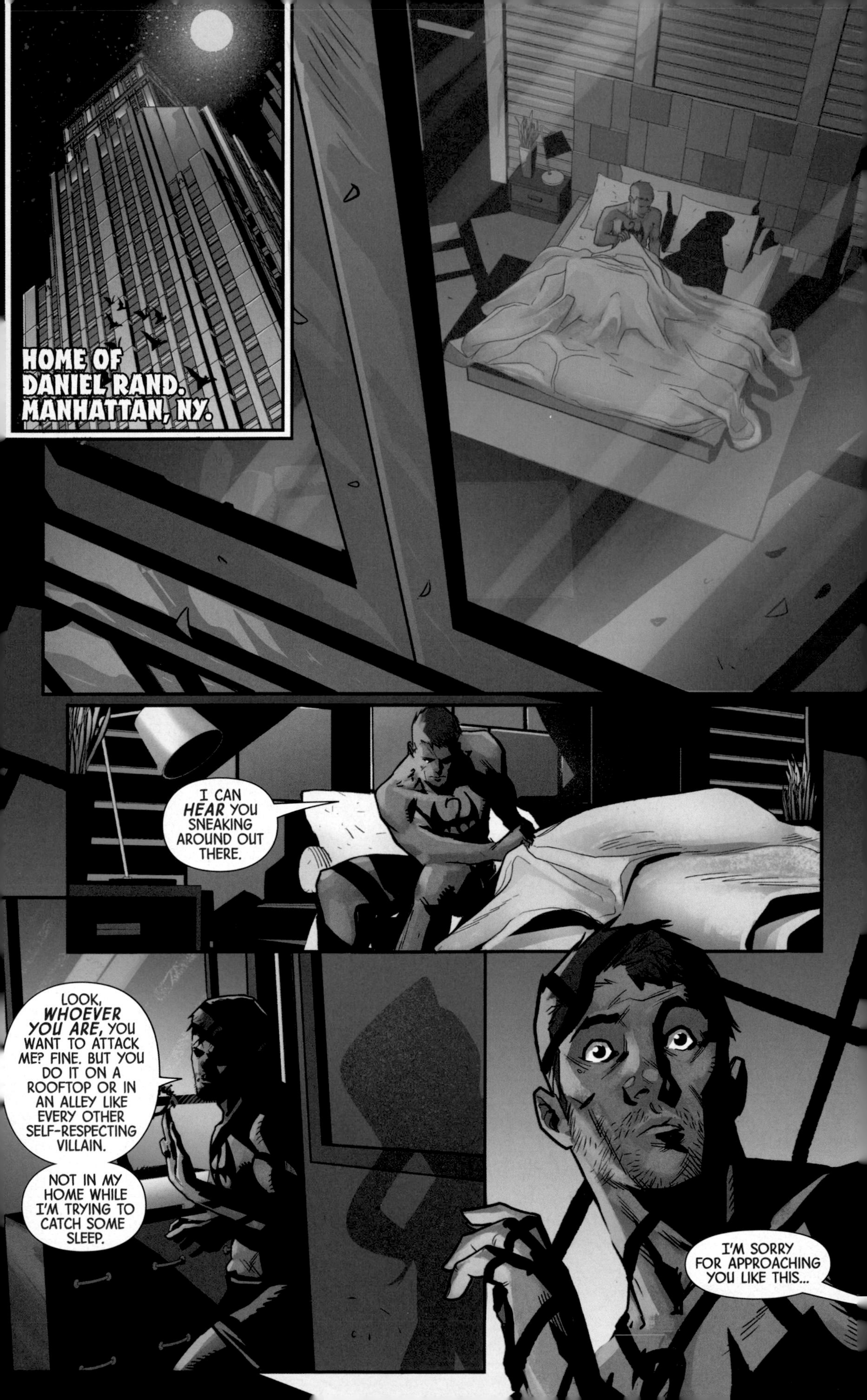
HOME OF DANIEL RAND. MANHATTAN, NY.
I CAN HEAR YOU SNEAKING AROUND OUT THERE.
LOOK, WHOEVER YOU ARE, YOU WANT TO ATTACK ME? FINE. BUT YOU DO IT ON A ROOFTOP OR IN AN ALLEY LIKE EVERY OTHER SELF-RESPECTING VILLAIN.
NOT IN MY HOME WHILE I'M TRYING TO CATCH SOME SLEEP.
I'M SORRY FOR APPROACHING YOU LIKE THIS...

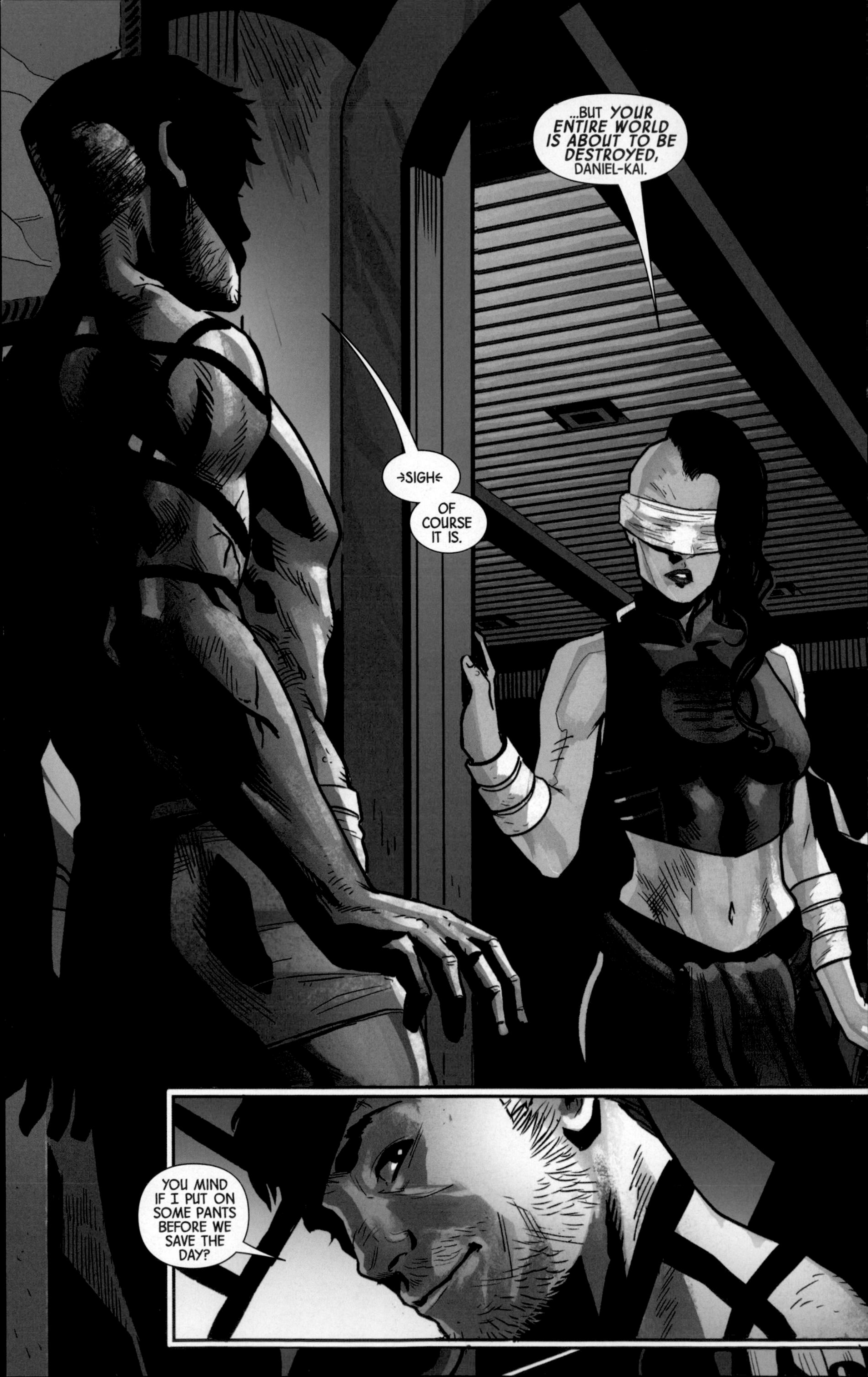
...BUT YOUR ENTIRE WORLD IS ABOUT TO BE DESTROYED, DANIEL-KAI.
>SIGH<
OF COURSE IT IS.
YOU MIND IF I PUT ON SOME PANTS BEFORE WE SAVE THE DAY?

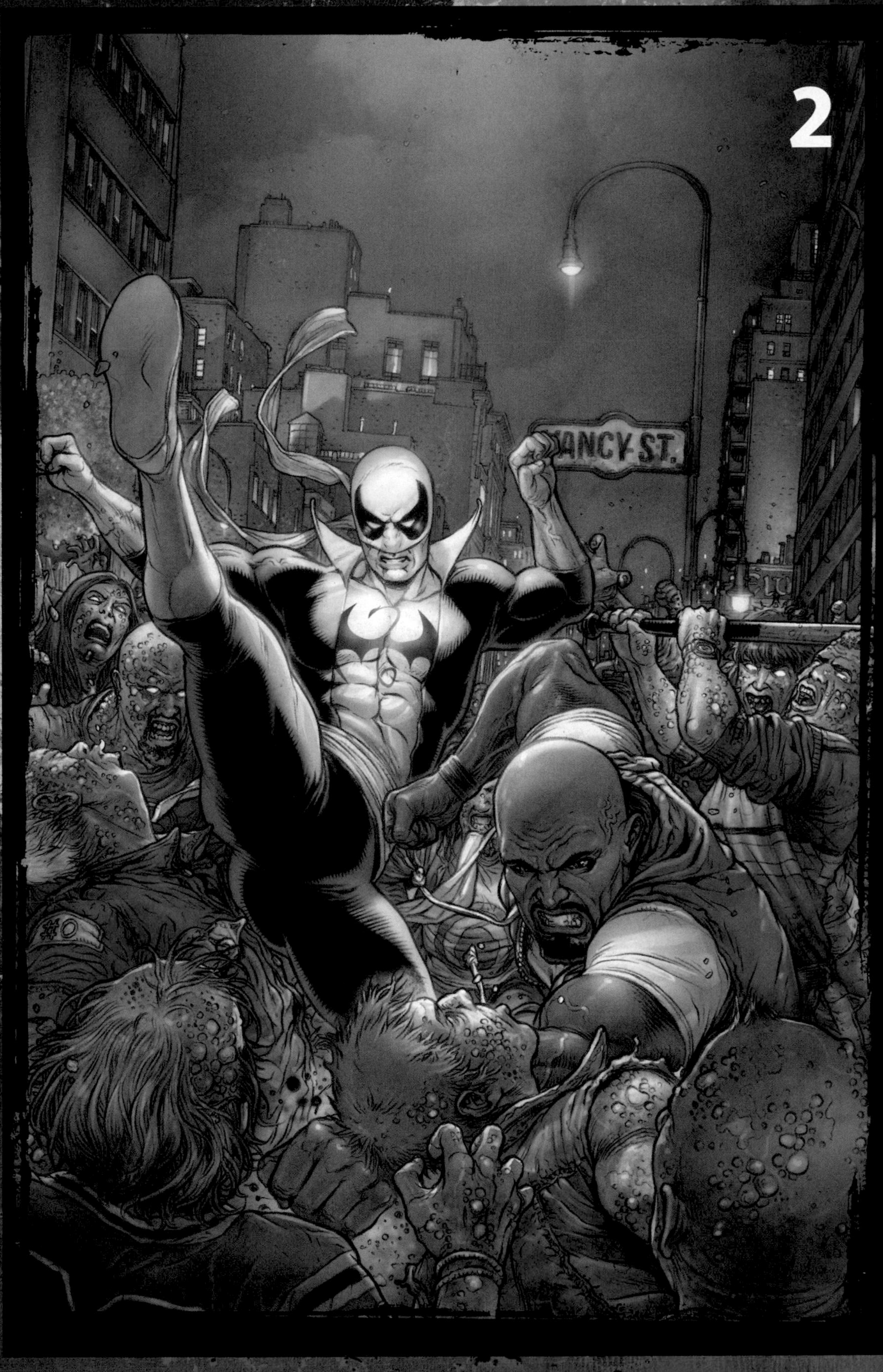
2
ANCY ST.

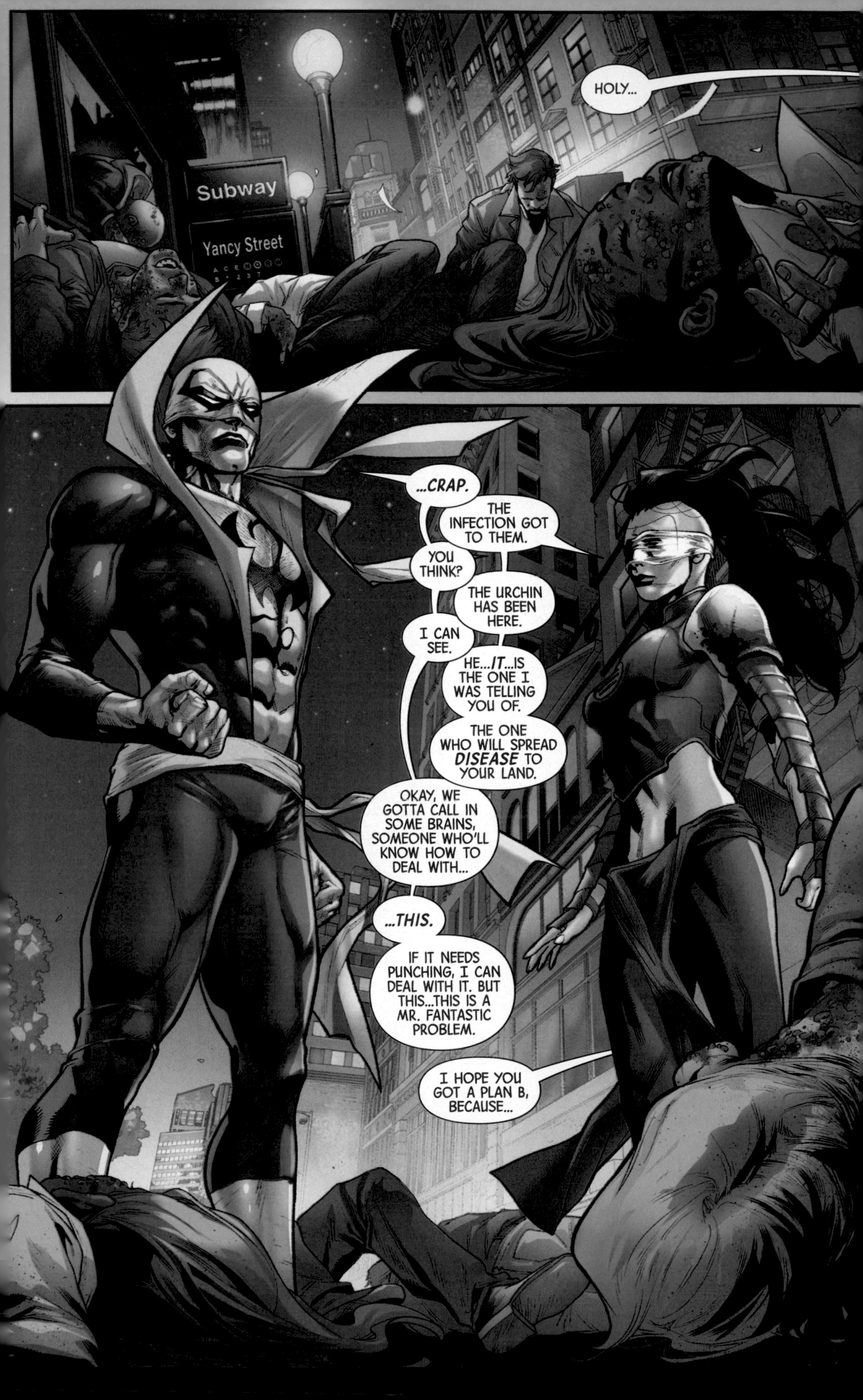

Subway
Yancy Street
HOLY...
...CRAP.
THE INFECTION GOT TO THEM.
YOU THINK?
THE URCHIN HAS BEEN HERE.
I CAN SEE.
HE...IT...IS THE ONE I WAS TELLING YOU OF.
THE ONE WHO WILL SPREAD DISEASE TO YOUR LAND.
OKAY, WE GOTTA CALL IN SOME BRAINS, SOMEONE WHO'LL KNOW HOW TO DEAL WITH...
...THIS.
IF IT NEEDS PUNCHING, I CAN DEAL WITH IT. BUT THIS...THIS IS A MR. FANTASTIC PROBLEM.
I HOPE YOU GOT A PLAN B, BECAUSE...

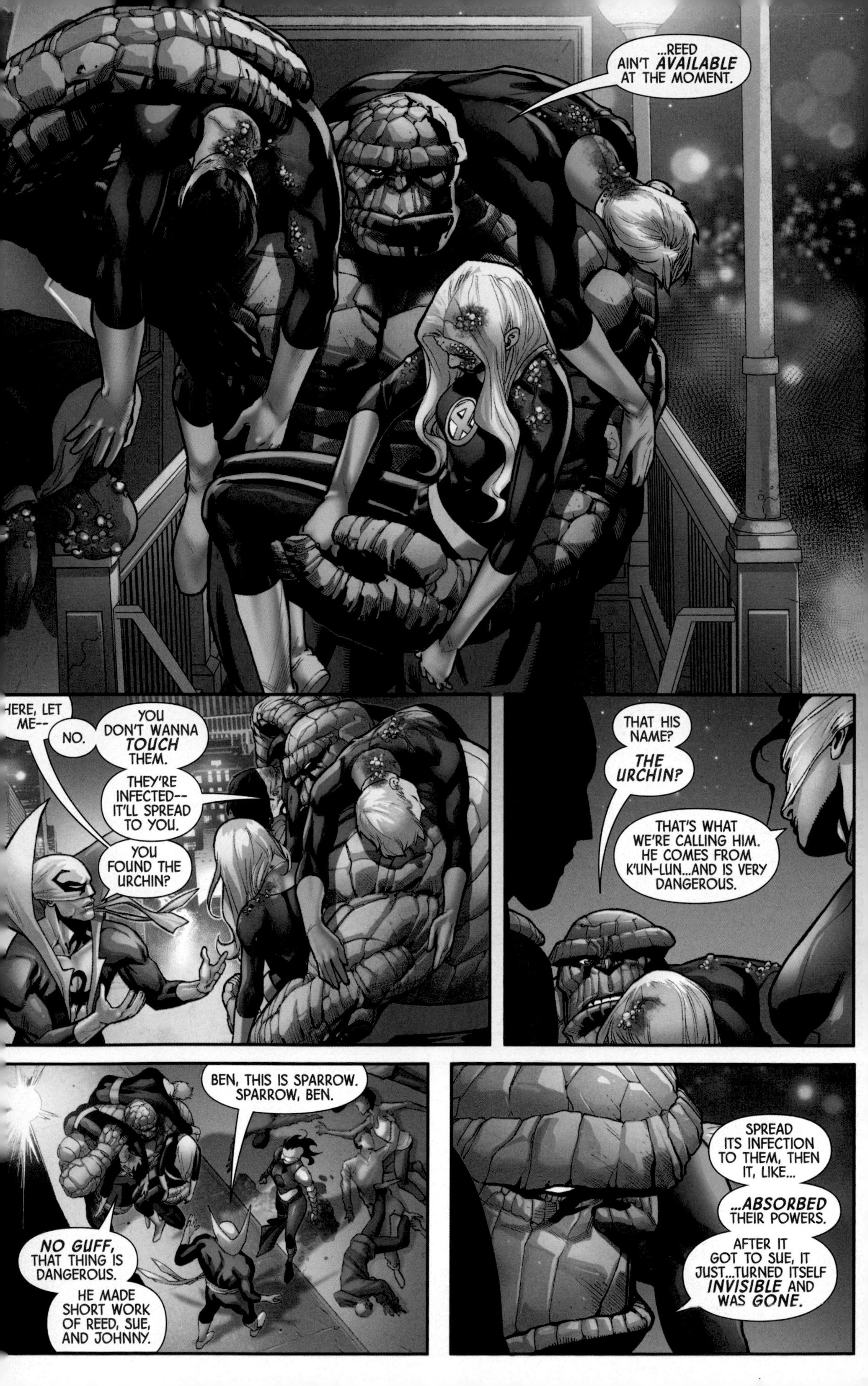
...REED AIN'T AVAILABLE AT THE MOMENT.
HERE, LET ME--
NO.
YOU DON'T WANNA TOUCH THEM.
THEY'RE INFECTED-- IT'LL SPREAD TO YOU.
YOU FOUND THE URCHIN?
THAT HIS NAME? THE URCHIN?
THAT'S WHAT WE'RE CALLING HIM. HE COMES FROM K'UN-LUN...AND IS VERY DANGEROUS.
BEN, THIS IS SPARROW. SPARROW, BEN.
NO GUFF, THAT THING IS DANGEROUS.
HE MADE SHORT WORK OF REED, SUE, AND JOHNNY.
SPREAD ITS INFECTION TO THEM, THEN IT, LIKE...
...ABSORBED THEIR POWERS.
AFTER IT GOT TO SUE, IT JUST...TURNED ITSELF INVISIBLE AND WAS GONE.

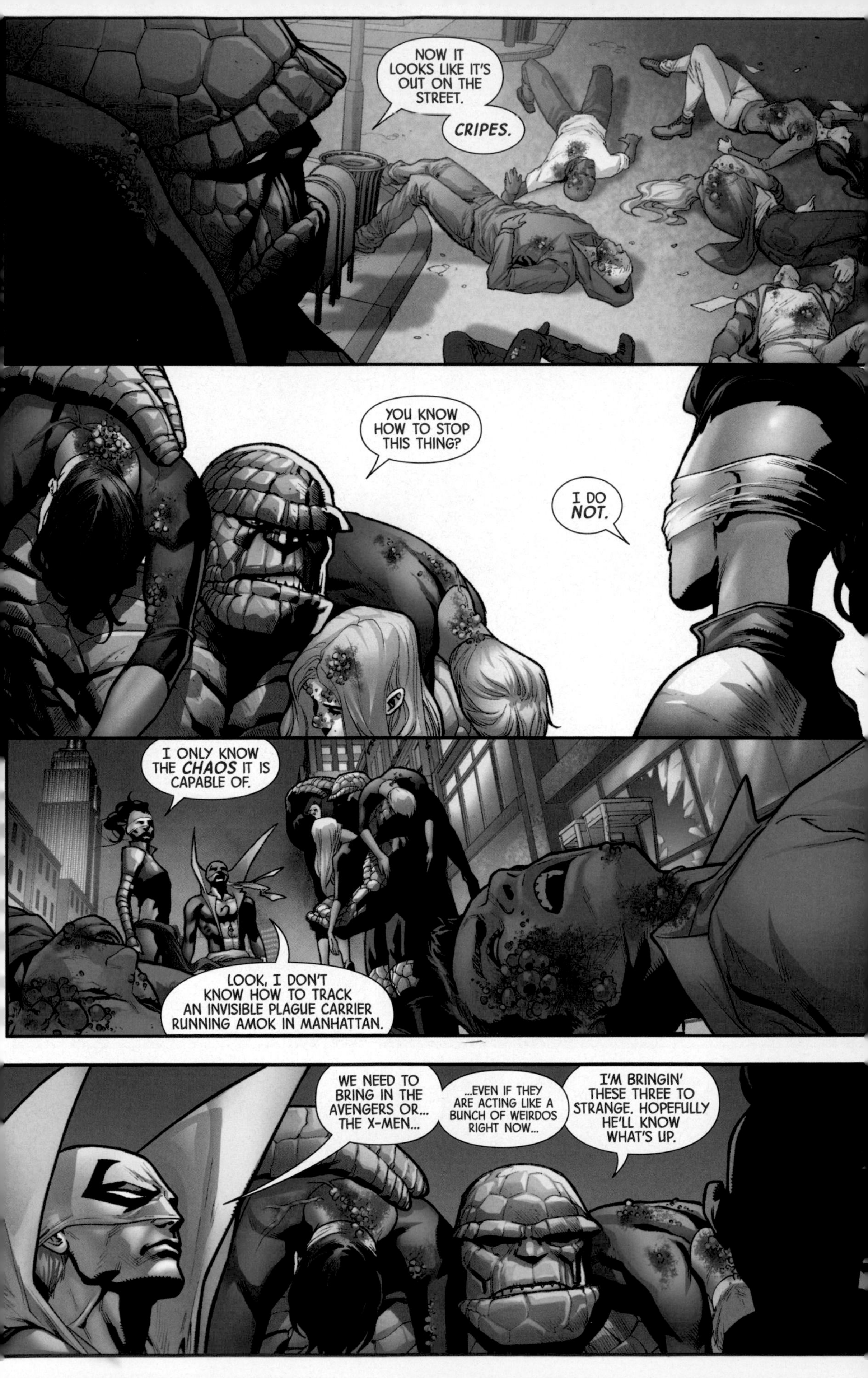
NOW IT LOOKS LIKE IT'S OUT ON THE STREET.
CRIPES.
YOU KNOW HOW TO STOP THIS THING?
I DO NOT.
I ONLY KNOW THE CHAOS IT IS CAPABLE OF.
LOOK, I DON'T KNOW HOW TO TRACK AN INVISIBLE PLAGUE CARRIER RUNNING AMOK IN MANHATTAN.
WE NEED TO BRING IN THE AVENGERS OR... THE X-MEN...
...EVEN IF THEY ARE ACTING LIKE A BUNCH OF WEIRDOS RIGHT NOW...
I'M BRINGIN' THESE THREE TO STRANGE. HOPEFULLY HE'LL KNOW WHAT'S UP.

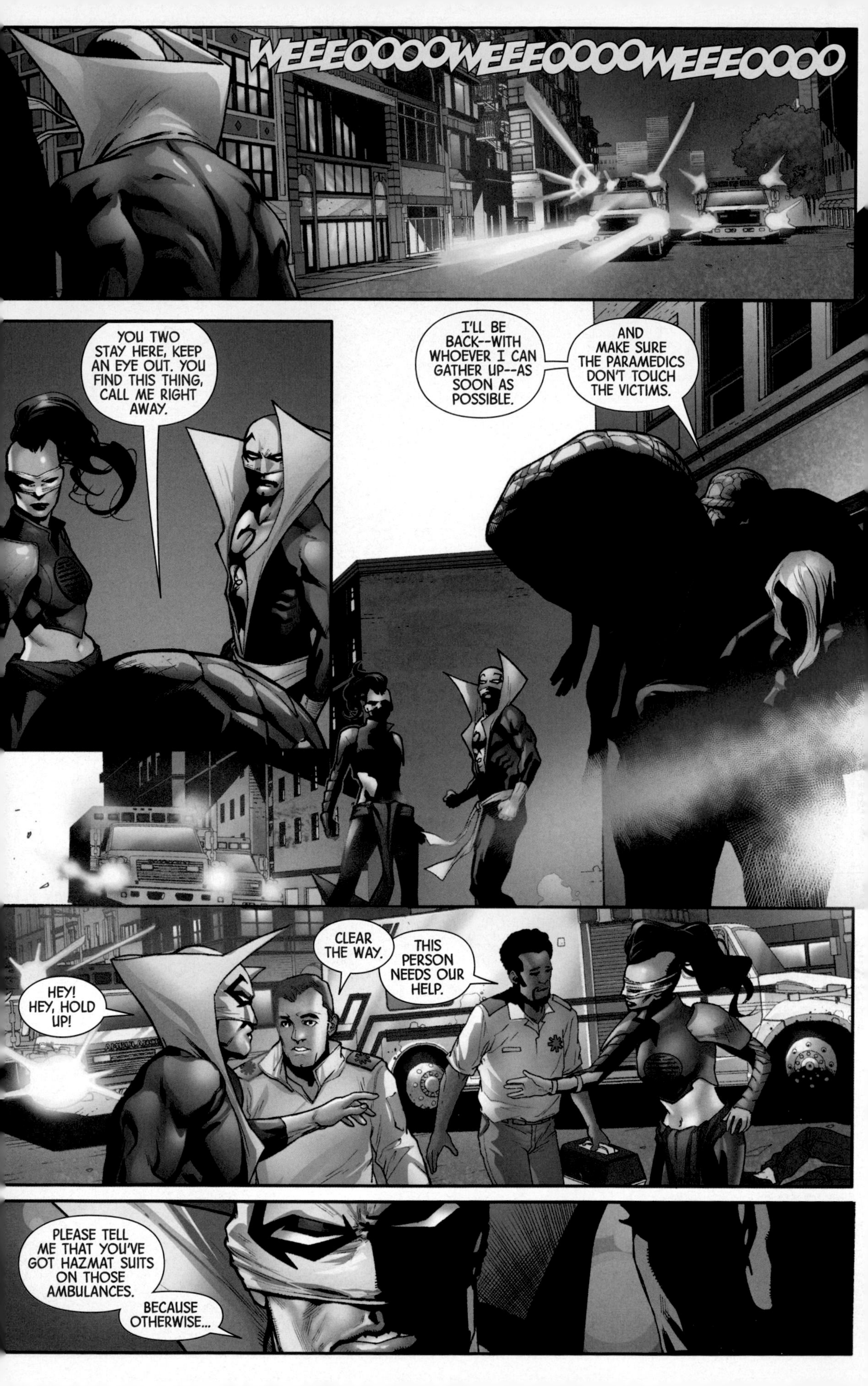
WEEEOOOOWEEEOOOOWEEEOOOO
YOU TWO STAY HERE, KEEP AN EYE OUT. YOU FIND THIS THING, CALL ME RIGHT AWAY.
I'LL BE BACK--WITH WHOEVER I CAN GATHER UP--AS SOON AS POSSIBLE.
AND MAKE SURE THE PARAMEDICS DON'T TOUCH THE VICTIMS.
HEY! HEY, HOLD UP!
CLEAR THE WAY.
THIS PERSON NEEDS OUR HELP.
PLEASE TELL ME THAT YOU'VE GOT HAZMAT SUITS ON THOSE AMBULANCES.
BECAUSE OTHERWISE...

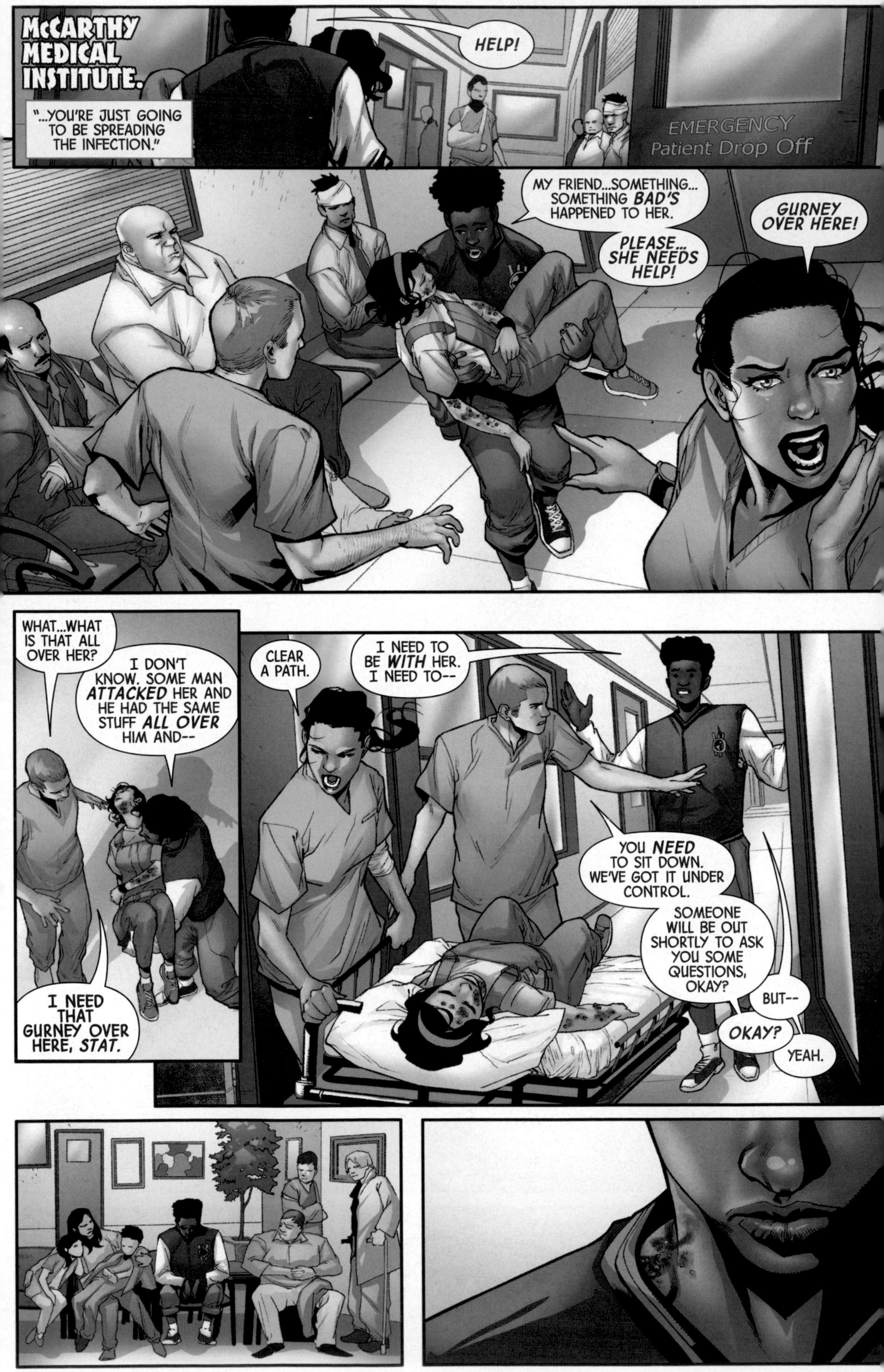
McCARTHY MEDICAL INSTITUTE.
"...YOU'RE JUST GOING TO BE SPREADING THE INFECTION."
HELP!
EMERGENCY Patient Drop Off
MY FRIEND...SOMETHING... SOMETHING BAD'S HAPPENED TO HER.
PLEASE... SHE NEEDS HELP!
GURNEY OVER HERE!
WHAT...WHAT IS THAT ALL OVER HER?
I DON'T KNOW. SOME MAN ATTACKED HER AND HE HAD THE SAME STUFF ALL OVER HIM AND--
I NEED THAT GURNEY OVER HERE, STAT.
CLEAR A PATH.
I NEED TO BE WITH HER. I NEED TO--
YOU NEED TO SIT DOWN. WE'VE GOT IT UNDER CONTROL.
SOMEONE WILL BE OUT SHORTLY TO ASK YOU SOME QUESTIONS, OKAY?
BUT--
OKAY?
YEAH.

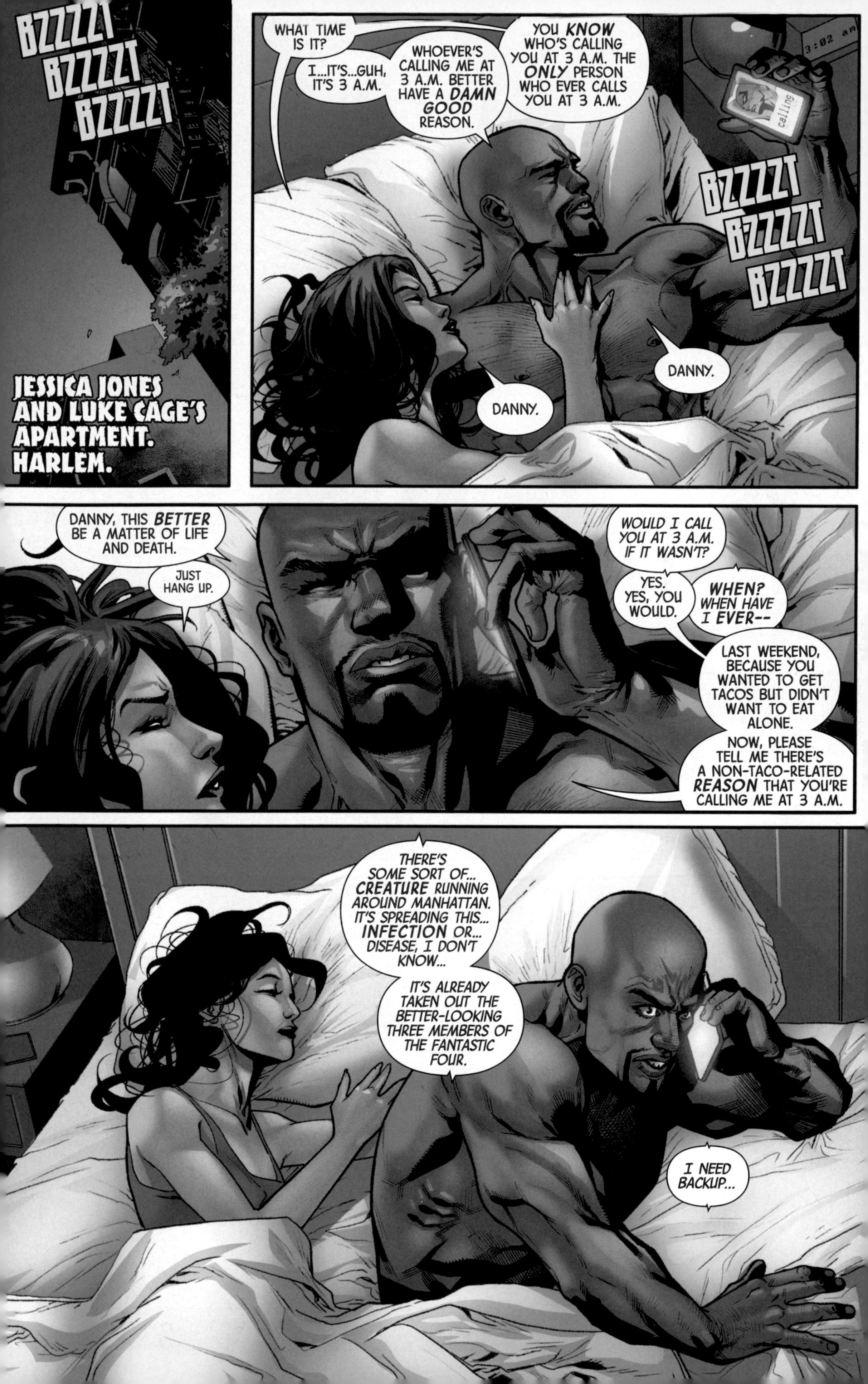
BZZZZT BZZZZT BZZZZT
JESSICA JONES AND LUKE CAGE'S APARTMENT. HARLEM.
WHAT TIME IS IT?
I...IT'S...GUH, IT'S 3 A.M.
WHOEVER'S CALLING ME AT 3 A.M. BETTER HAVE A DAMN GOOD REASON.
YOU KNOW WHO'S CALLING YOU AT 3 A.M. THE ONLY PERSON WHO EVER CALLS YOU AT 3 A.M.
3:02 am
calling
BZZZZT BZZZZT BZZZZT
DANNY.
DANNY.
DANNY, THIS BETTER BE A MATTER OF LIFE AND DEATH.
JUST HANG UP.
WOULD I CALL YOU AT 3 A.M. IF IT WASN'T?
YES. YES, YOU WOULD.
WHEN? WHEN HAVE I EVER--
LAST WEEKEND, BECAUSE YOU WANTED TO GET TACOS BUT DIDN'T WANT TO EAT ALONE.
NOW, PLEASE TELL ME THERE'S A NON-TACO-RELATED REASON THAT YOU'RE CALLING ME AT 3 A.M.
THERE'S SOME SORT OF... CREATURE RUNNING AROUND MANHATTAN. IT'S SPREADING THIS... INFECTION OR... DISEASE, I DON'T KNOW...
IT'S ALREADY TAKEN OUT THE BETTER-LOOKING THREE MEMBERS OF THE FANTASTIC FOUR.
I NEED BACKUP...

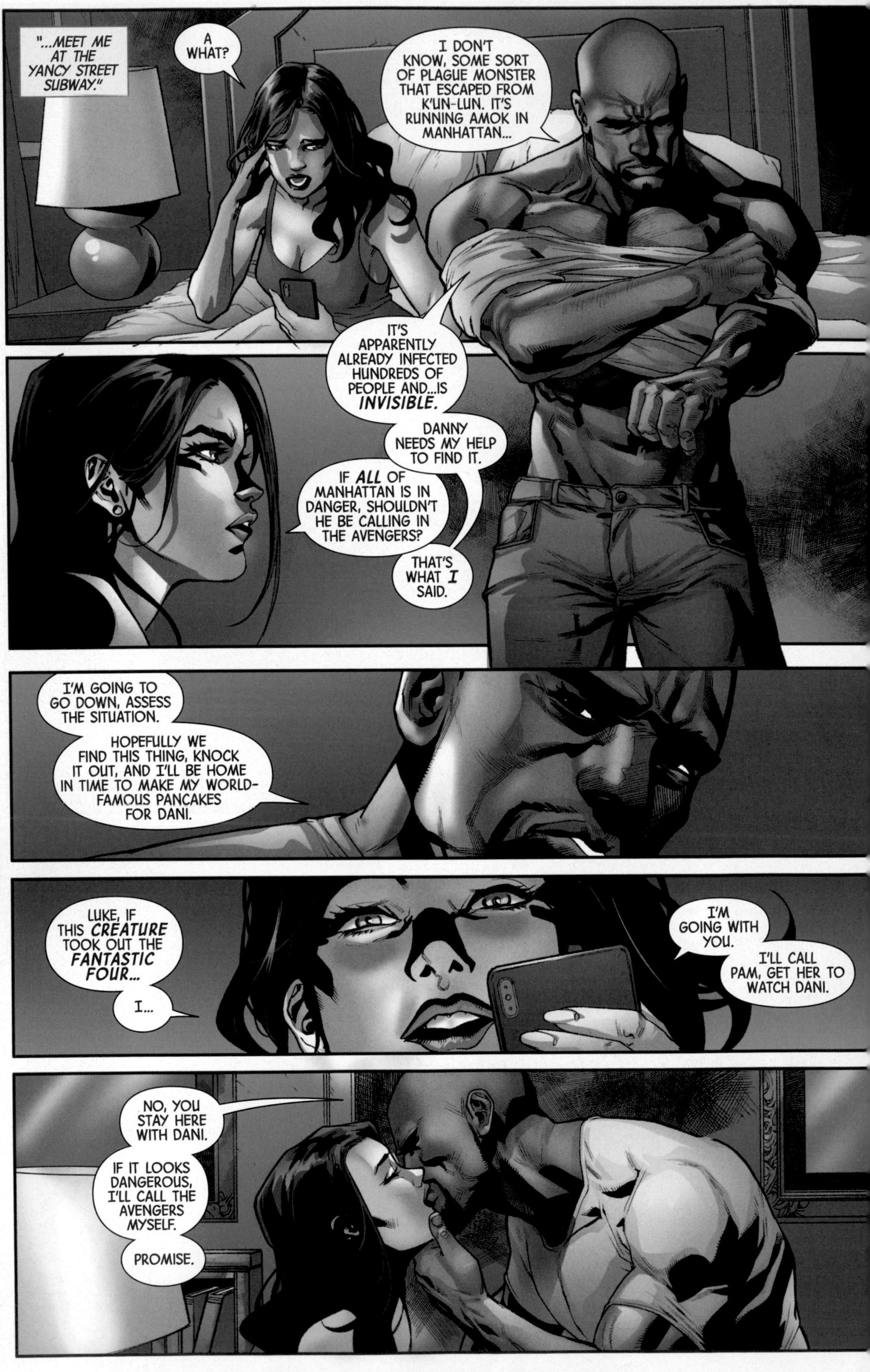
"...MEET ME AT THE YANCY STREET SUBWAY."
A WHAT?
I DON'T KNOW, SOME SORT OF PLAGUE MONSTER THAT ESCAPED FROM K'UN-LUN. IT'S RUNNING AMOK IN MANHATTAN...
IT'S APPARENTLY ALREADY INFECTED HUNDREDS OF PEOPLE AND...IS INVISIBLE.
DANNY NEEDS MY HELP TO FIND IT.
IF ALL OF MANHATTAN IS IN DANGER, SHOULDN'T HE BE CALLING IN THE AVENGERS?
THAT'S WHAT I SAID.
I'M GOING TO GO DOWN, ASSESS THE SITUATION.
HOPEFULLY WE FIND THIS THING, KNOCK IT OUT, AND I'LL BE HOME IN TIME TO MAKE MY WORLD-FAMOUS PANCAKES FOR DANI.
LUKE, IF THIS CREATURE TOOK OUT THE FANTASTIC FOUR...
I...
I'M GOING WITH YOU.
I'LL CALL PAM, GET HER TO WATCH DANI.
NO, YOU STAY HERE WITH DANI.
IF IT LOOKS DANGEROUS, I'LL CALL THE AVENGERS MYSELF.
PROMISE.

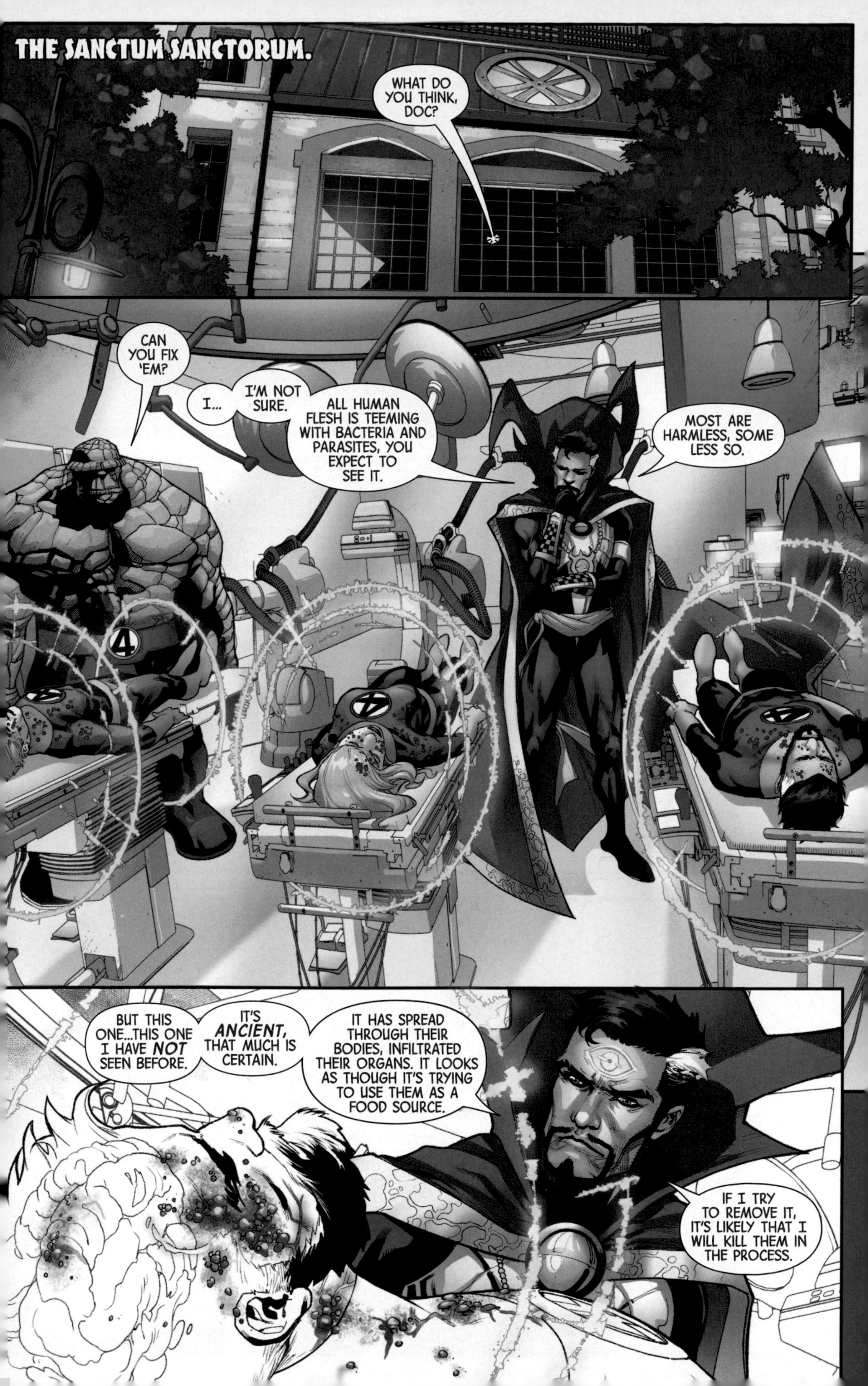
THE SANCTUM SANCTORUM.
WHAT DO YOU THINK, DOC?
CAN YOU FIX 'EM?
I...
I'M NOT SURE.
ALL HUMAN FLESH IS TEEMING WITH BACTERIA AND PARASITES, YOU EXPECT TO SEE IT.
MOST ARE HARMLESS, SOME LESS SO.
BUT THIS ONE...THIS ONE I HAVE NOT SEEN BEFORE.
IT'S ANCIENT, THAT MUCH IS CERTAIN.
IT HAS SPREAD THROUGH THEIR BODIES, INFILTRATED THEIR ORGANS. IT LOOKS AS THOUGH IT'S TRYING TO USE THEM AS A FOOD SOURCE.
IF I TRY TO REMOVE IT, IT'S LIKELY THAT I WILL KILL THEM IN THE PROCESS.

YOU SAID THAT IT CAME FROM K'UN-LUN?

YEAH... THAT'S WHAT IRON FIST'S LADY FRIEND WAS SAYIN'.

THIS FUNGUS HAS BEEN *ENHANCED.* *MAGICALLY SUPERCHARGED.* I'M FAMILIAR WITH K'UN-LUN MYSTICISM, BUT THIS DOESN'T LINE UP WITH ANY I'VE SEEN. AND...IT SEEMS OLDER THAN K'UN-LUN ITSELF.

BRING ME TO WHERE YOU SAW THIS CREATURE.

YOU'RE JUST GONNA *LEAVE* THEM LIKE THIS?

I NEED A SAMPLE FROM THE SOURCE. THIS FUNGUS IS COMMUNICATING WITH ITS HOST. IF I CAN STUDY THE HOST, THEN PERHAPS I CAN DISCOVER HOW TO...HOW TO UNDO THIS BEFORE IT'S TOO--

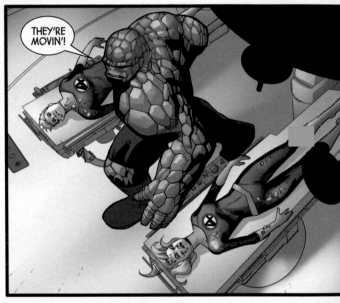

THEY'RE MOVIN'!

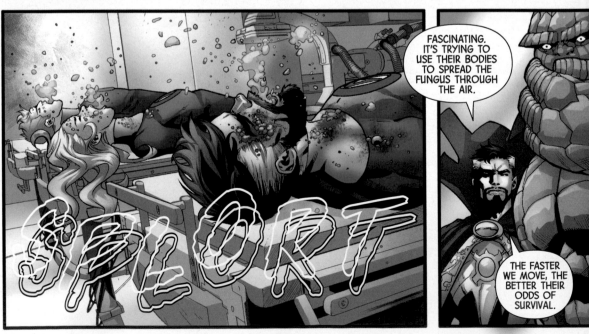

SPLORT

FASCINATING. IT'S TRYING TO USE THEIR BODIES TO SPREAD THE FUNGUS THROUGH THE AIR.

THE FASTER WE MOVE, THE BETTER THEIR ODDS OF SURVIVAL.

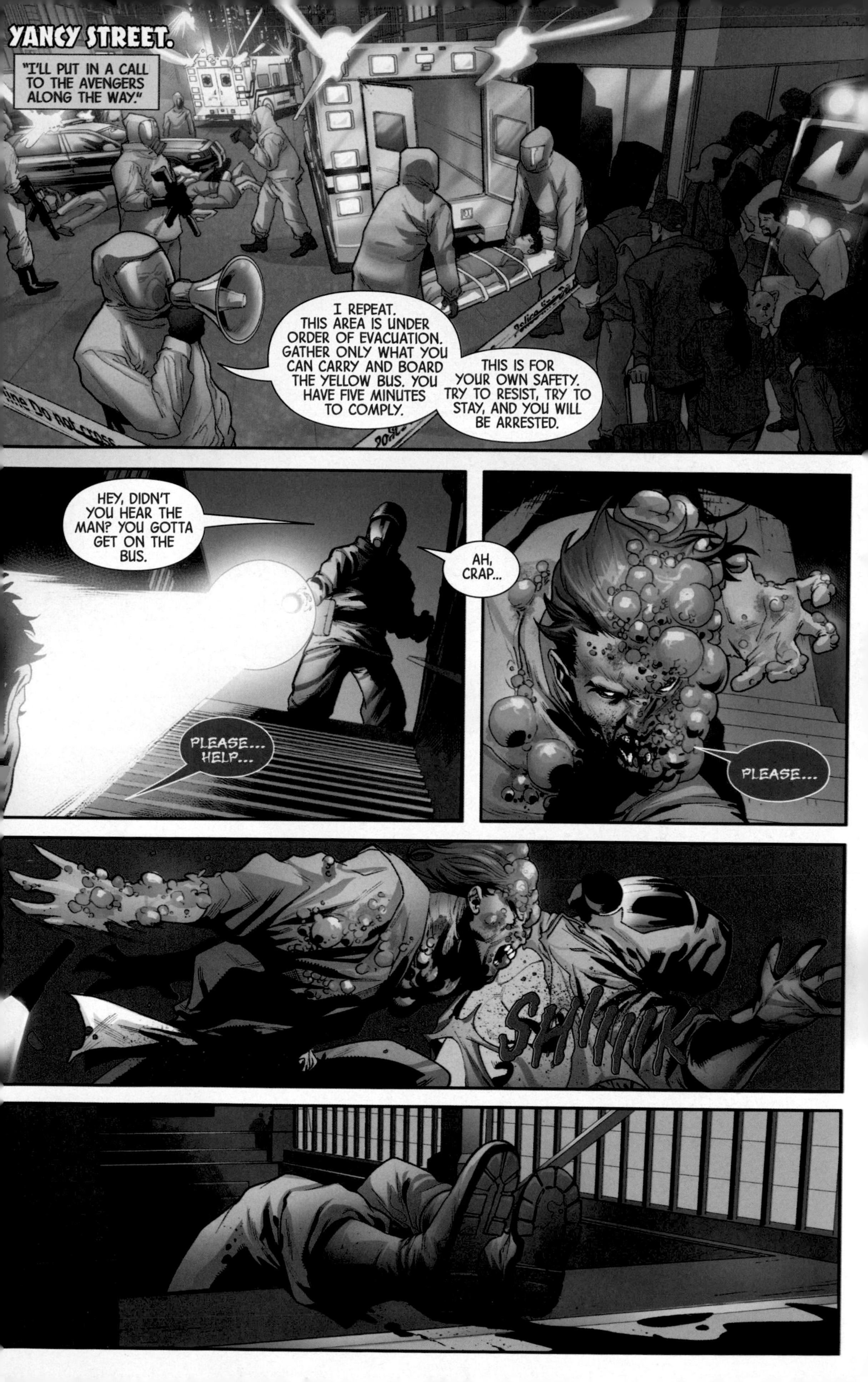
YANCY STREET.
"I'LL PUT IN A CALL TO THE AVENGERS ALONG THE WAY."
I REPEAT. THIS AREA IS UNDER ORDER OF EVACUATION. GATHER ONLY WHAT YOU CAN CARRY AND BOARD THE YELLOW BUS. YOU HAVE FIVE MINUTES TO COMPLY.
THIS IS FOR YOUR OWN SAFETY. TRY TO RESIST, TRY TO STAY, AND YOU WILL BE ARRESTED.
HEY, DIDN'T YOU HEAR THE MAN? YOU GOTTA GET ON THE BUS.
AH, CRAP...
PLEASE... HELP...
PLEASE...
SHIIIK

AAAAAAAAAAAAAAAAAAAAHH!!!!!

DID YOU HEAR THAT?

I GOT EARS, DON'T I?

IT IS THE URCHIN.

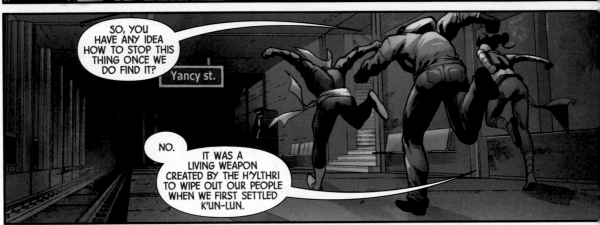

SO, YOU HAVE ANY IDEA HOW TO STOP THIS THING ONCE WE DO FIND IT?

Yancy st.

NO.

IT WAS A LIVING WEAPON CREATED BY THE H'YLTHRI TO WIPE OUT OUR PEOPLE WHEN WE FIRST SETTLED K'UN-LUN.

Yancy st.

BUT IT TURNED ON THEM, NEARLY WIPING OUT *THEIR* POPULATION.

THEY WERE ONLY ABLE TO STOP IT BY CONTAINING IT. ENTOMBING IT.

SWEET CHRISTMAS.

WE NEED TO DO THE SAME.

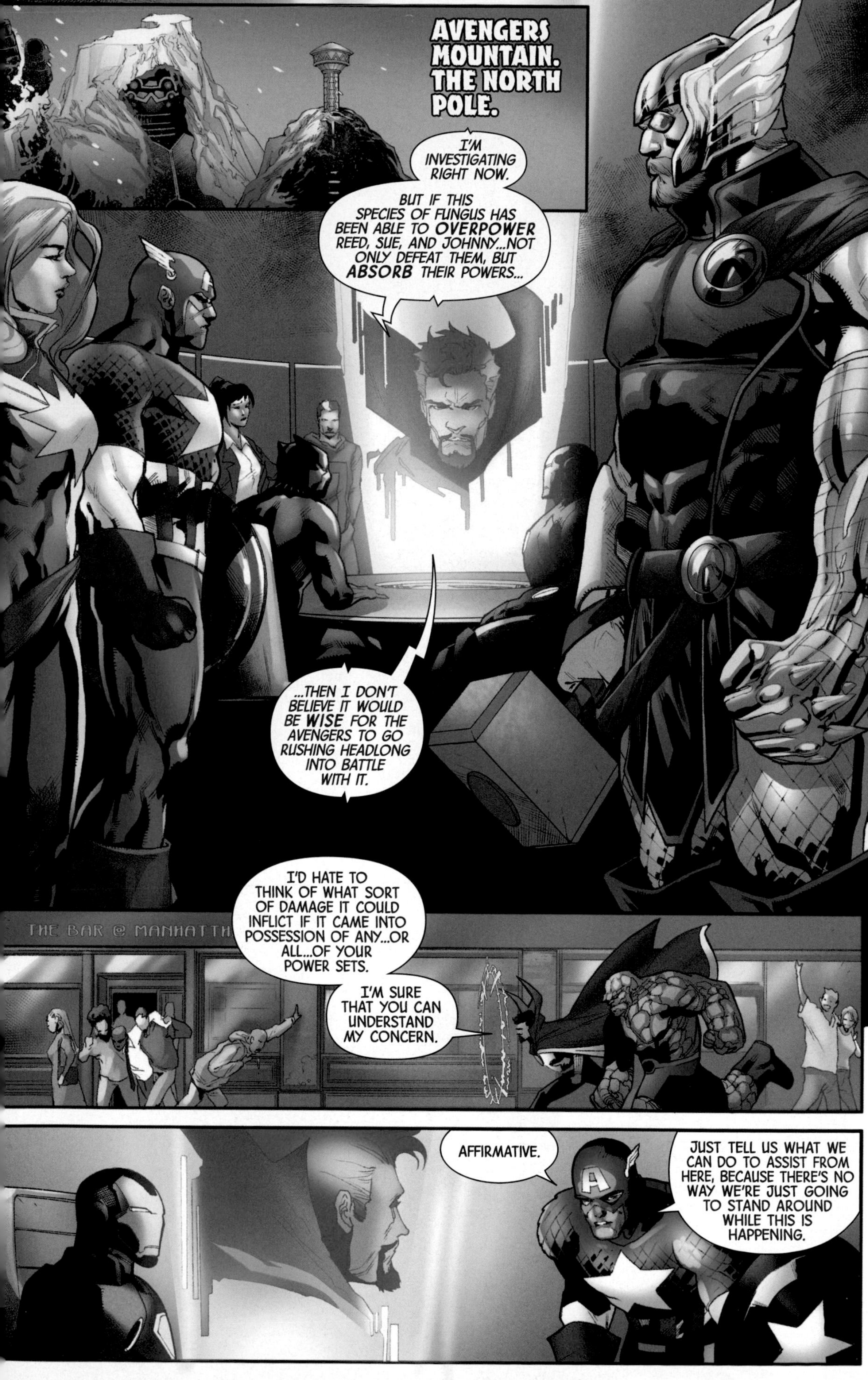
AVENGERS MOUNTAIN. THE NORTH POLE.
I'M INVESTIGATING RIGHT NOW.
BUT IF THIS SPECIES OF FUNGUS HAS BEEN ABLE TO OVERPOWER REED, SUE, AND JOHNNY...NOT ONLY DEFEAT THEM, BUT ABSORB THEIR POWERS...
...THEN I DON'T BELIEVE IT WOULD BE WISE FOR THE AVENGERS TO GO RUSHING HEADLONG INTO BATTLE WITH IT.
I'D HATE TO THINK OF WHAT SORT OF DAMAGE IT COULD INFLICT IF IT CAME INTO POSSESSION OF ANY...OR ALL...OF YOUR POWER SETS.
THE BAR @ MANHATTA
I'M SURE THAT YOU CAN UNDERSTAND MY CONCERN.
AFFIRMATIVE.
JUST TELL US WHAT WE CAN DO TO ASSIST FROM HERE, BECAUSE THERE'S NO WAY WE'RE JUST GOING TO STAND AROUND WHILE THIS IS HAPPENING.

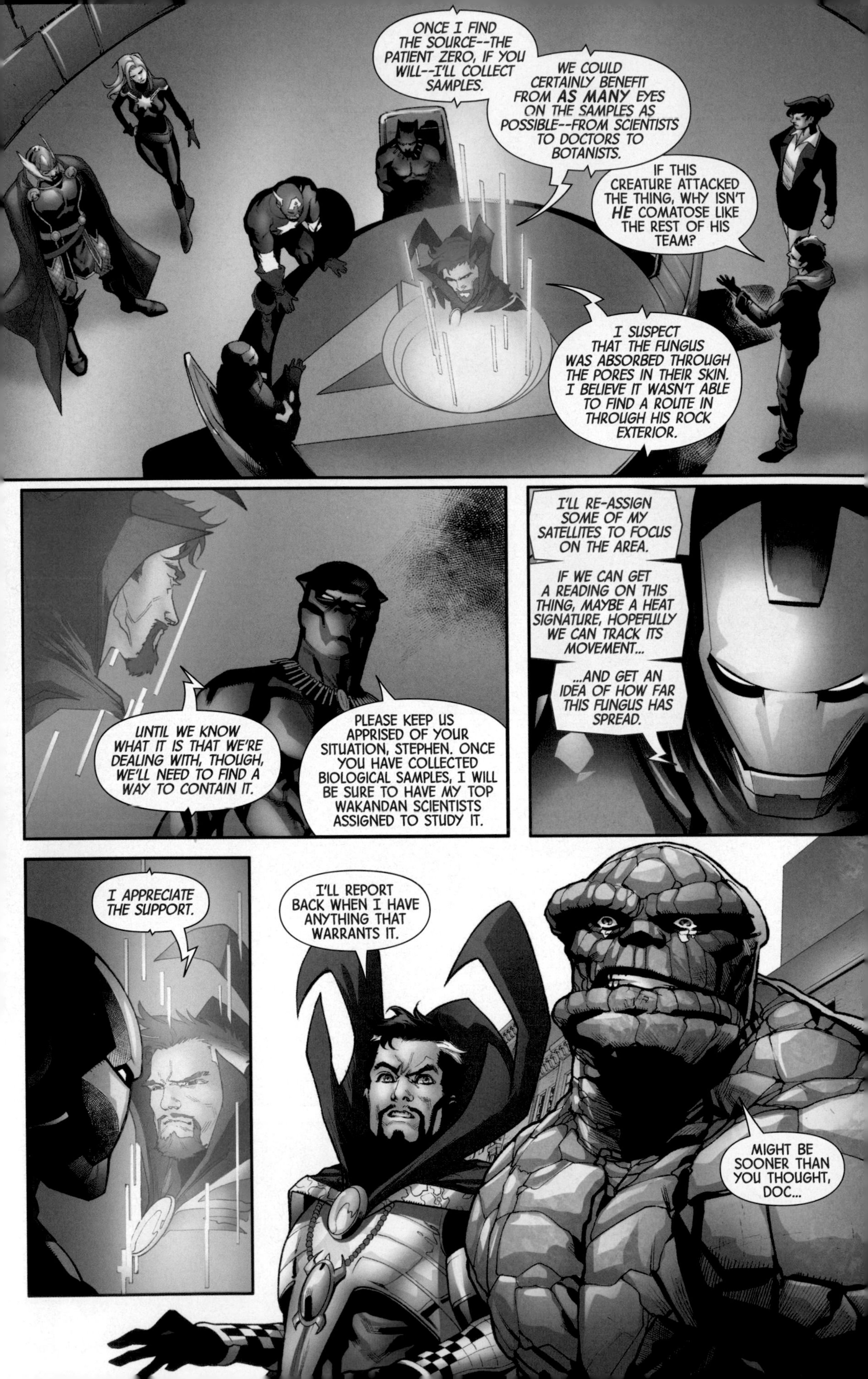
ONCE I FIND THE SOURCE--THE PATIENT ZERO, IF YOU WILL--I'LL COLLECT SAMPLES.
WE COULD CERTAINLY BENEFIT FROM AS MANY EYES ON THE SAMPLES AS POSSIBLE--FROM SCIENTISTS TO DOCTORS TO BOTANISTS.
IF THIS CREATURE ATTACKED THE THING, WHY ISN'T HE COMATOSE LIKE THE REST OF HIS TEAM?
I SUSPECT THAT THE FUNGUS WAS ABSORBED THROUGH THE PORES IN THEIR SKIN. I BELIEVE IT WASN'T ABLE TO FIND A ROUTE IN THROUGH HIS ROCK EXTERIOR.
UNTIL WE KNOW WHAT IT IS THAT WE'RE DEALING WITH, THOUGH, WE'LL NEED TO FIND A WAY TO CONTAIN IT.
PLEASE KEEP US APPRISED OF YOUR SITUATION, STEPHEN. ONCE YOU HAVE COLLECTED BIOLOGICAL SAMPLES, I WILL BE SURE TO HAVE MY TOP WAKANDAN SCIENTISTS ASSIGNED TO STUDY IT.
I'LL RE-ASSIGN SOME OF MY SATELLITES TO FOCUS ON THE AREA.
IF WE CAN GET A READING ON THIS THING, MAYBE A HEAT SIGNATURE, HOPEFULLY WE CAN TRACK ITS MOVEMENT...
...AND GET AN IDEA OF HOW FAR THIS FUNGUS HAS SPREAD.
I APPRECIATE THE SUPPORT.
I'LL REPORT BACK WHEN I HAVE ANYTHING THAT WARRANTS IT.
MIGHT BE SOONER THAN YOU THOUGHT, DOC...

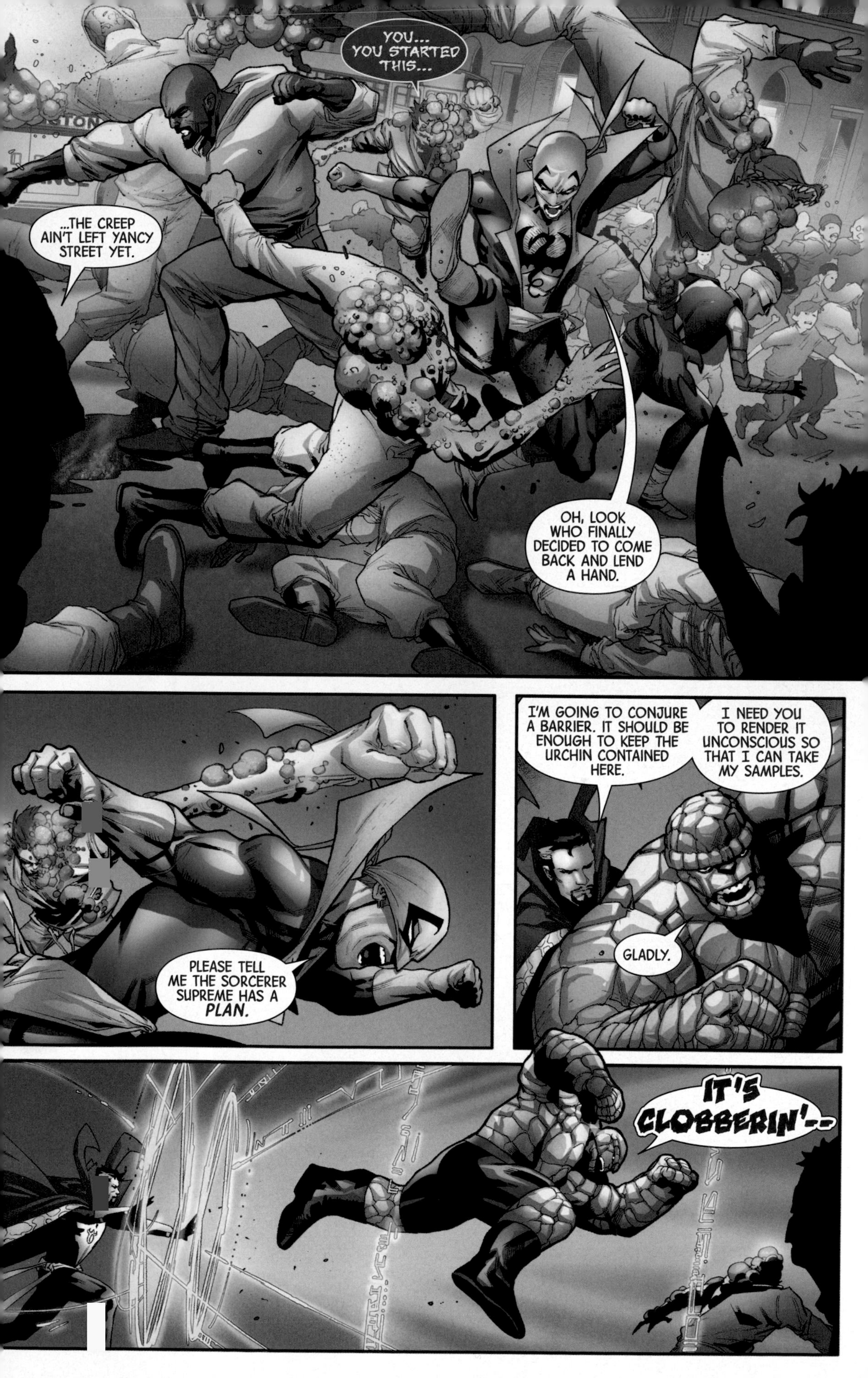
YOU... YOU STARTED THIS...
...THE CREEP AIN'T LEFT YANCY STREET YET.
OH, LOOK WHO FINALLY DECIDED TO COME BACK AND LEND A HAND.
PLEASE TELL ME THE SORCERER SUPREME HAS A *PLAN.*
I'M GOING TO CONJURE A BARRIER. IT SHOULD BE ENOUGH TO KEEP THE URCHIN CONTAINED HERE.
I NEED YOU TO RENDER IT UNCONSCIOUS SO THAT I CAN TAKE MY SAMPLES.
GLADLY.
IT'S CLOBBERIN'--

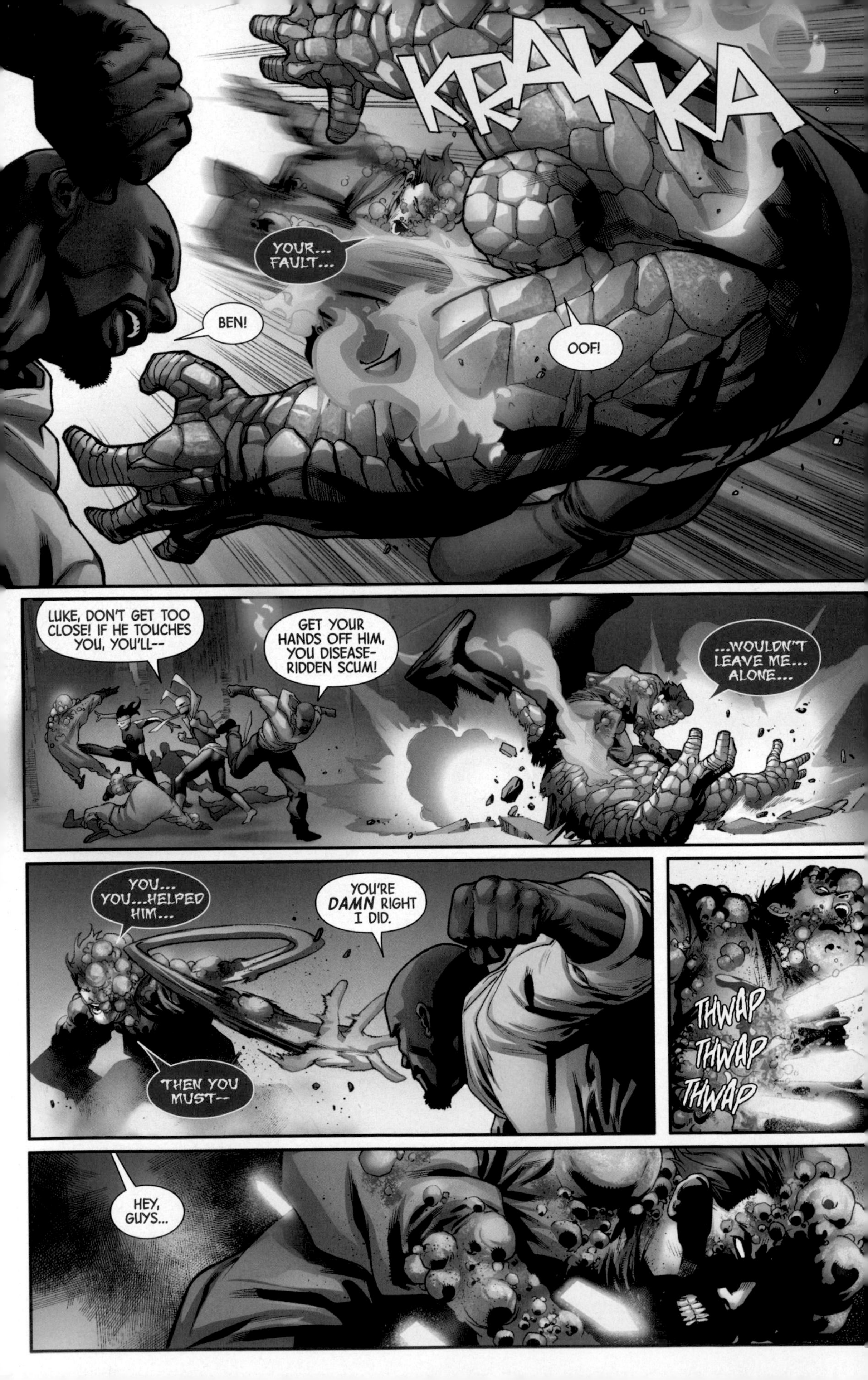
KRAKKA
YOUR... FAULT...
BEN!
OOF!
LUKE, DON'T GET TOO CLOSE! IF HE TOUCHES YOU, YOU'LL--
GET YOUR HANDS OFF HIM, YOU DISEASE-RIDDEN SCUM!
...WOULDN'T LEAVE ME... ALONE...
YOU... YOU...HELPED HIM...
YOU'RE DAMN RIGHT I DID.
THEN YOU MUST--
THWAP
THWAP
THWAP
HEY, GUYS...

...LOOKS LIKE YOU COULD USE A LITTLE HELP.
CLOAK AND DAGGER?
NONE OTHER.

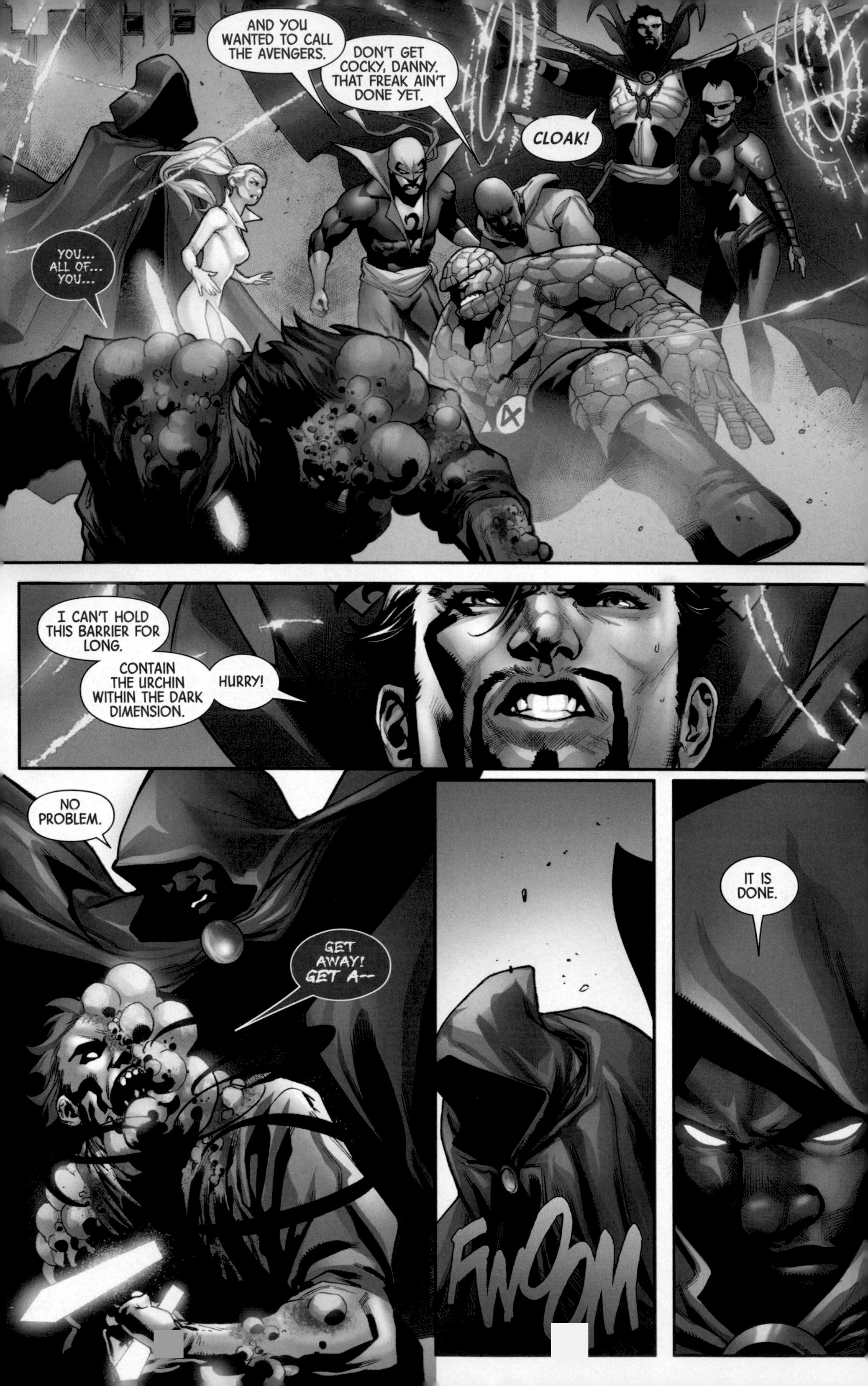

AND YOU WANTED TO CALL THE AVENGERS.
DON'T GET COCKY, DANNY. THAT FREAK AIN'T DONE YET.
CLOAK!
YOU... ALL OF... YOU...
I CAN'T HOLD THIS BARRIER FOR LONG.
CONTAIN THE URCHIN WITHIN THE DARK DIMENSION.
HURRY!
NO PROBLEM.
GET AWAY! GET A--
FWOOM
IT IS DONE.

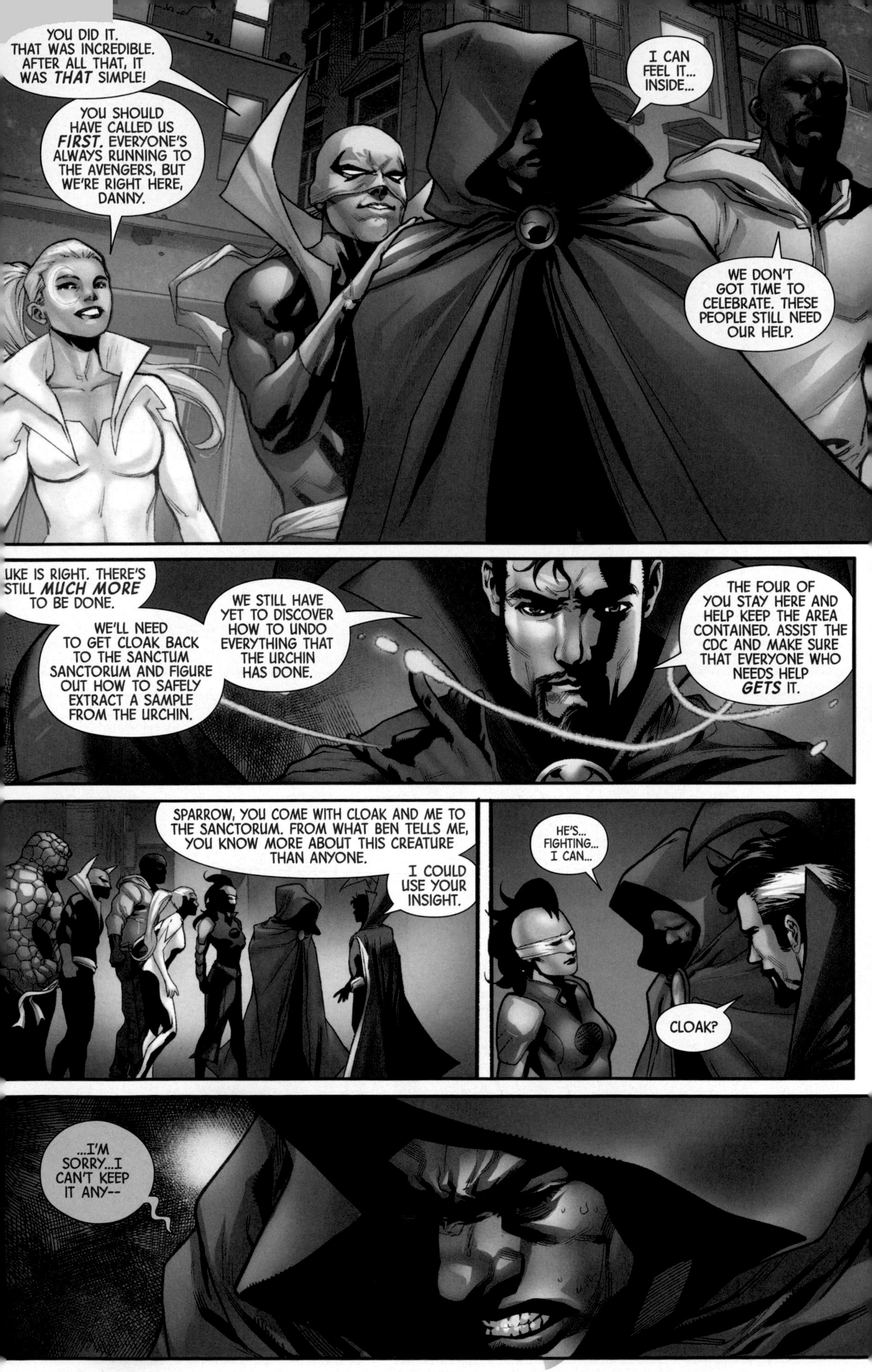
YOU DID IT. THAT WAS INCREDIBLE. AFTER ALL THAT, IT WAS THAT SIMPLE!
YOU SHOULD HAVE CALLED US FIRST. EVERYONE'S ALWAYS RUNNING TO THE AVENGERS, BUT WE'RE RIGHT HERE, DANNY.
I CAN FEEL IT... INSIDE...
WE DON'T GOT TIME TO CELEBRATE. THESE PEOPLE STILL NEED OUR HELP.
LUKE IS RIGHT. THERE'S STILL MUCH MORE TO BE DONE.
WE'LL NEED TO GET CLOAK BACK TO THE SANCTUM SANCTORUM AND FIGURE OUT HOW TO SAFELY EXTRACT A SAMPLE FROM THE URCHIN.
WE STILL HAVE YET TO DISCOVER HOW TO UNDO EVERYTHING THAT THE URCHIN HAS DONE.
THE FOUR OF YOU STAY HERE AND HELP KEEP THE AREA CONTAINED. ASSIST THE CDC AND MAKE SURE THAT EVERYONE WHO NEEDS HELP GETS IT.
SPARROW, YOU COME WITH CLOAK AND ME TO THE SANCTORUM. FROM WHAT BEN TELLS ME, YOU KNOW MORE ABOUT THIS CREATURE THAN ANYONE.
I COULD USE YOUR INSIGHT.
HE'S... FIGHTING... I CAN...
CLOAK?
...I'M SORRY...I CAN'T KEEP IT ANY--

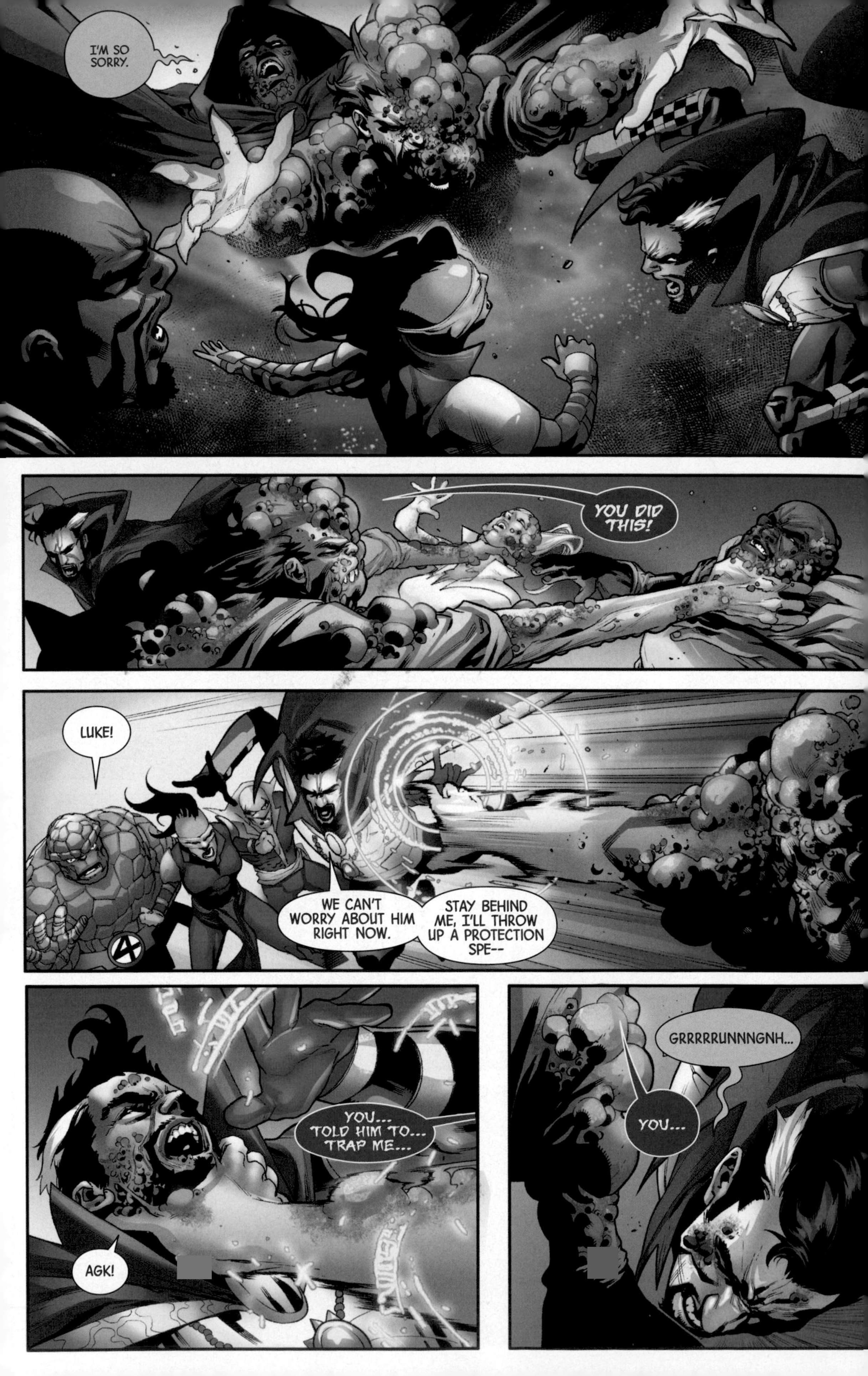
I'M SO SORRY.
YOU DID THIS!
LUKE!
WE CAN'T WORRY ABOUT HIM RIGHT NOW.
STAY BEHIND ME, I'LL THROW UP A PROTECTION SPE--
YOU... TOLD HIM TO... TRAP ME...
AGK!
GRRRRRUNNNGNH...
YOU...

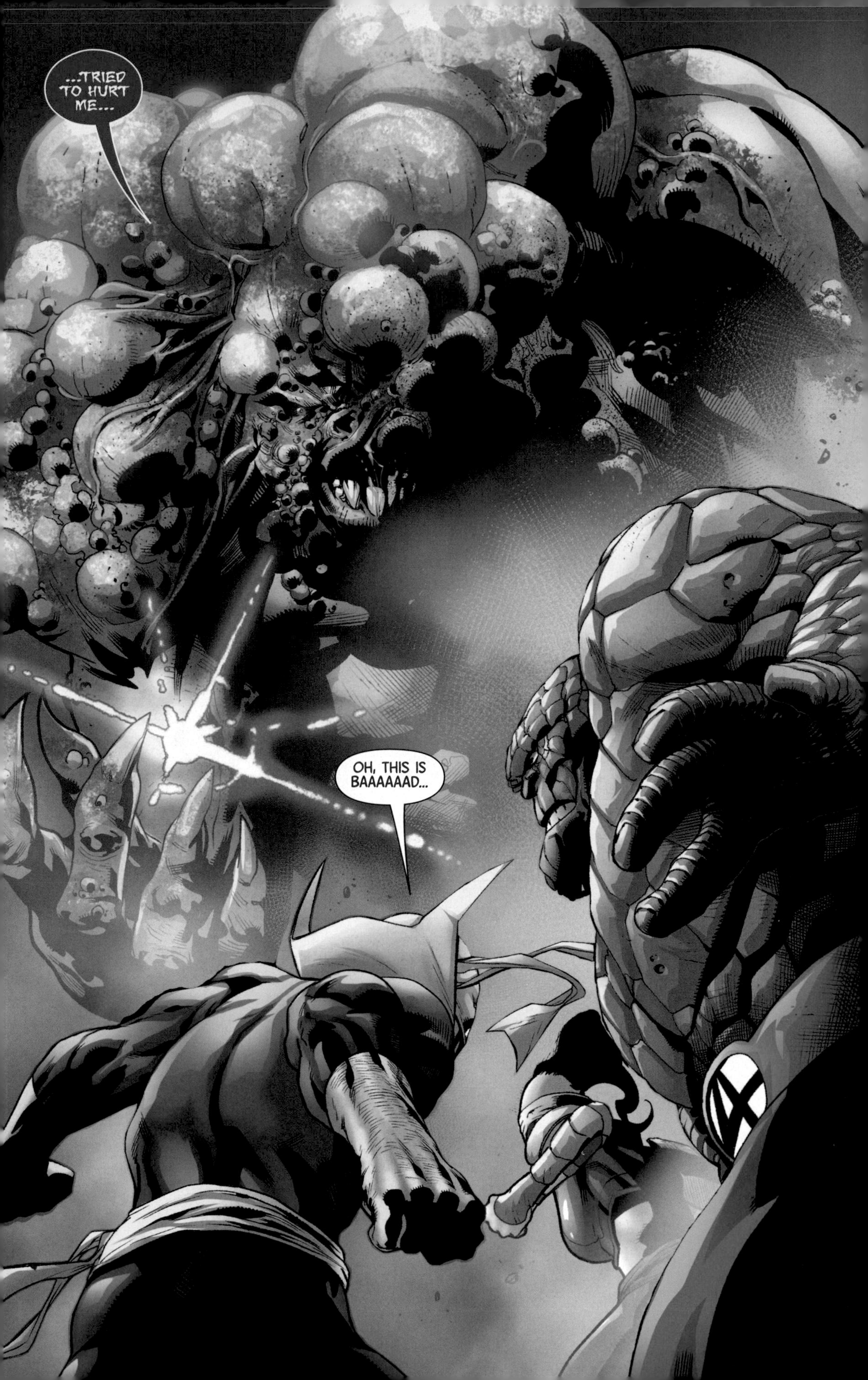
...TRIED TO HURT ME...
OH, THIS IS BAAAAAAD...

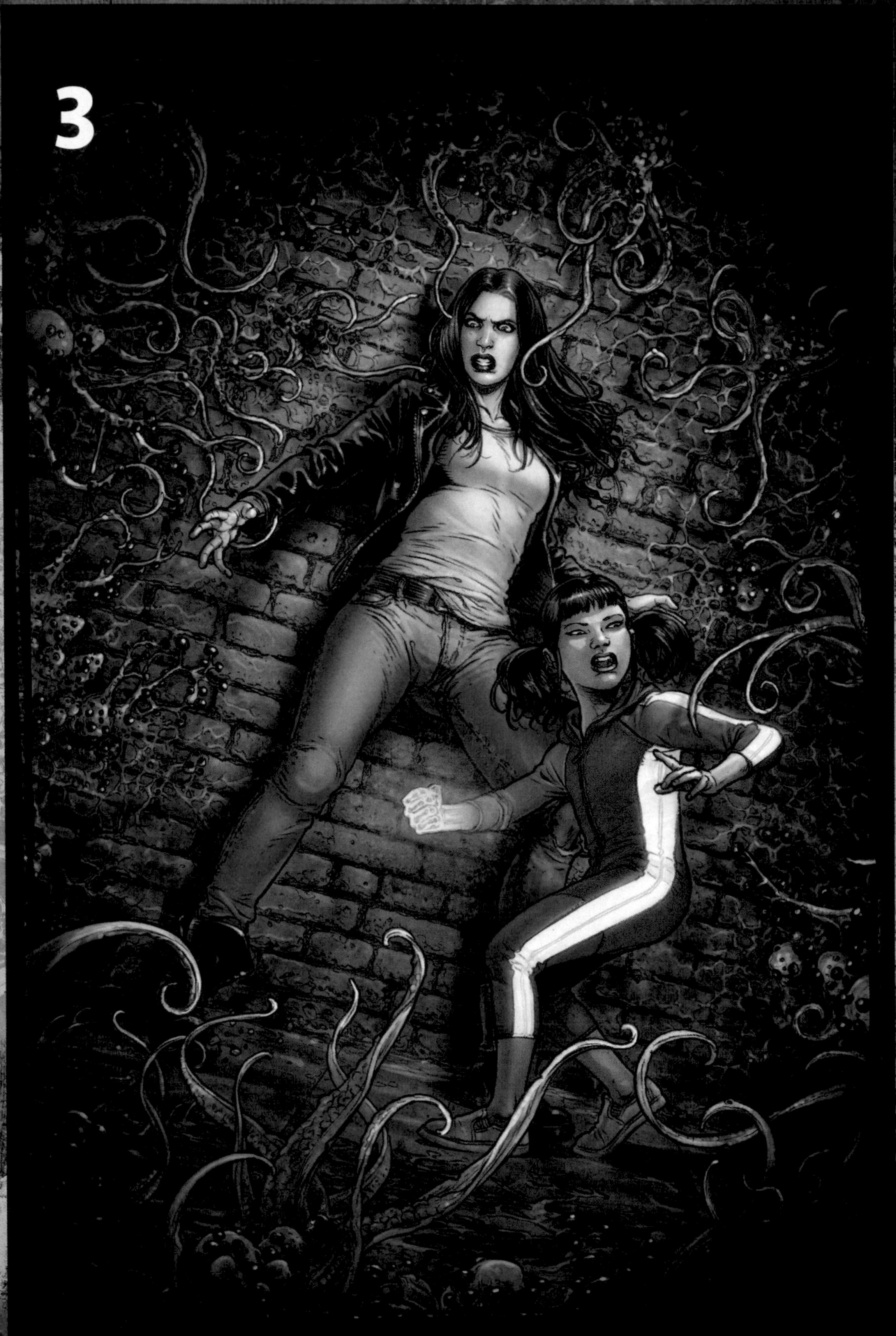
3

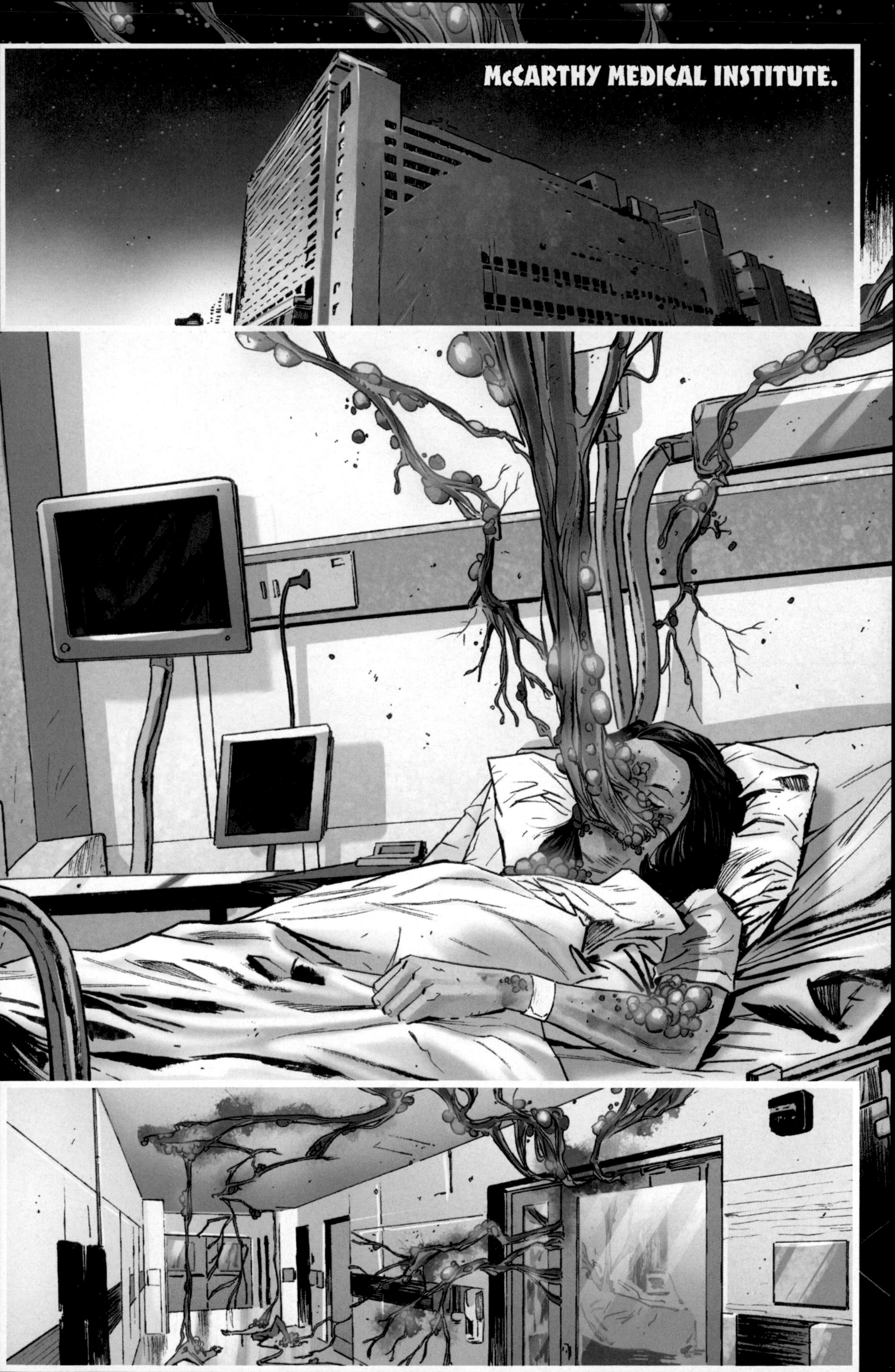
McCARTHY MEDICAL INSTITUTE.

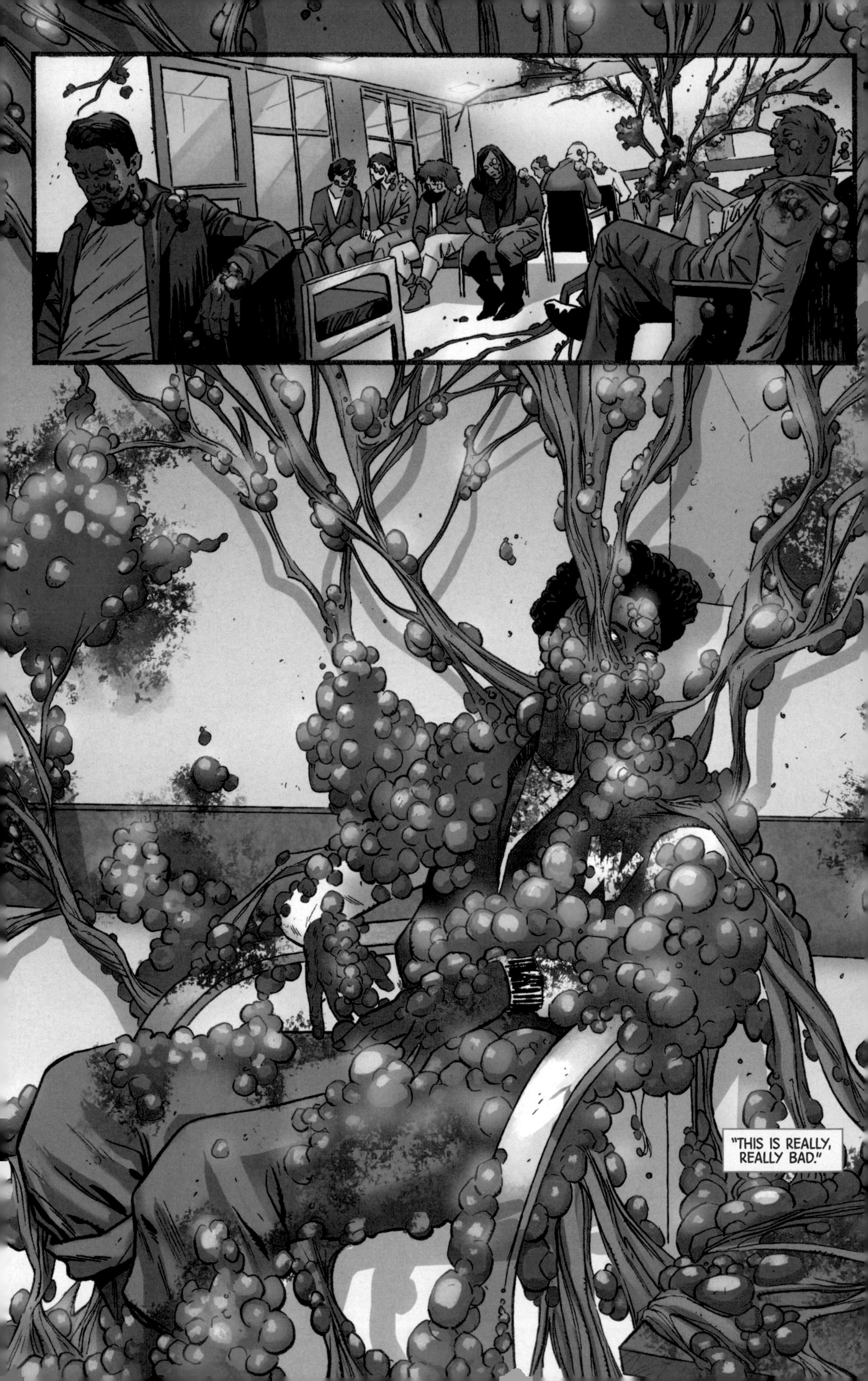
"THIS IS REALLY, REALLY BAD."

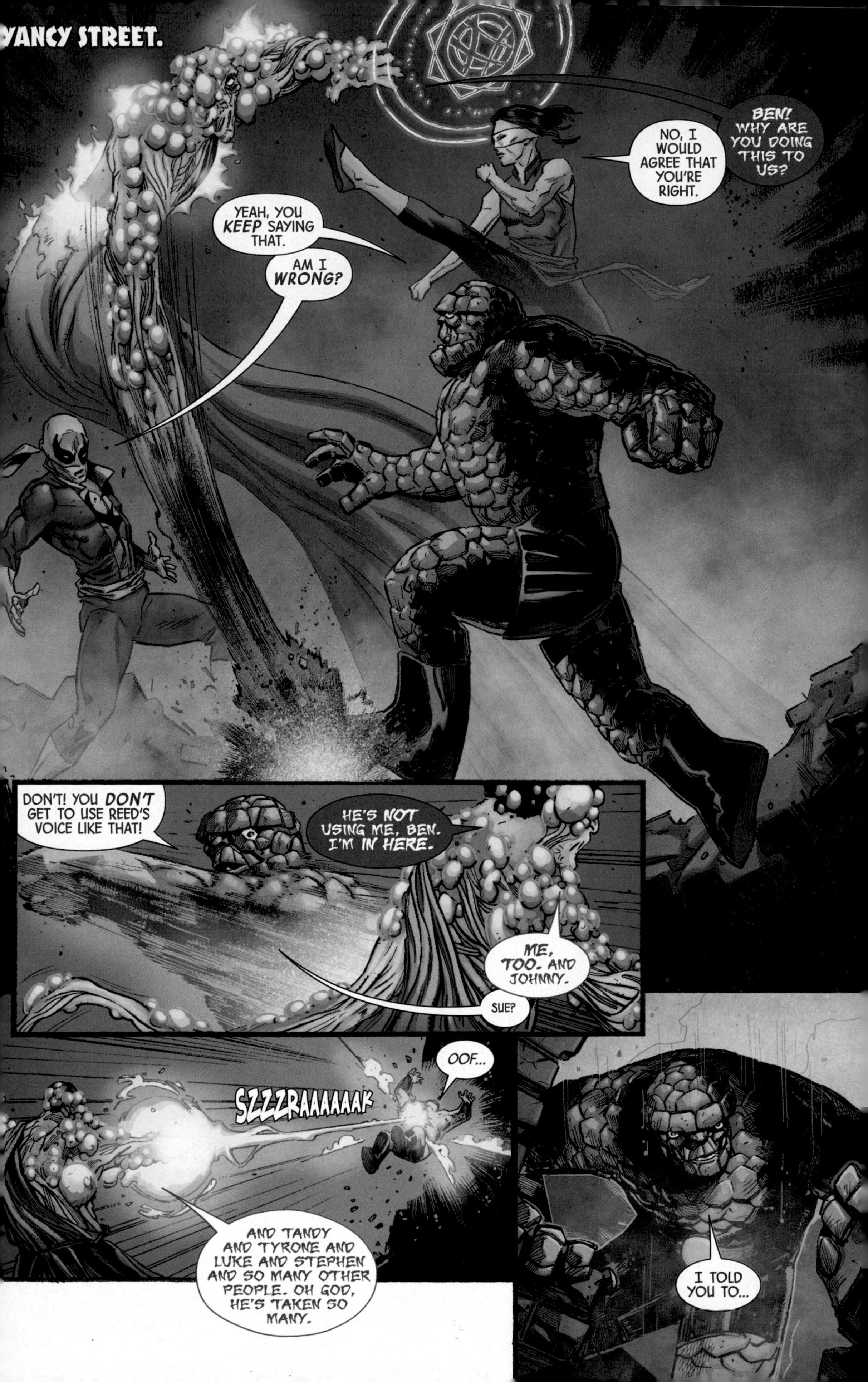
YANCY STREET.
BEN! WHY ARE YOU DOING THIS TO US?
NO, I WOULD AGREE THAT YOU'RE RIGHT.
YEAH, YOU KEEP SAYING THAT.
AM I WRONG?
DON'T! YOU DON'T GET TO USE REED'S VOICE LIKE THAT!
HE'S NOT USING ME, BEN. I'M IN HERE.
SUE?
ME, TOO. AND JOHNNY.
OOF...
SZZZRAAAAAAK
AND TANDY AND TYRONE AND LUKE AND STEPHEN AND SO MANY OTHER PEOPLE. OH GOD, HE'S TAKEN SO MANY.
I TOLD YOU TO...

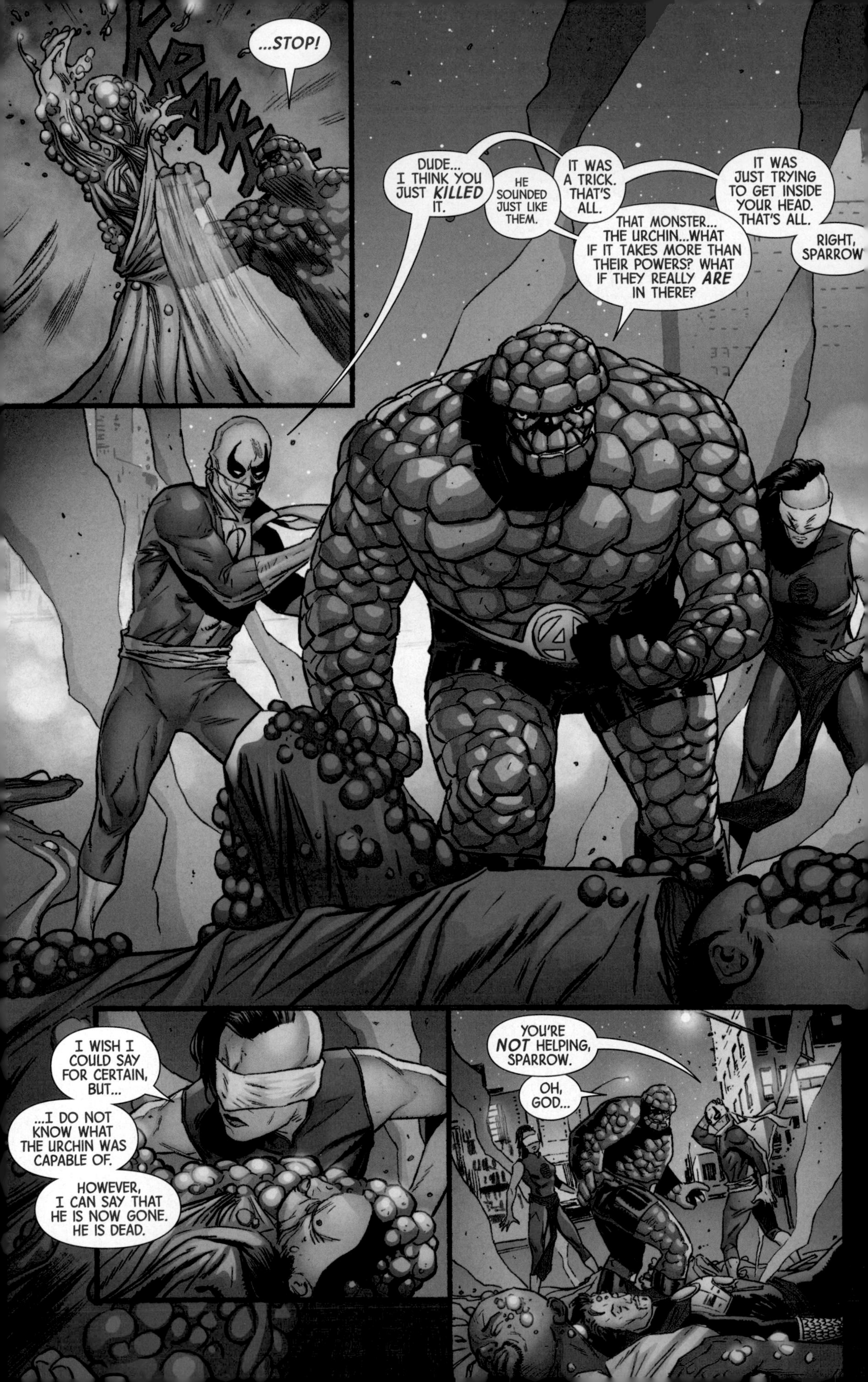
KRAKK!
...STOP!
DUDE... I THINK YOU JUST KILLED IT.
HE SOUNDED JUST LIKE THEM.
IT WAS A TRICK. THAT'S ALL.
IT WAS JUST TRYING TO GET INSIDE YOUR HEAD. THAT'S ALL.
RIGHT, SPARROW
THAT MONSTER... THE URCHIN...WHAT IF IT TAKES MORE THAN THEIR POWERS? WHAT IF THEY REALLY ARE IN THERE?
I WISH I COULD SAY FOR CERTAIN, BUT...
...I DO NOT KNOW WHAT THE URCHIN WAS CAPABLE OF.
HOWEVER, I CAN SAY THAT HE IS NOW GONE. HE IS DEAD.
YOU'RE NOT HELPING, SPARROW.
OH, GOD...

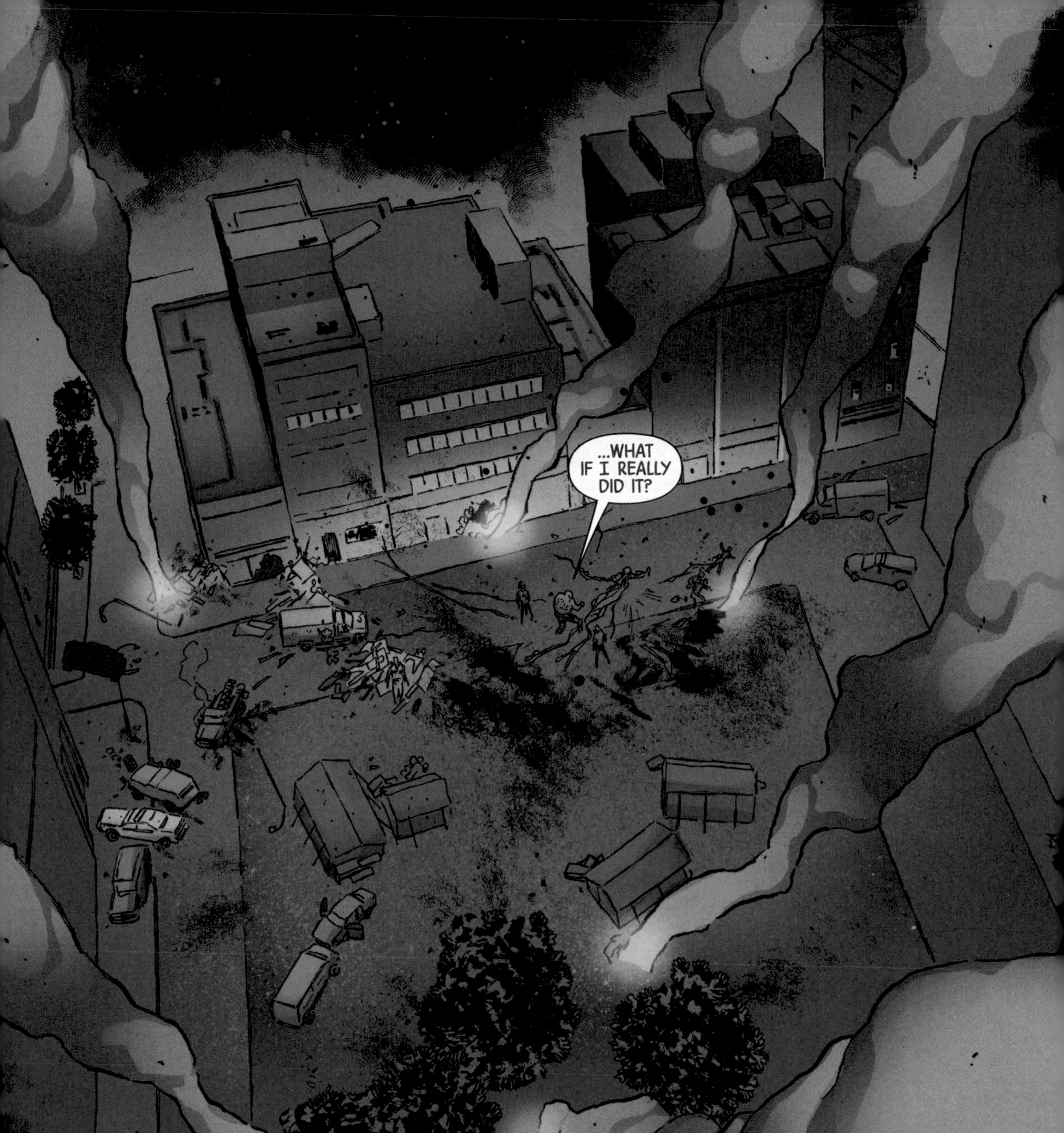
...WHAT IF I REALLY DID IT?

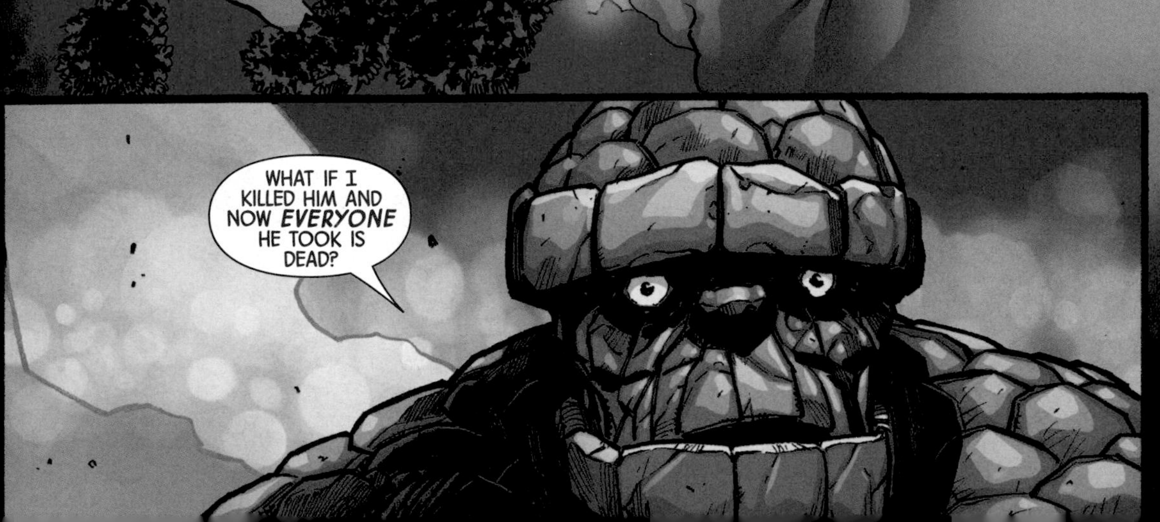
WHAT IF I KILLED HIM AND NOW *EVERYONE* HE TOOK IS DEAD?

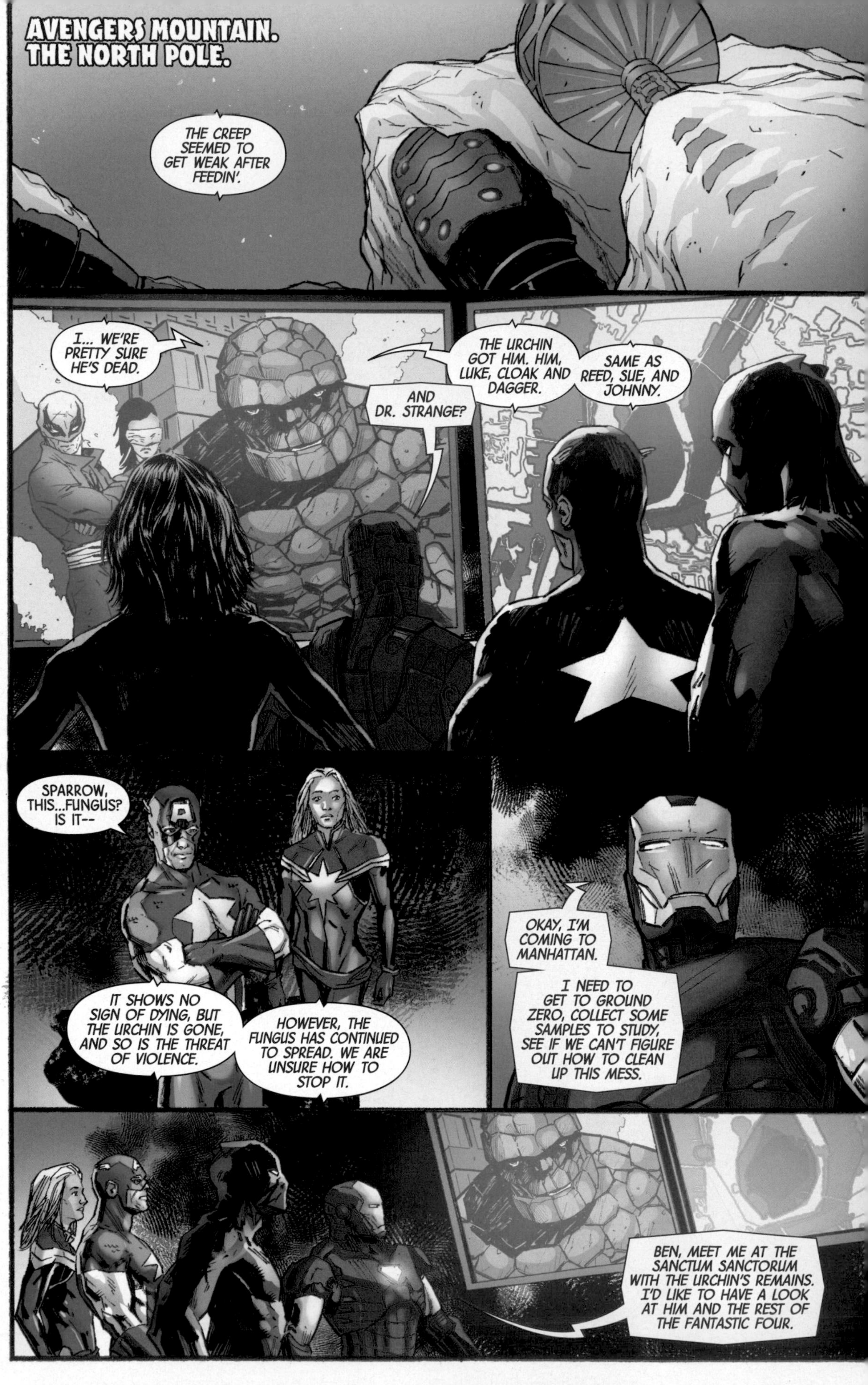
AVENGERS MOUNTAIN. THE NORTH POLE.
THE CREEP SEEMED TO GET WEAK AFTER FEEDIN'.
I... WE'RE PRETTY SURE HE'S DEAD.
AND DR. STRANGE?
THE URCHIN GOT HIM. HIM, LUKE, CLOAK AND DAGGER.
SAME AS REED, SUE, AND JOHNNY.
SPARROW, THIS...FUNGUS? IS IT--
IT SHOWS NO SIGN OF DYING, BUT THE URCHIN IS GONE, AND SO IS THE THREAT OF VIOLENCE.
HOWEVER, THE FUNGUS HAS CONTINUED TO SPREAD. WE ARE UNSURE HOW TO STOP IT.
OKAY, I'M COMING TO MANHATTAN.
I NEED TO GET TO GROUND ZERO, COLLECT SOME SAMPLES TO STUDY, SEE IF WE CAN'T FIGURE OUT HOW TO CLEAN UP THIS MESS.
BEN, MEET ME AT THE SANCTUM SANCTORUM WITH THE URCHIN'S REMAINS. I'D LIKE TO HAVE A LOOK AT HIM AND THE REST OF THE FANTASTIC FOUR.

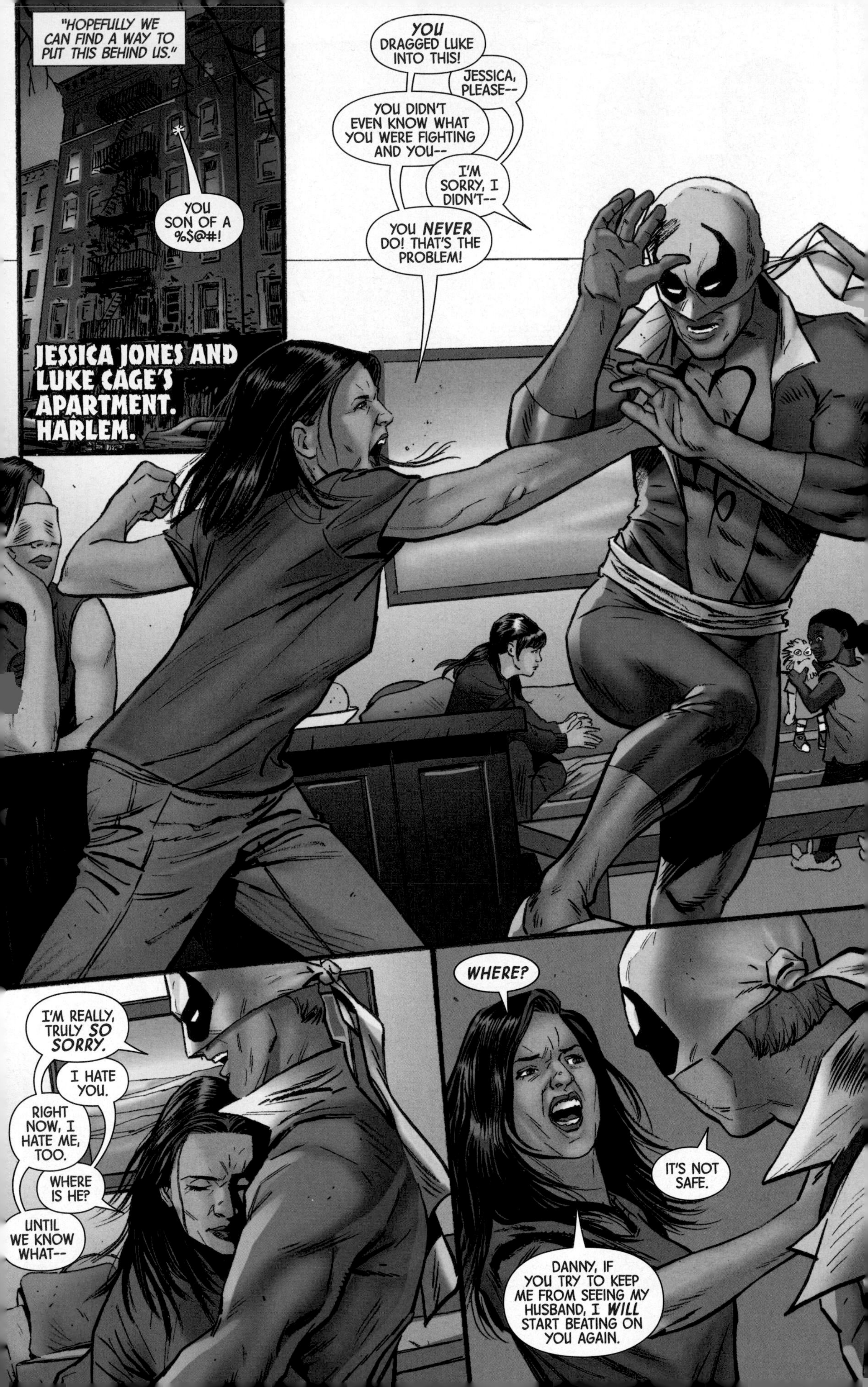
"HOPEFULLY WE CAN FIND A WAY TO PUT THIS BEHIND US."
YOU SON OF A %$@#!
JESSICA JONES AND LUKE CAGE'S APARTMENT. HARLEM.
YOU DRAGGED LUKE INTO THIS!
JESSICA, PLEASE--
YOU DIDN'T EVEN KNOW WHAT YOU WERE FIGHTING AND YOU--
I'M SORRY, I DIDN'T--
YOU NEVER DO! THAT'S THE PROBLEM!
I'M REALLY, TRULY SO SORRY.
I HATE YOU.
RIGHT NOW, I HATE ME, TOO.
WHERE IS HE?
UNTIL WE KNOW WHAT--
WHERE?
IT'S NOT SAFE.
DANNY, IF YOU TRY TO KEEP ME FROM SEEING MY HUSBAND, I WILL START BEATING ON YOU AGAIN.

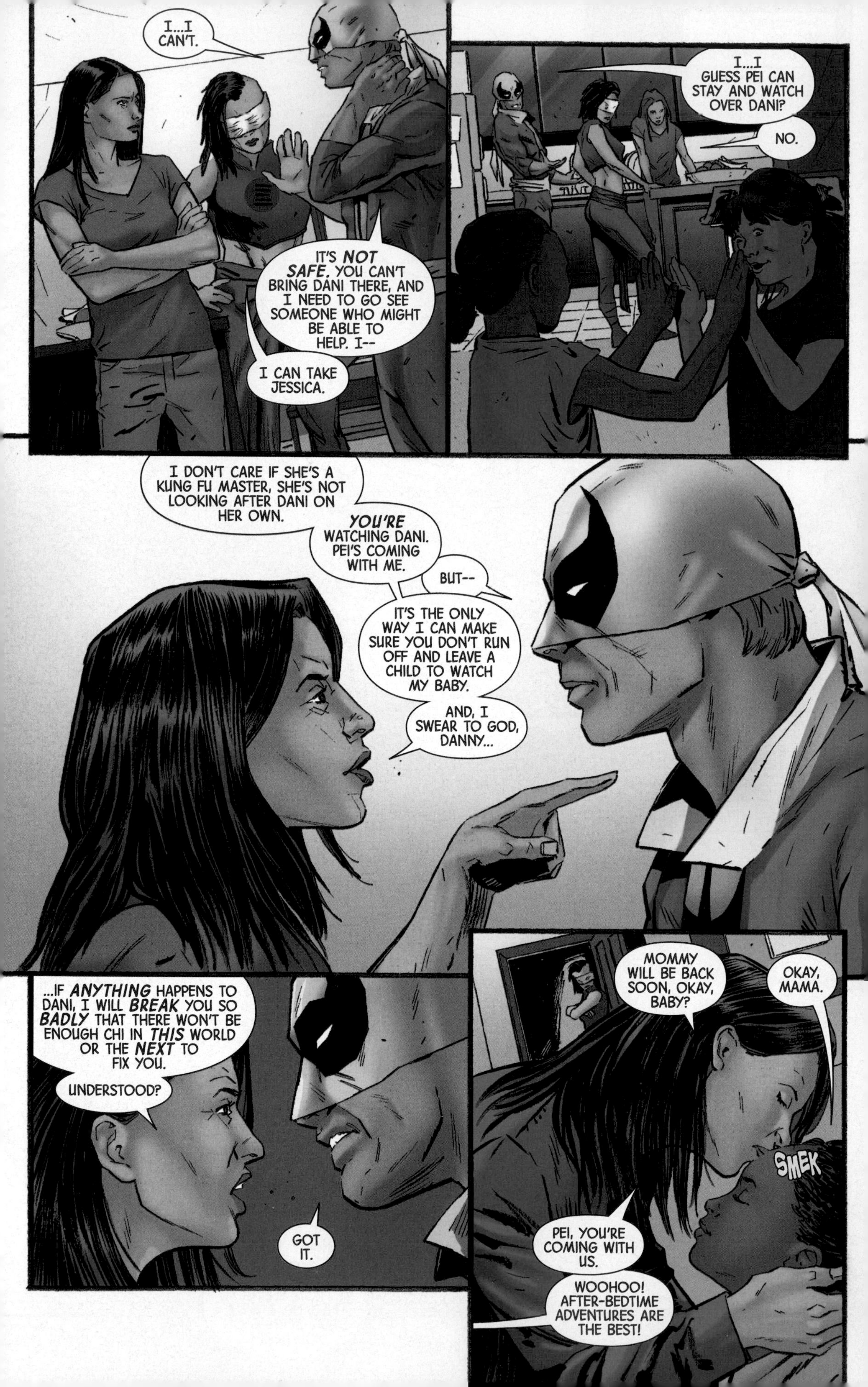
I...I CAN'T.
IT'S NOT SAFE. YOU CAN'T BRING DANI THERE, AND I NEED TO GO SEE SOMEONE WHO MIGHT BE ABLE TO HELP. I--
I CAN TAKE JESSICA.
I...I GUESS PEI CAN STAY AND WATCH OVER DANI?
NO.
I DON'T CARE IF SHE'S A KUNG FU MASTER, SHE'S NOT LOOKING AFTER DANI ON HER OWN.
YOU'RE WATCHING DANI. PEI'S COMING WITH ME.
BUT--
IT'S THE ONLY WAY I CAN MAKE SURE YOU DON'T RUN OFF AND LEAVE A CHILD TO WATCH MY BABY.
AND, I SWEAR TO GOD, DANNY...
...IF ANYTHING HAPPENS TO DANI, I WILL BREAK YOU SO BADLY THAT THERE WON'T BE ENOUGH CHI IN THIS WORLD OR THE NEXT TO FIX YOU.
UNDERSTOOD?
GOT IT.
MOMMY WILL BE BACK SOON, OKAY, BABY?
OKAY, MAMA.
SMEK
PEI, YOU'RE COMING WITH US.
WOOHOO! AFTER-BEDTIME ADVENTURES ARE THE BEST!

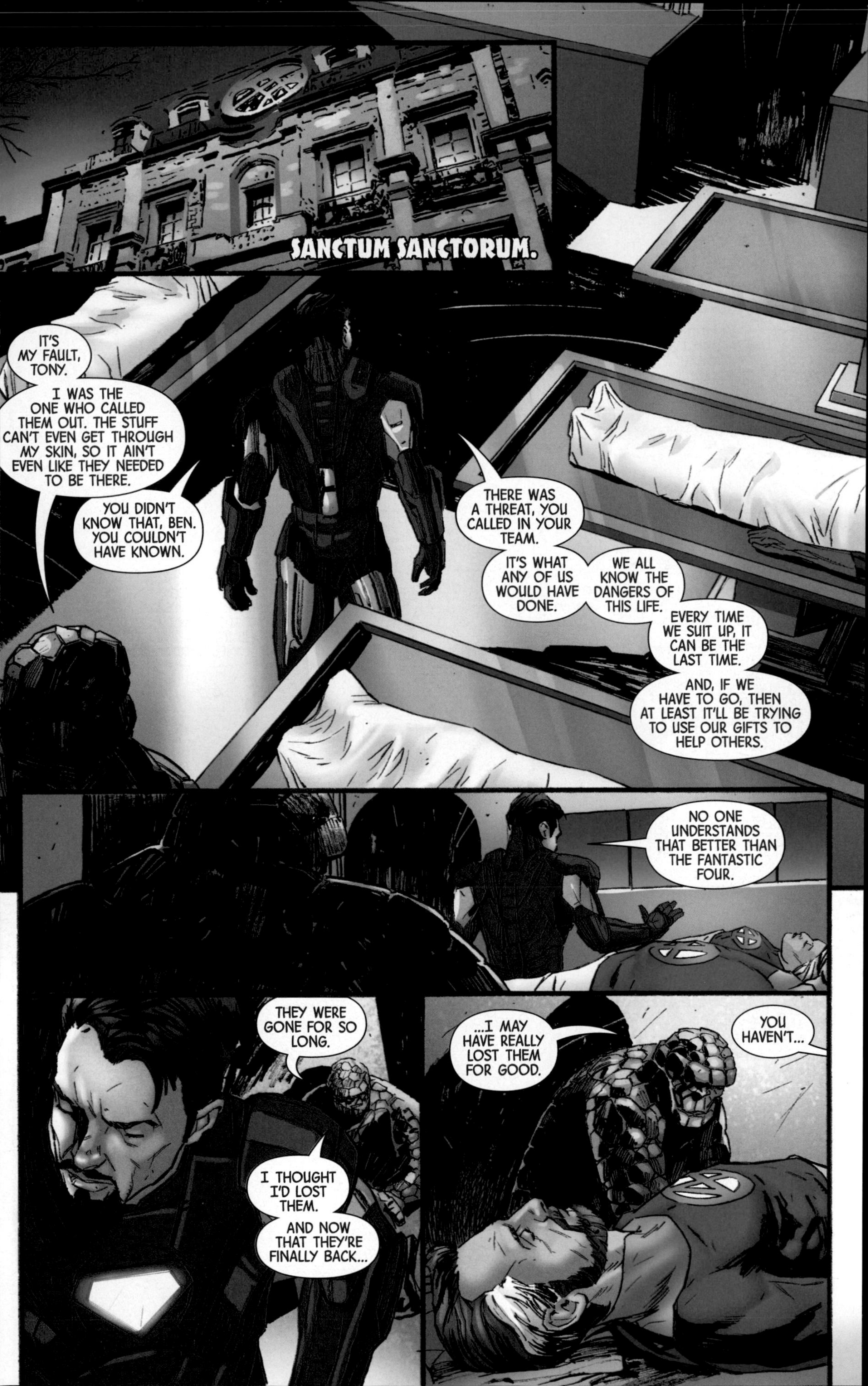
SANCTUM SANCTORUM.
IT'S MY FAULT, TONY.
I WAS THE ONE WHO CALLED THEM OUT. THE STUFF CAN'T EVEN GET THROUGH MY SKIN, SO IT AIN'T EVEN LIKE THEY NEEDED TO BE THERE.
YOU DIDN'T KNOW THAT, BEN. YOU COULDN'T HAVE KNOWN.
THERE WAS A THREAT, YOU CALLED IN YOUR TEAM.
IT'S WHAT ANY OF US WOULD HAVE DONE.
WE ALL KNOW THE DANGERS OF THIS LIFE.
EVERY TIME WE SUIT UP, IT CAN BE THE LAST TIME.
AND, IF WE HAVE TO GO, THEN AT LEAST IT'LL BE TRYING TO USE OUR GIFTS TO HELP OTHERS.
NO ONE UNDERSTANDS THAT BETTER THAN THE FANTASTIC FOUR.
THEY WERE GONE FOR SO LONG.
I THOUGHT I'D LOST THEM.
AND NOW THAT THEY'RE FINALLY BACK...
...I MAY HAVE REALLY LOST THEM FOR GOOD.
YOU HAVEN'T...

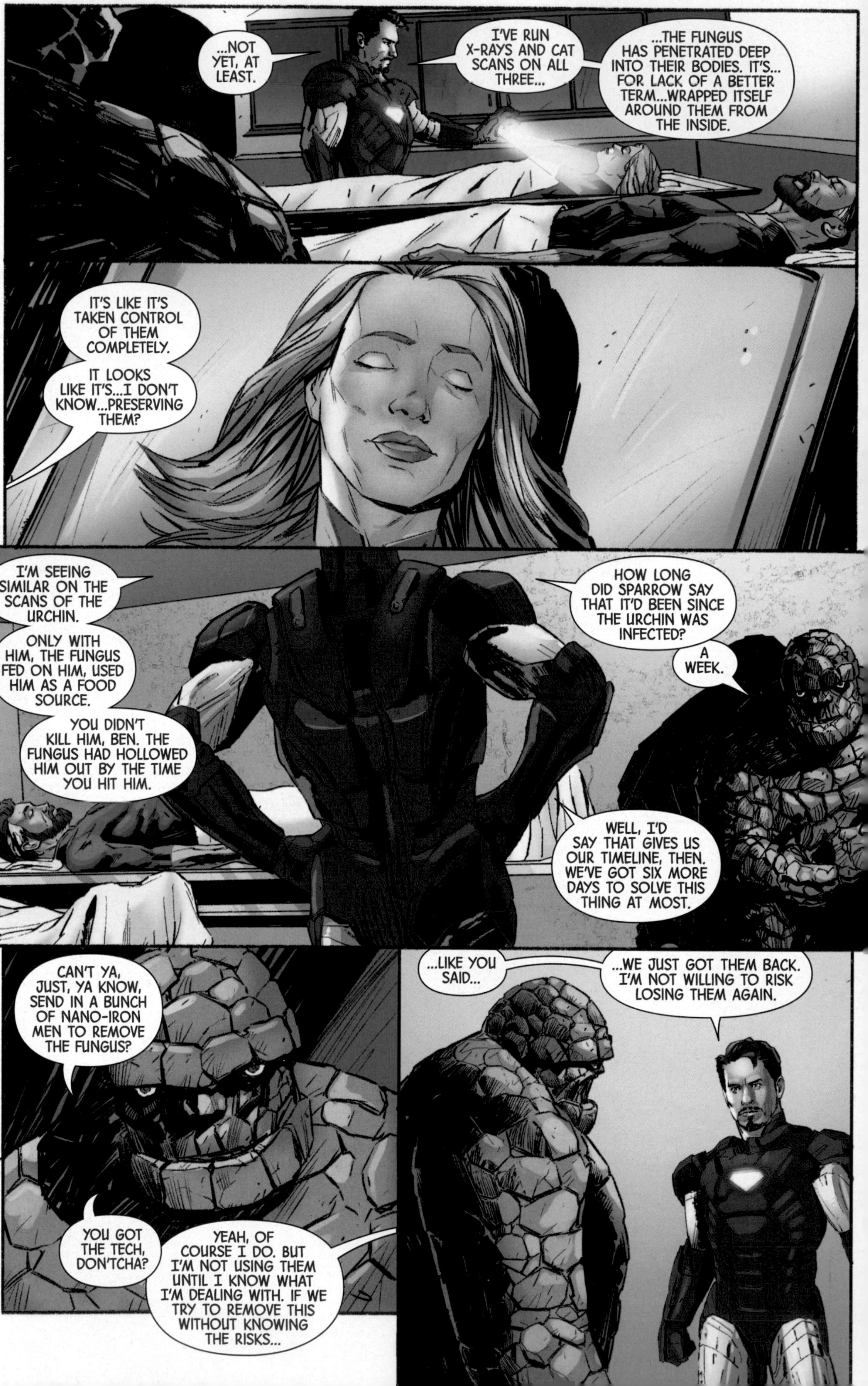
...NOT YET, AT LEAST.
I'VE RUN X-RAYS AND CAT SCANS ON ALL THREE...
...THE FUNGUS HAS PENETRATED DEEP INTO THEIR BODIES. IT'S... FOR LACK OF A BETTER TERM...WRAPPED ITSELF AROUND THEM FROM THE INSIDE.
IT'S LIKE IT'S TAKEN CONTROL OF THEM COMPLETELY.
IT LOOKS LIKE IT'S...I DON'T KNOW...PRESERVING THEM?
I'M SEEING SIMILAR ON THE SCANS OF THE URCHIN.
ONLY WITH HIM, THE FUNGUS FED ON HIM, USED HIM AS A FOOD SOURCE.
YOU DIDN'T KILL HIM, BEN. THE FUNGUS HAD HOLLOWED HIM OUT BY THE TIME YOU HIT HIM.
HOW LONG DID SPARROW SAY THAT IT'D BEEN SINCE THE URCHIN WAS INFECTED?
A WEEK.
WELL, I'D SAY THAT GIVES US OUR TIMELINE, THEN. WE'VE GOT SIX MORE DAYS TO SOLVE THIS THING AT MOST.
CAN'T YA, JUST, YA KNOW, SEND IN A BUNCH OF NANO-IRON MEN TO REMOVE THE FUNGUS?
YOU GOT THE TECH, DON'TCHA?
YEAH, OF COURSE I DO. BUT I'M NOT USING THEM UNTIL I KNOW WHAT I'M DEALING WITH. IF WE TRY TO REMOVE THIS WITHOUT KNOWING THE RISKS...
...LIKE YOU SAID...
...WE JUST GOT THEM BACK. I'M NOT WILLING TO RISK LOSING THEM AGAIN.

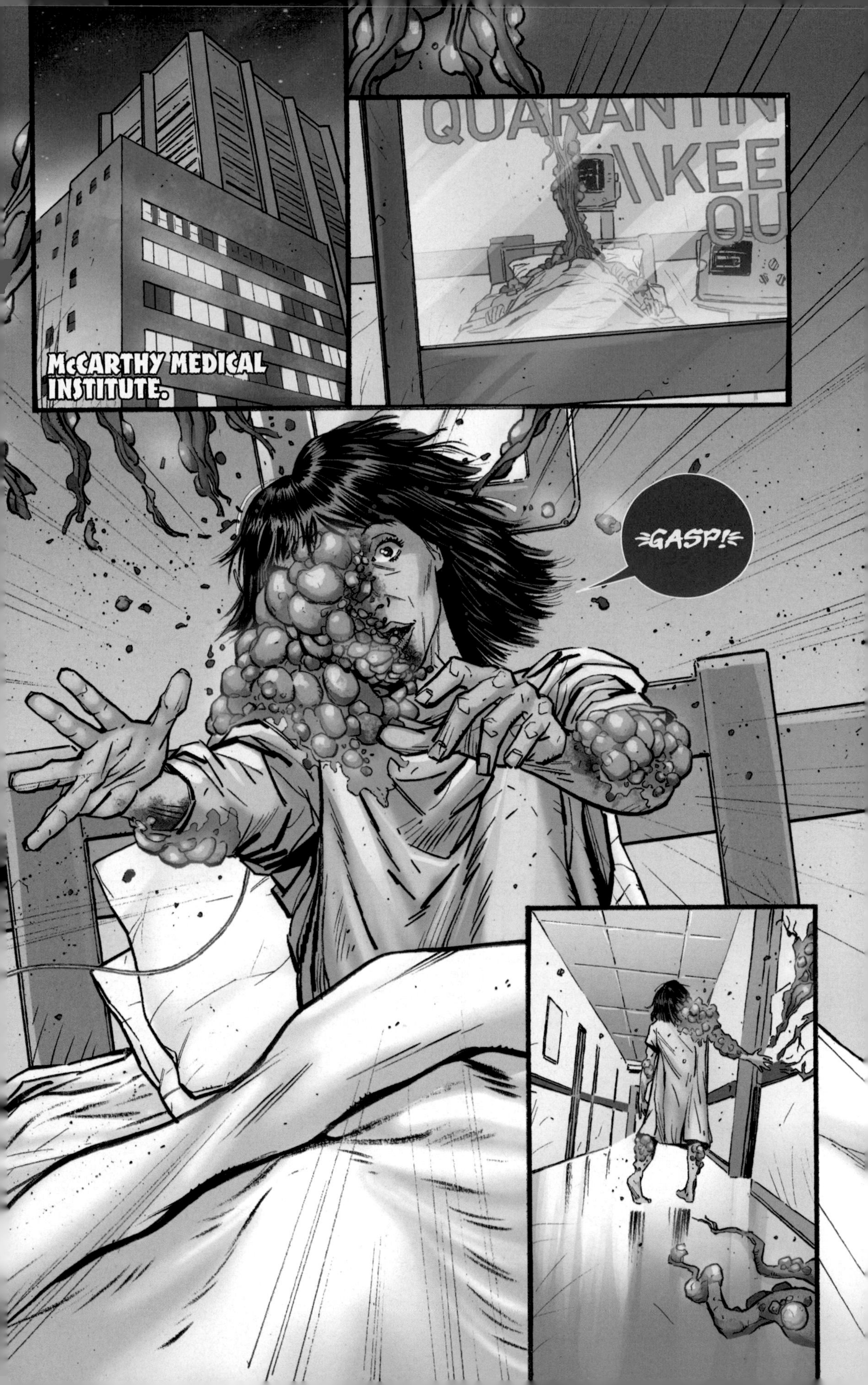
McCARTHY MEDICAL INSTITUTE.
QUARANTIN
KEE
OU
GASP!

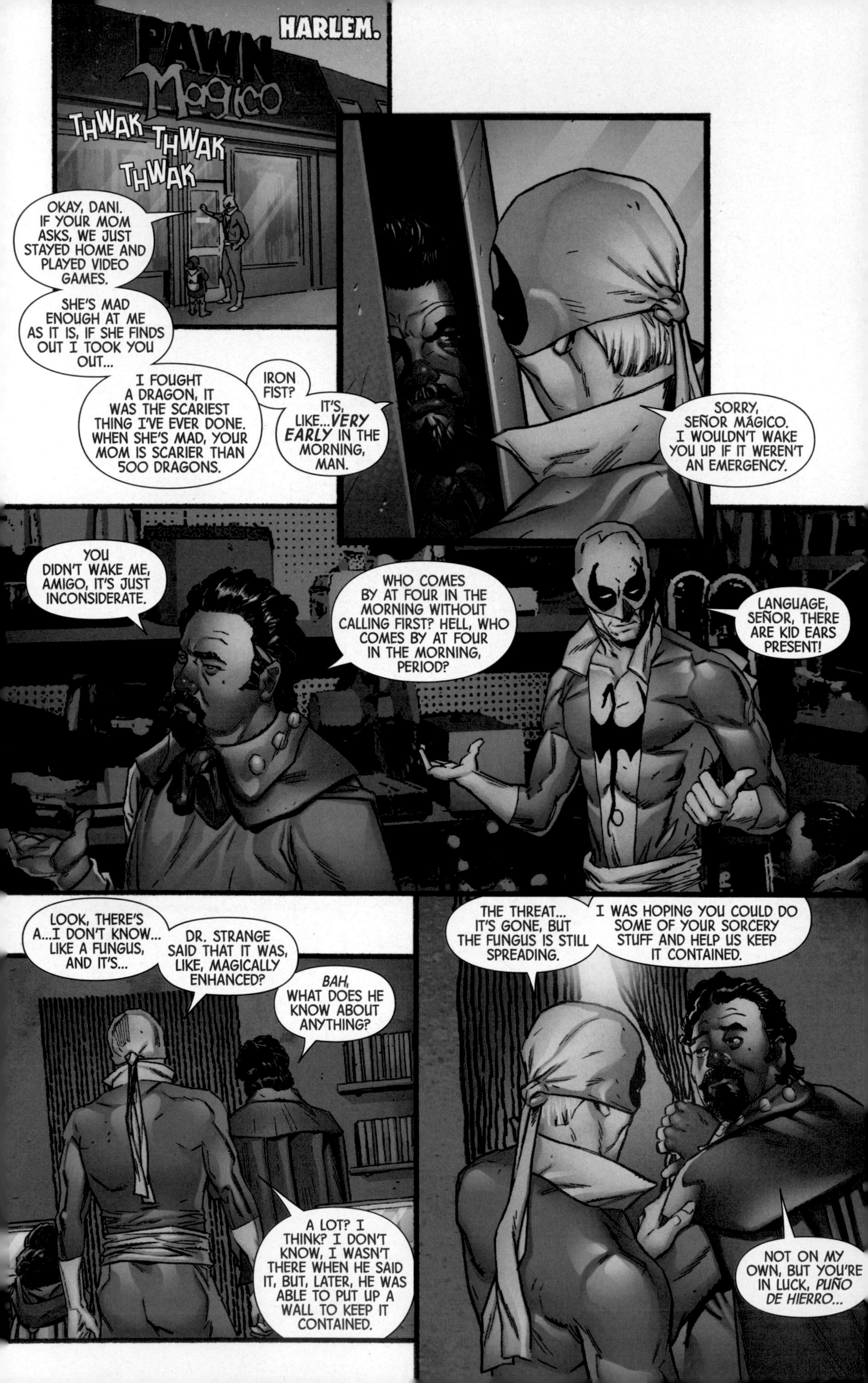
HARLEM.
PAWN
Magico
THWAK THWAK
THWAK
OKAY, DANI. IF YOUR MOM ASKS, WE JUST STAYED HOME AND PLAYED VIDEO GAMES.
SHE'S MAD ENOUGH AT ME AS IT IS, IF SHE FINDS OUT I TOOK YOU OUT...
I FOUGHT A DRAGON, IT WAS THE SCARIEST THING I'VE EVER DONE. WHEN SHE'S MAD, YOUR MOM IS SCARIER THAN 500 DRAGONS.
IRON FIST?
IT'S, LIKE...*VERY EARLY* IN THE MORNING, MAN.
SORRY, SEÑOR MÁGICO. I WOULDN'T WAKE YOU UP IF IT WEREN'T AN EMERGENCY.
YOU DIDN'T WAKE ME, AMIGO, IT'S JUST INCONSIDERATE.
WHO COMES BY AT FOUR IN THE MORNING WITHOUT CALLING FIRST? HELL, WHO COMES BY AT FOUR IN THE MORNING, PERIOD?
LANGUAGE, SEÑOR, THERE ARE KID EARS PRESENT!
LOOK, THERE'S A...I DON'T KNOW... LIKE A FUNGUS, AND IT'S...
DR. STRANGE SAID THAT IT WAS, LIKE, MAGICALLY ENHANCED?
BAH, WHAT DOES HE KNOW ABOUT ANYTHING?
A LOT? I THINK? I DON'T KNOW, I WASN'T THERE WHEN HE SAID IT, BUT, LATER, HE WAS ABLE TO PUT UP A WALL TO KEEP IT CONTAINED.
THE THREAT... IT'S GONE, BUT THE FUNGUS IS STILL SPREADING.
I WAS HOPING YOU COULD DO SOME OF YOUR SORCERY STUFF AND HELP US KEEP IT CONTAINED.
NOT ON MY OWN, BUT YOU'RE IN LUCK, *PUÑO DE HIERRO*...

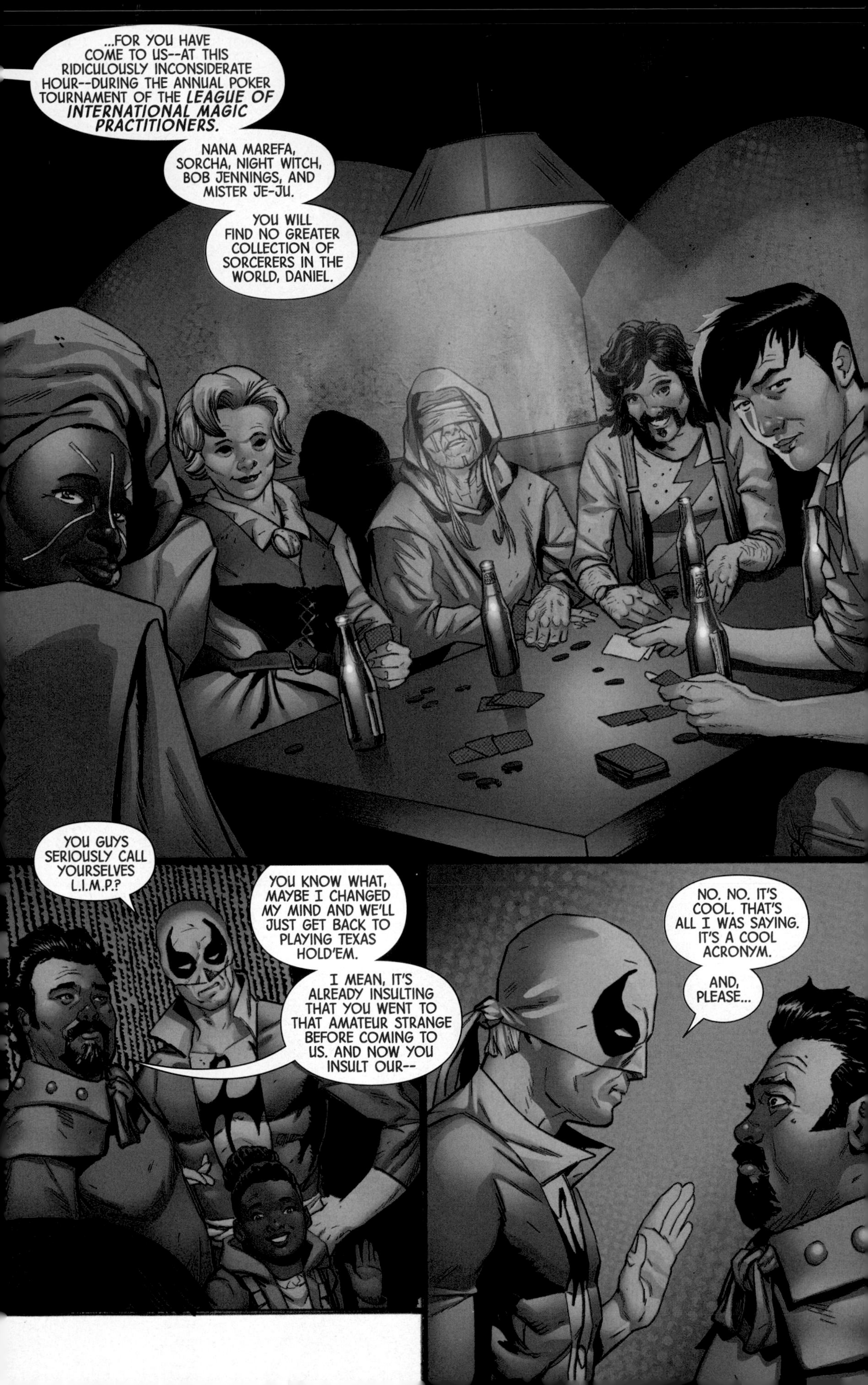
...FOR YOU HAVE COME TO US--AT THIS RIDICULOUSLY INCONSIDERATE HOUR--DURING THE ANNUAL POKER TOURNAMENT OF THE LEAGUE OF INTERNATIONAL MAGIC PRACTITIONERS.
NANA MAREFA, SORCHA, NIGHT WITCH, BOB JENNINGS, AND MISTER JE-JU.
YOU WILL FIND NO GREATER COLLECTION OF SORCERERS IN THE WORLD, DANIEL.
YOU GUYS SERIOUSLY CALL YOURSELVES L.I.M.P.?
YOU KNOW WHAT, MAYBE I CHANGED MY MIND AND WE'LL JUST GET BACK TO PLAYING TEXAS HOLD'EM.
I MEAN, IT'S ALREADY INSULTING THAT YOU WENT TO THAT AMATEUR STRANGE BEFORE COMING TO US. AND NOW YOU INSULT OUR--
NO. NO. IT'S COOL. THAT'S ALL I WAS SAYING. IT'S A COOL ACRONYM.
AND, PLEASE...

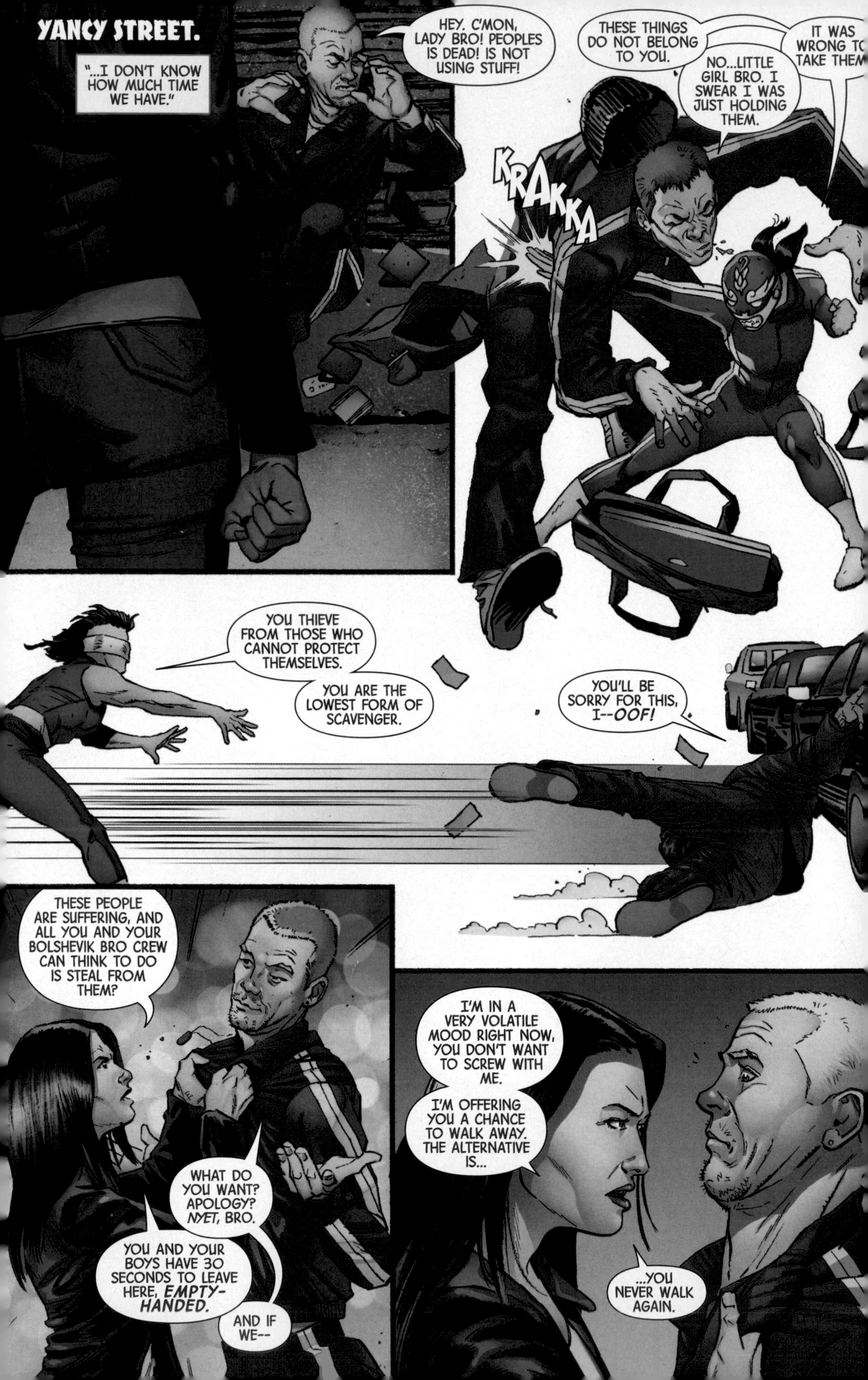

YANCY STREET.
"...I DON'T KNOW HOW MUCH TIME WE HAVE."
HEY. C'MON, LADY BRO! PEOPLES IS DEAD! IS NOT USING STUFF!
THESE THINGS DO NOT BELONG TO YOU.
IT WAS WRONG TO TAKE THEM
NO...LITTLE GIRL BRO. I SWEAR I WAS JUST HOLDING THEM.
KRAKKA
YOU THIEVE FROM THOSE WHO CANNOT PROTECT THEMSELVES.
YOU ARE THE LOWEST FORM OF SCAVENGER.
YOU'LL BE SORRY FOR THIS, I--OOF!
THESE PEOPLE ARE SUFFERING, AND ALL YOU AND YOUR BOLSHEVIK BRO CREW CAN THINK TO DO IS STEAL FROM THEM?
WHAT DO YOU WANT? APOLOGY? NYET, BRO.
YOU AND YOUR BOYS HAVE 30 SECONDS TO LEAVE HERE, EMPTY-HANDED.
AND IF WE--
I'M IN A VERY VOLATILE MOOD RIGHT NOW, YOU DON'T WANT TO SCREW WITH ME.
I'M OFFERING YOU A CHANCE TO WALK AWAY. THE ALTERNATIVE IS...
...YOU NEVER WALK AGAIN.

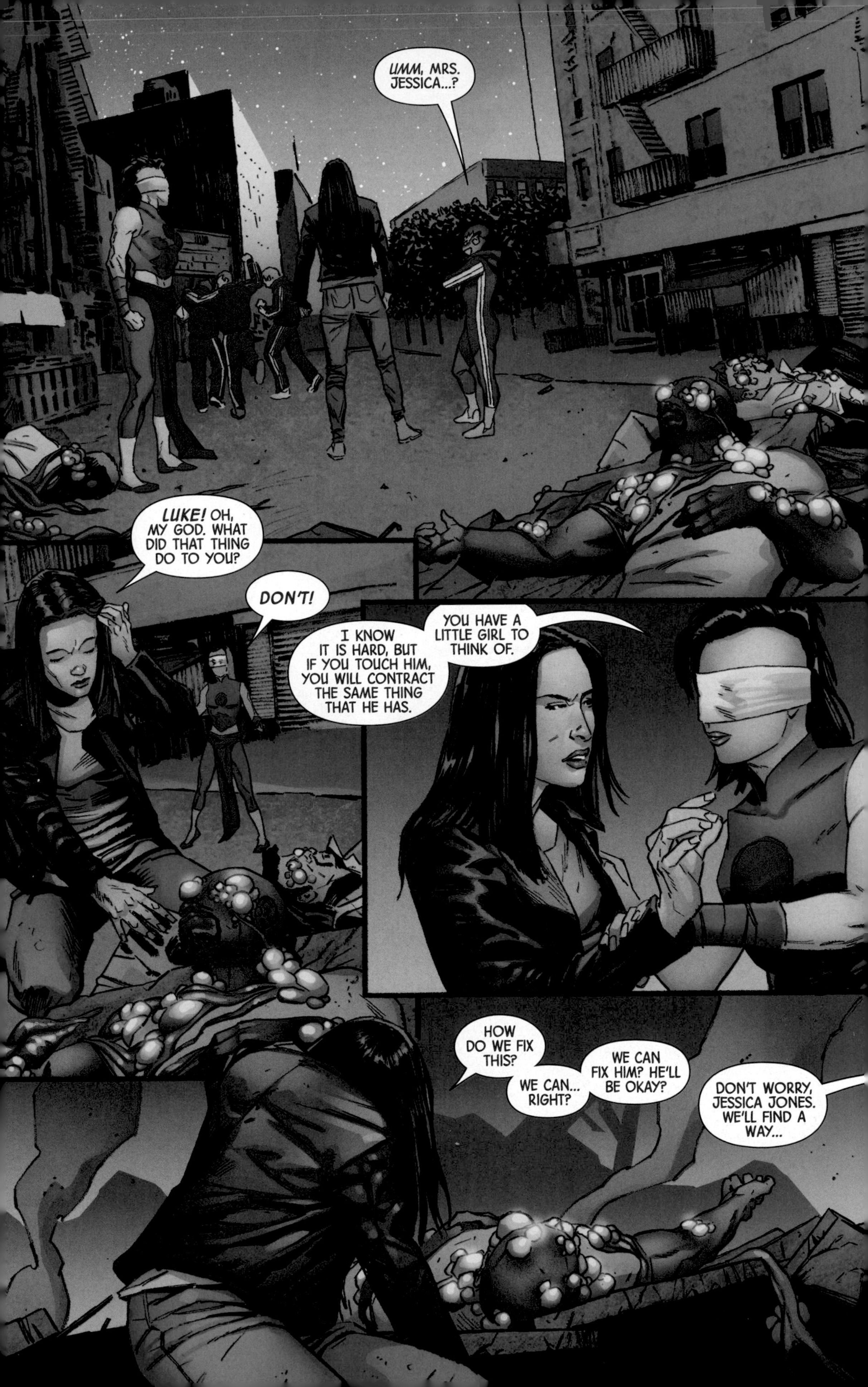
UMM, MRS. JESSICA...?
LUKE! OH, MY GOD. WHAT DID THAT THING DO TO YOU?
DON'T!
I KNOW IT IS HARD, BUT IF YOU TOUCH HIM, YOU WILL CONTRACT THE SAME THING THAT HE HAS.
YOU HAVE A LITTLE GIRL TO THINK OF.
HOW DO WE FIX THIS?
WE CAN... RIGHT?
WE CAN FIX HIM? HE'LL BE OKAY?
DON'T WORRY, JESSICA JONES. WE'LL FIND A WAY...

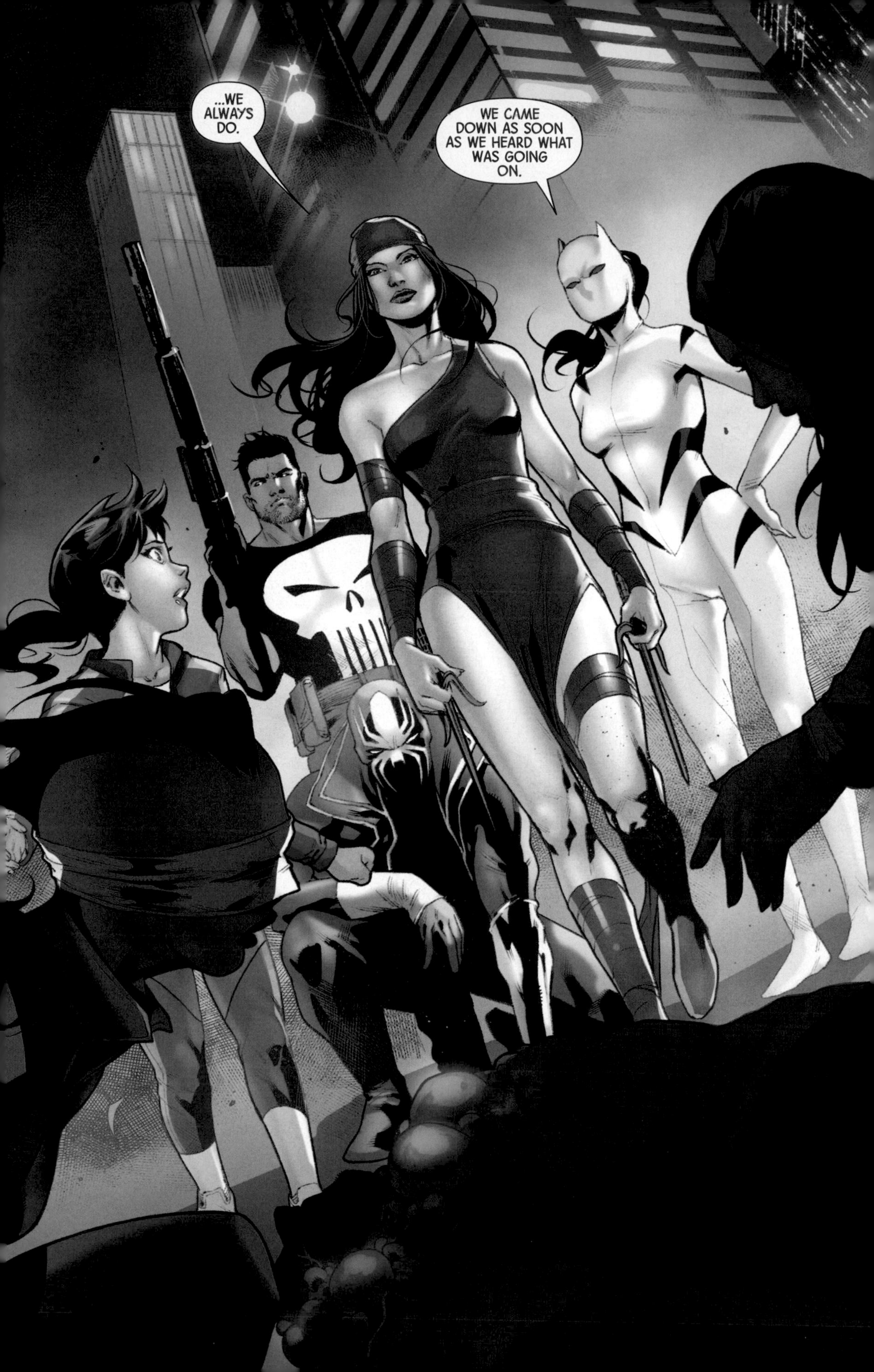
...WE ALWAYS DO.
WE CAME DOWN AS SOON AS WE HEARD WHAT WAS GOING ON.

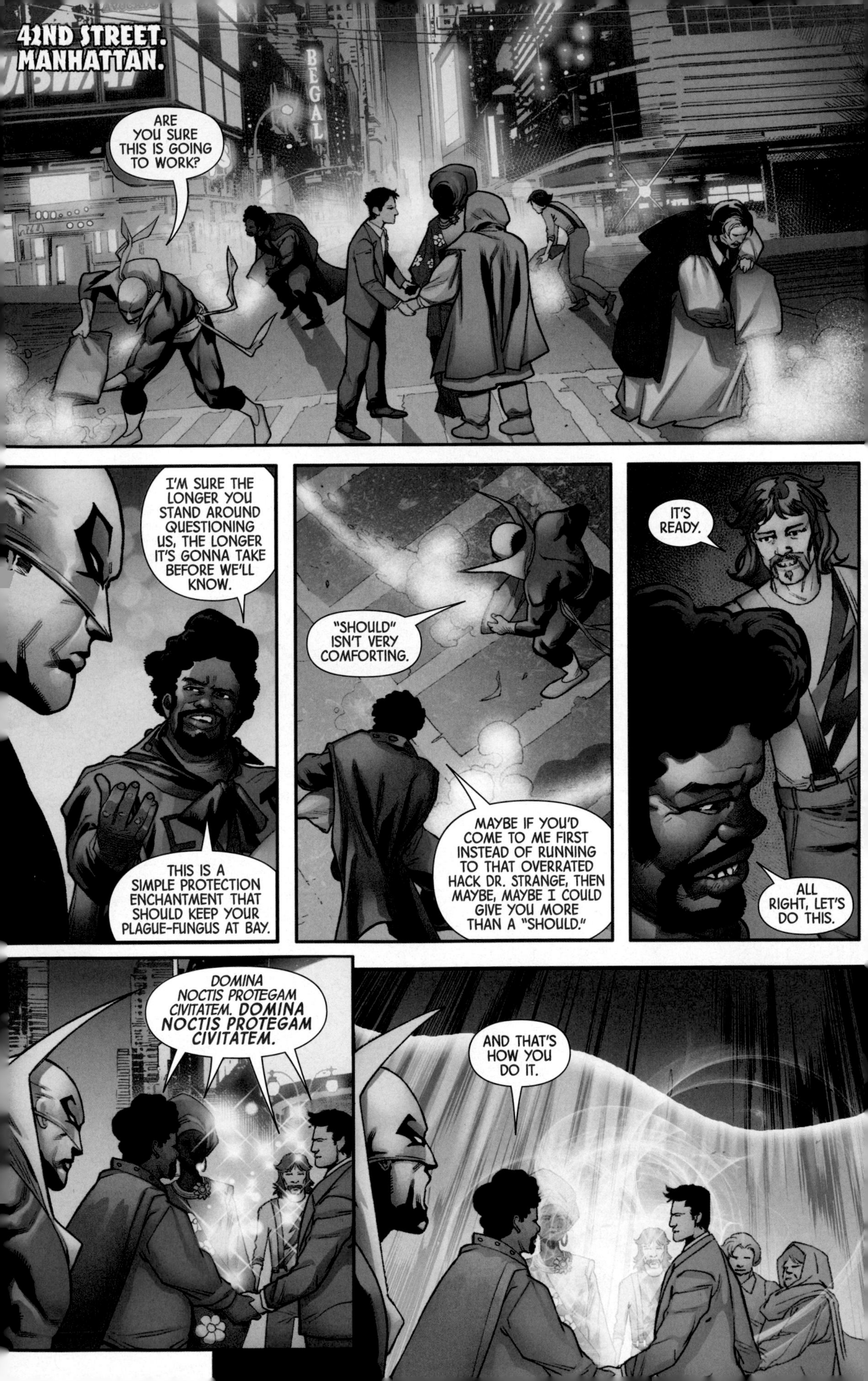
42ND STREET. MANHATTAN.
ARE YOU SURE THIS IS GOING TO WORK?
I'M SURE THE LONGER YOU STAND AROUND QUESTIONING US, THE LONGER IT'S GONNA TAKE BEFORE WE'LL KNOW.
THIS IS A SIMPLE PROTECTION ENCHANTMENT THAT SHOULD KEEP YOUR PLAGUE-FUNGUS AT BAY.
"SHOULD" ISN'T VERY COMFORTING.
MAYBE IF YOU'D COME TO ME FIRST INSTEAD OF RUNNING TO THAT OVERRATED HACK DR. STRANGE, THEN MAYBE, MAYBE I COULD GIVE YOU MORE THAN A "SHOULD."
IT'S READY.
ALL RIGHT, LET'S DO THIS.
DOMINA NOCTIS PROTEGAM CIVITATEM. DOMINA NOCTIS PROTEGAM CIVITATEM.
AND THAT'S HOW YOU DO IT.

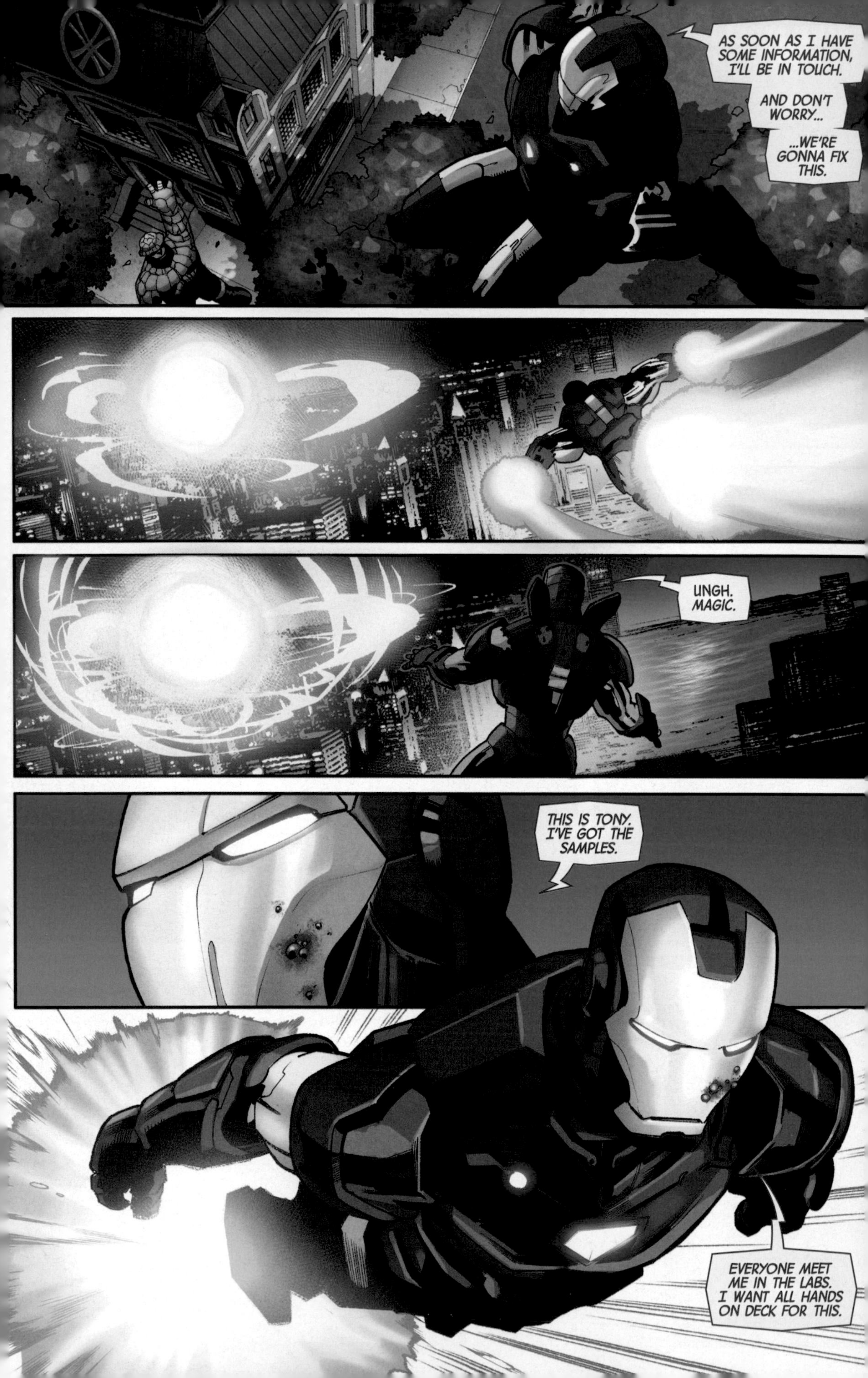
AS SOON AS I HAVE SOME INFORMATION, I'LL BE IN TOUCH.
AND DON'T WORRY...
...WE'RE GONNA FIX THIS.
UNGH. MAGIC.
THIS IS TONY. I'VE GOT THE SAMPLES.
EVERYONE MEET ME IN THE LABS. I WANT ALL HANDS ON DECK FOR THIS.

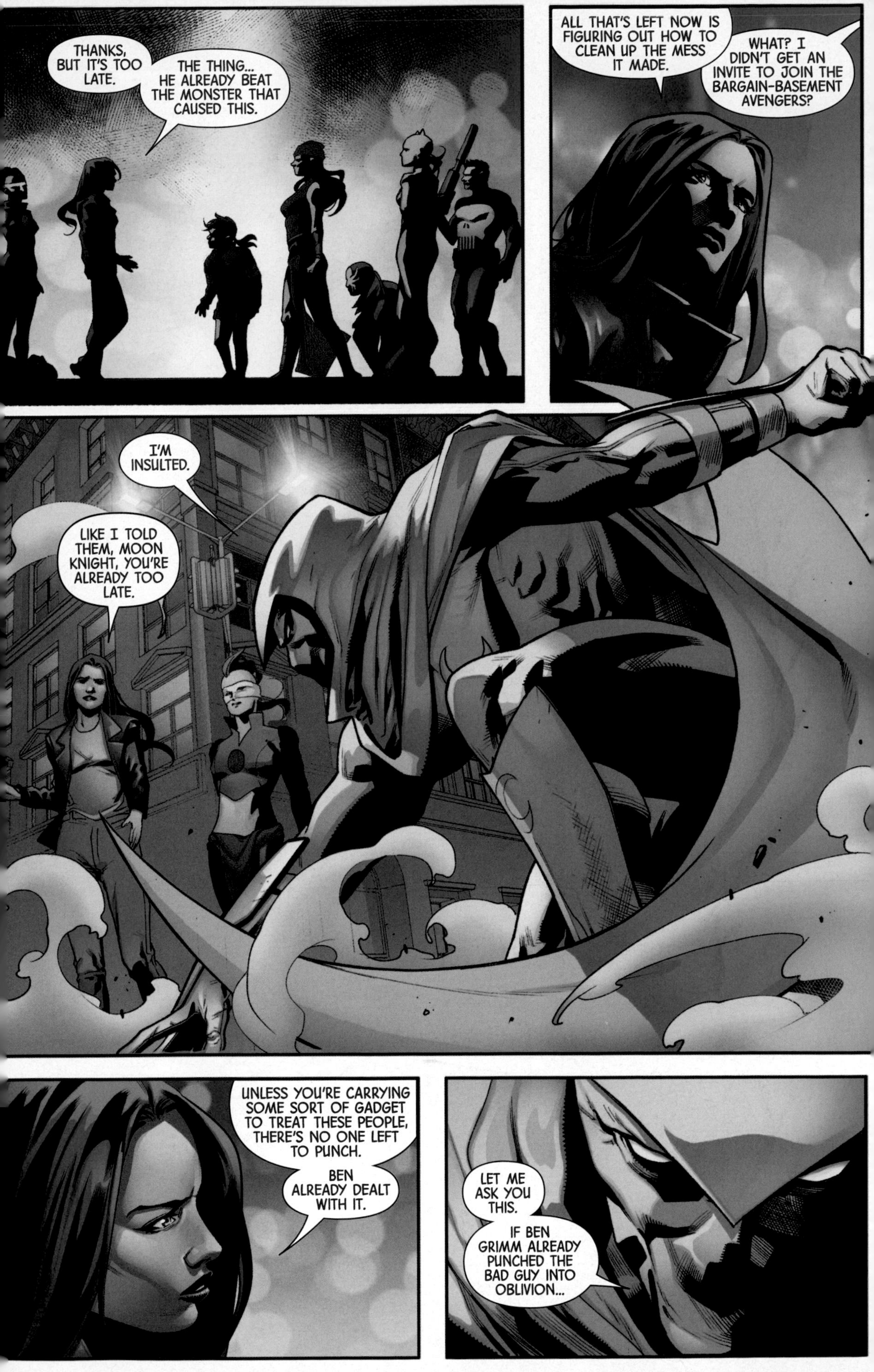
THANKS, BUT IT'S TOO LATE.
THE THING... HE ALREADY BEAT THE MONSTER THAT CAUSED THIS.
ALL THAT'S LEFT NOW IS FIGURING OUT HOW TO CLEAN UP THE MESS IT MADE.
WHAT? I DIDN'T GET AN INVITE TO JOIN THE BARGAIN-BASEMENT AVENGERS?
I'M INSULTED.
LIKE I TOLD THEM, MOON KNIGHT, YOU'RE ALREADY TOO LATE.
UNLESS YOU'RE CARRYING SOME SORT OF GADGET TO TREAT THESE PEOPLE, THERE'S NO ONE LEFT TO PUNCH.
BEN ALREADY DEALT WITH IT.
LET ME ASK YOU THIS.
IF BEN GRIMM ALREADY PUNCHED THE BAD GUY INTO OBLIVION...

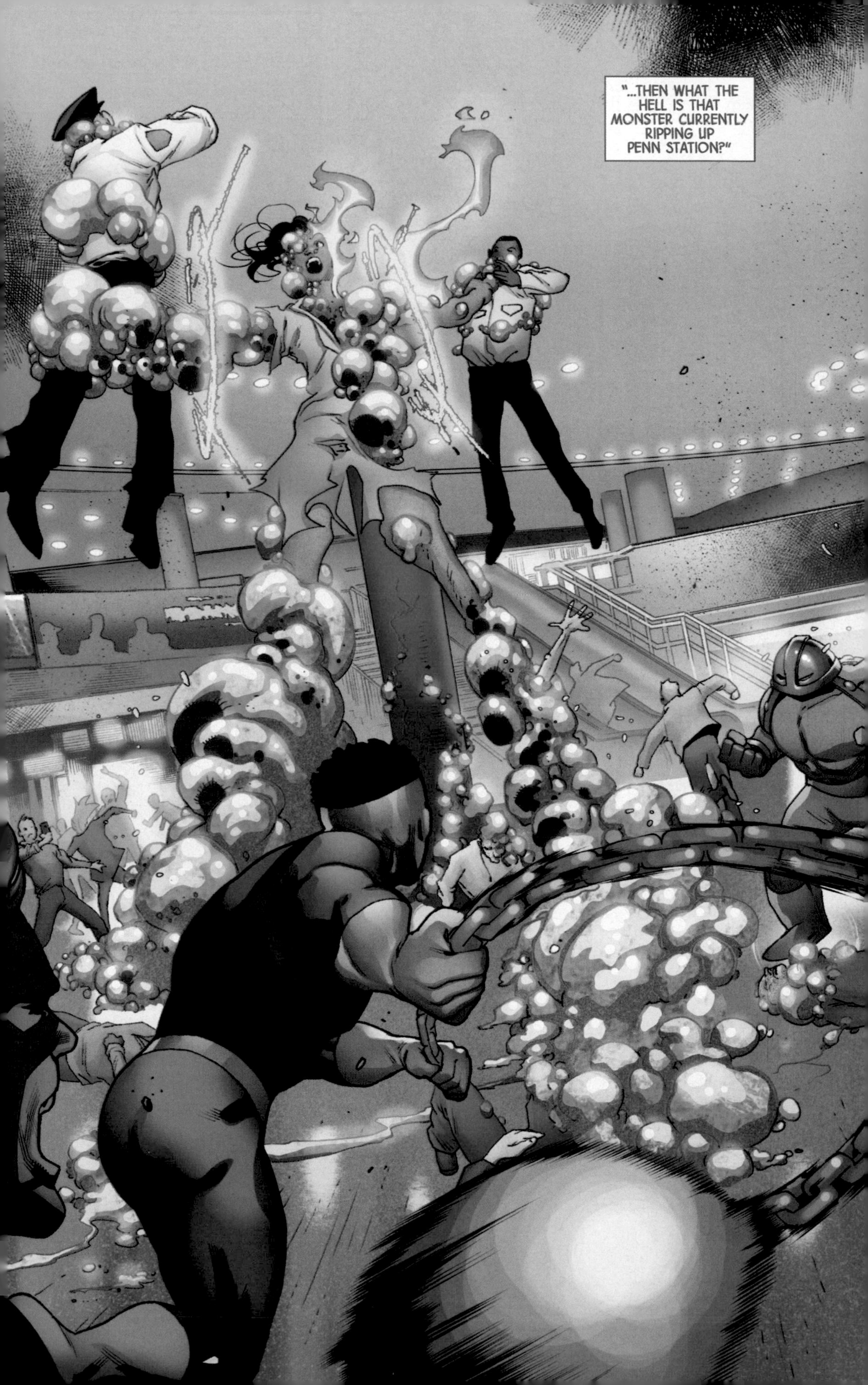
"...THEN WHAT THE HELL IS THAT MONSTER CURRENTLY RIPPING UP PENN STATION?"

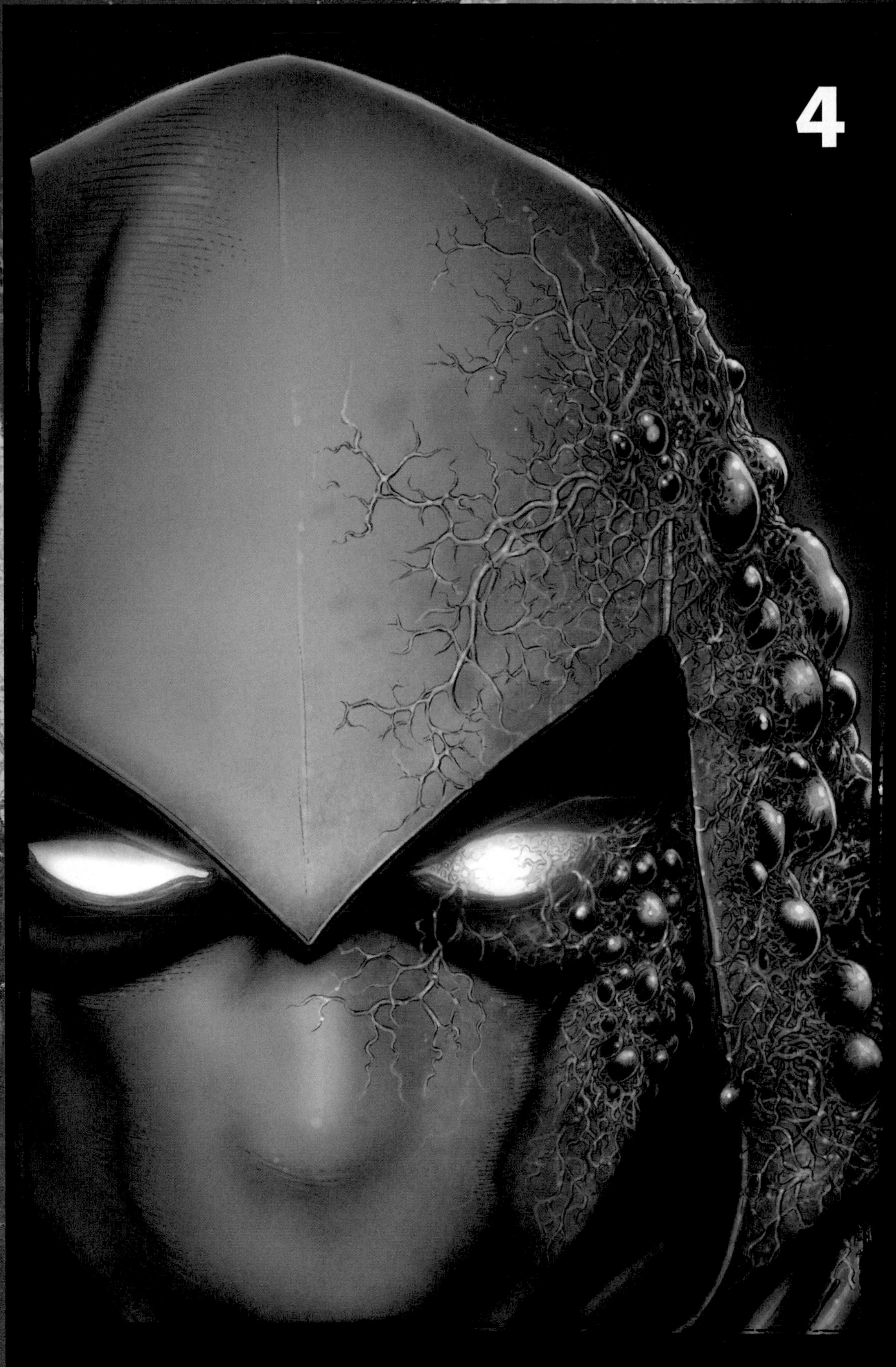
4

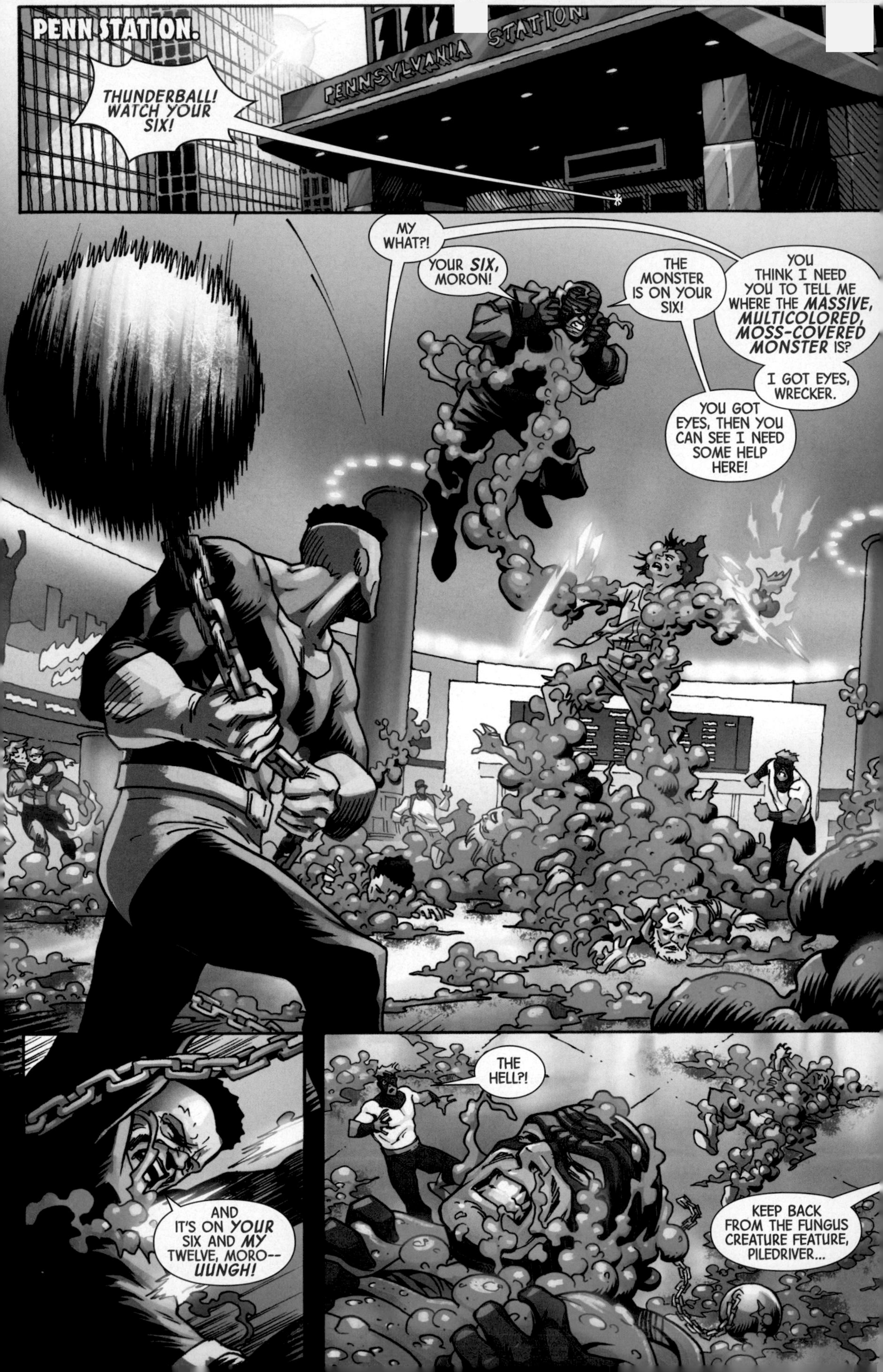
PENN STATION.
PENNSYLVANIA STATION
THUNDERBALL! WATCH YOUR SIX!
MY WHAT?!
YOUR *SIX*, MORON!
THE MONSTER IS ON YOUR SIX!
YOU THINK I NEED YOU TO TELL ME WHERE THE *MASSIVE, MULTICOLORED, MOSS-COVERED MONSTER* IS?
I GOT EYES, WRECKER.
YOU GOT EYES, THEN YOU CAN SEE I NEED SOME HELP HERE!
AND IT'S ON *YOUR* SIX AND *MY* TWELVE, MORO-- *UUNGH!*
THE HELL?!
KEEP BACK FROM THE FUNGUS CREATURE FEATURE, PILEDRIVER...

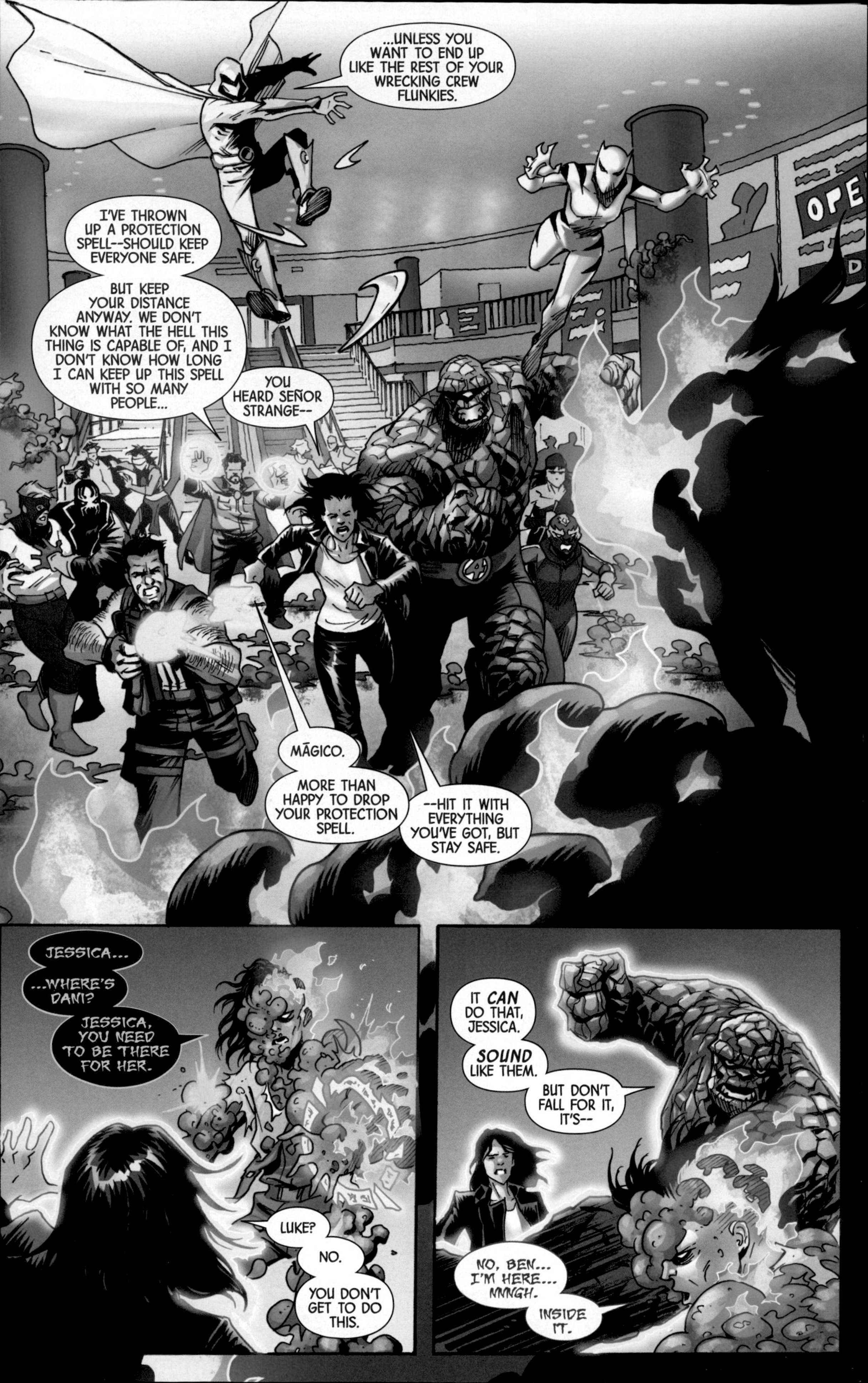
...UNLESS YOU WANT TO END UP LIKE THE REST OF YOUR WRECKING CREW FLUNKIES.
I'VE THROWN UP A PROTECTION SPELL--SHOULD KEEP EVERYONE SAFE.
BUT KEEP YOUR DISTANCE ANYWAY. WE DON'T KNOW WHAT THE HELL THIS THING IS CAPABLE OF, AND I DON'T KNOW HOW LONG I CAN KEEP UP THIS SPELL WITH SO MANY PEOPLE...
YOU HEARD SEÑOR STRANGE--
MÁGICO.
MORE THAN HAPPY TO DROP YOUR PROTECTION SPELL.
--HIT IT WITH EVERYTHING YOU'VE GOT, BUT STAY SAFE.
JESSICA...
...WHERE'S DANI?
JESSICA, YOU NEED TO BE THERE FOR HER.
LUKE?
NO.
YOU DON'T GET TO DO THIS.
IT CAN DO THAT, JESSICA.
SOUND LIKE THEM.
BUT DON'T FALL FOR IT, IT'S--
NO, BEN... I'M HERE... NNNGH.
INSIDE IT.

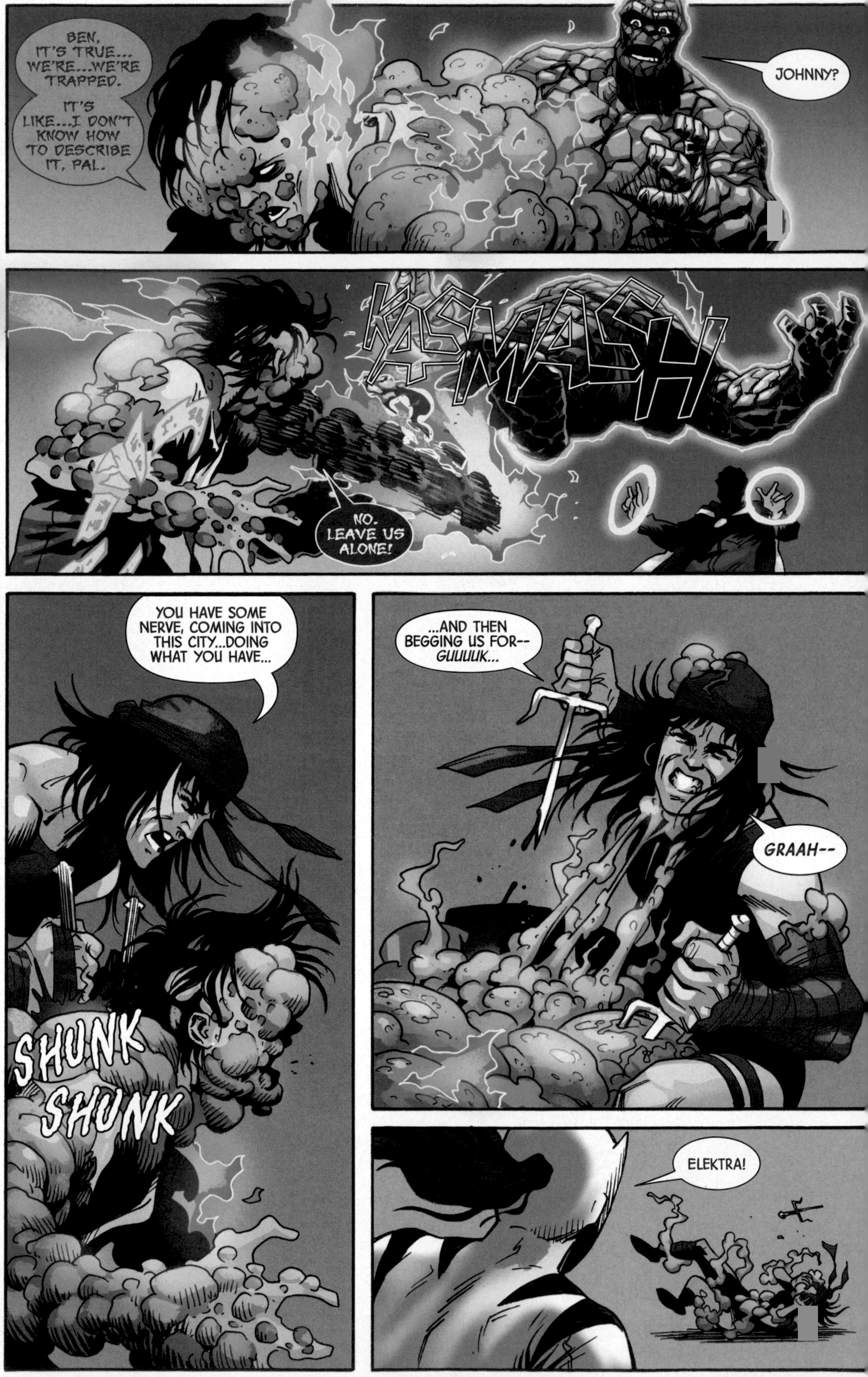
BEN, IT'S TRUE... WE'RE...WE'RE TRAPPED.
IT'S LIKE...I DON'T KNOW HOW TO DESCRIBE IT, PAL.
JOHNNY?
KASMASH
NO. LEAVE US ALONE!
YOU HAVE SOME NERVE, COMING INTO THIS CITY...DOING WHAT YOU HAVE...
SHUNK
SHUNK
...AND THEN BEGGING US FOR-- GUUUUK...
GRAAH--
ELEKTRA!

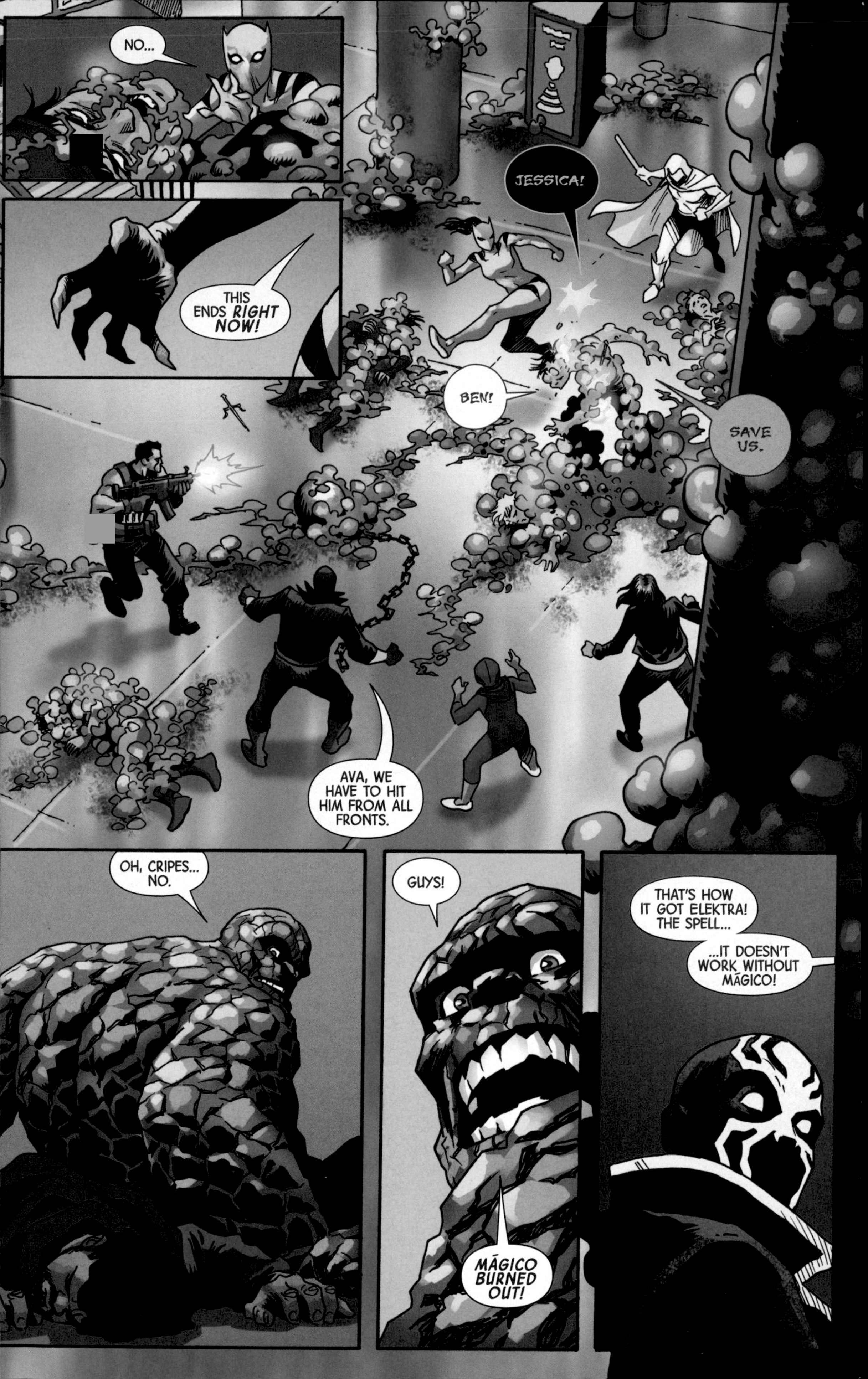
NO...
THIS ENDS RIGHT NOW!
JESSICA!
BEN!
SAVE US.
AVA, WE HAVE TO HIT HIM FROM ALL FRONTS.
OH, CRIPES... NO.
GUYS!
MÁGICO BURNED OUT!
THAT'S HOW IT GOT ELEKTRA! THE SPELL...
...IT DOESN'T WORK WITHOUT MÁGICO!

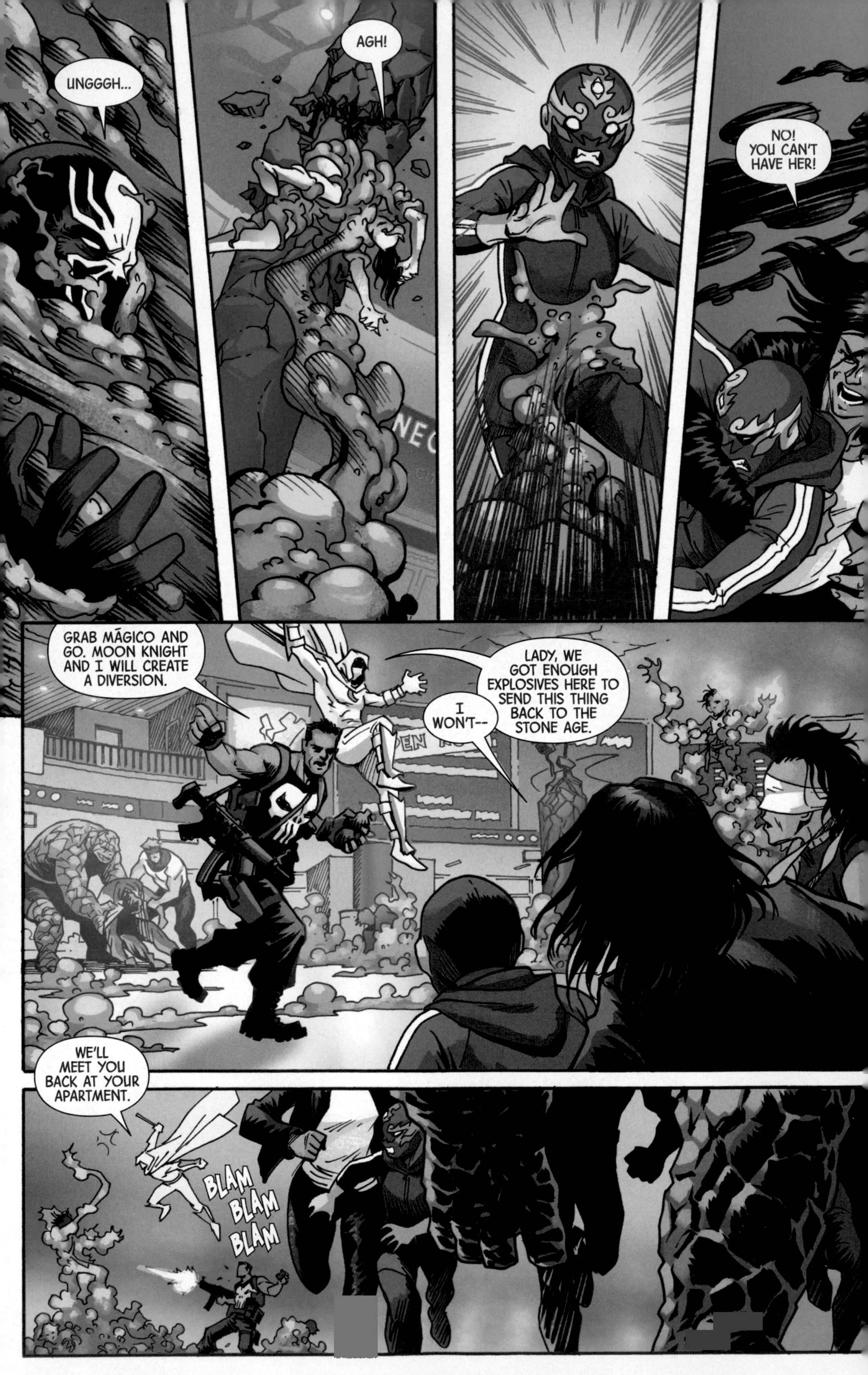

UNGGGH...
AGH!
NO! YOU CAN'T HAVE HER!
GRAB MÁGICO AND GO. MOON KNIGHT AND I WILL CREATE A DIVERSION.
LADY, WE GOT ENOUGH EXPLOSIVES HERE TO SEND THIS THING BACK TO THE STONE AGE.
I WON'T--
WE'LL MEET YOU BACK AT YOUR APARTMENT.
BLAM
BLAM
BLAM

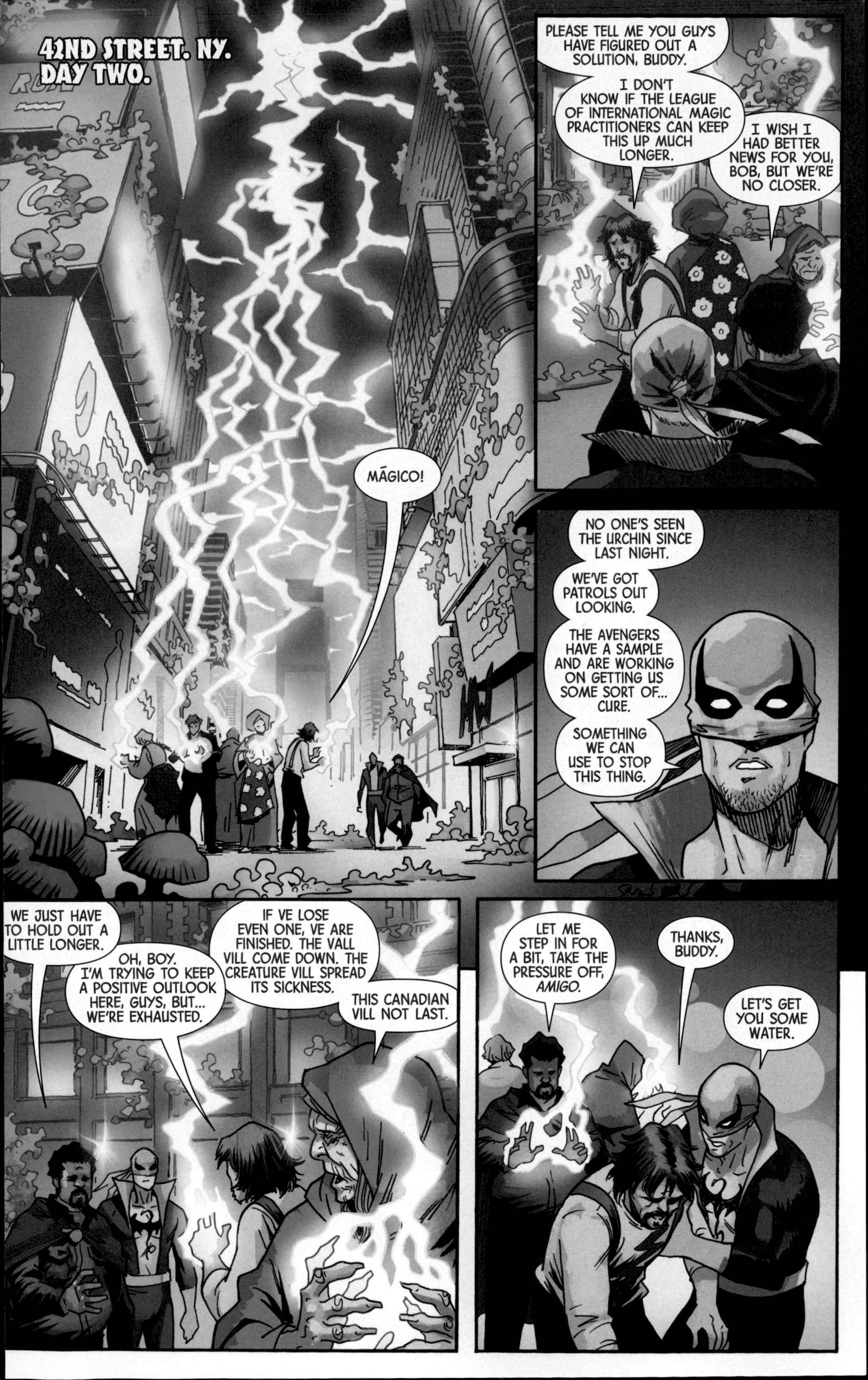
42ND STREET. NY.
DAY TWO.
MÁGICO!
PLEASE TELL ME YOU GUYS HAVE FIGURED OUT A SOLUTION, BUDDY.
I DON'T KNOW IF THE LEAGUE OF INTERNATIONAL MAGIC PRACTITIONERS CAN KEEP THIS UP MUCH LONGER.
I WISH I HAD BETTER NEWS FOR YOU, BOB, BUT WE'RE NO CLOSER.
NO ONE'S SEEN THE URCHIN SINCE LAST NIGHT.
WE'VE GOT PATROLS OUT LOOKING.
THE AVENGERS HAVE A SAMPLE AND ARE WORKING ON GETTING US SOME SORT OF... CURE.
SOMETHING WE CAN USE TO STOP THIS THING.
WE JUST HAVE TO HOLD OUT A LITTLE LONGER.
OH, BOY. I'M TRYING TO KEEP A POSITIVE OUTLOOK HERE, GUYS, BUT... WE'RE EXHAUSTED.
IF VE LOSE EVEN ONE, VE ARE FINISHED. THE VALL VILL COME DOWN. THE CREATURE VILL SPREAD ITS SICKNESS.
THIS CANADIAN VILL NOT LAST.
LET ME STEP IN FOR A BIT, TAKE THE PRESSURE OFF, *AMIGO.*
THANKS, BUDDY.
LET'S GET YOU SOME WATER.

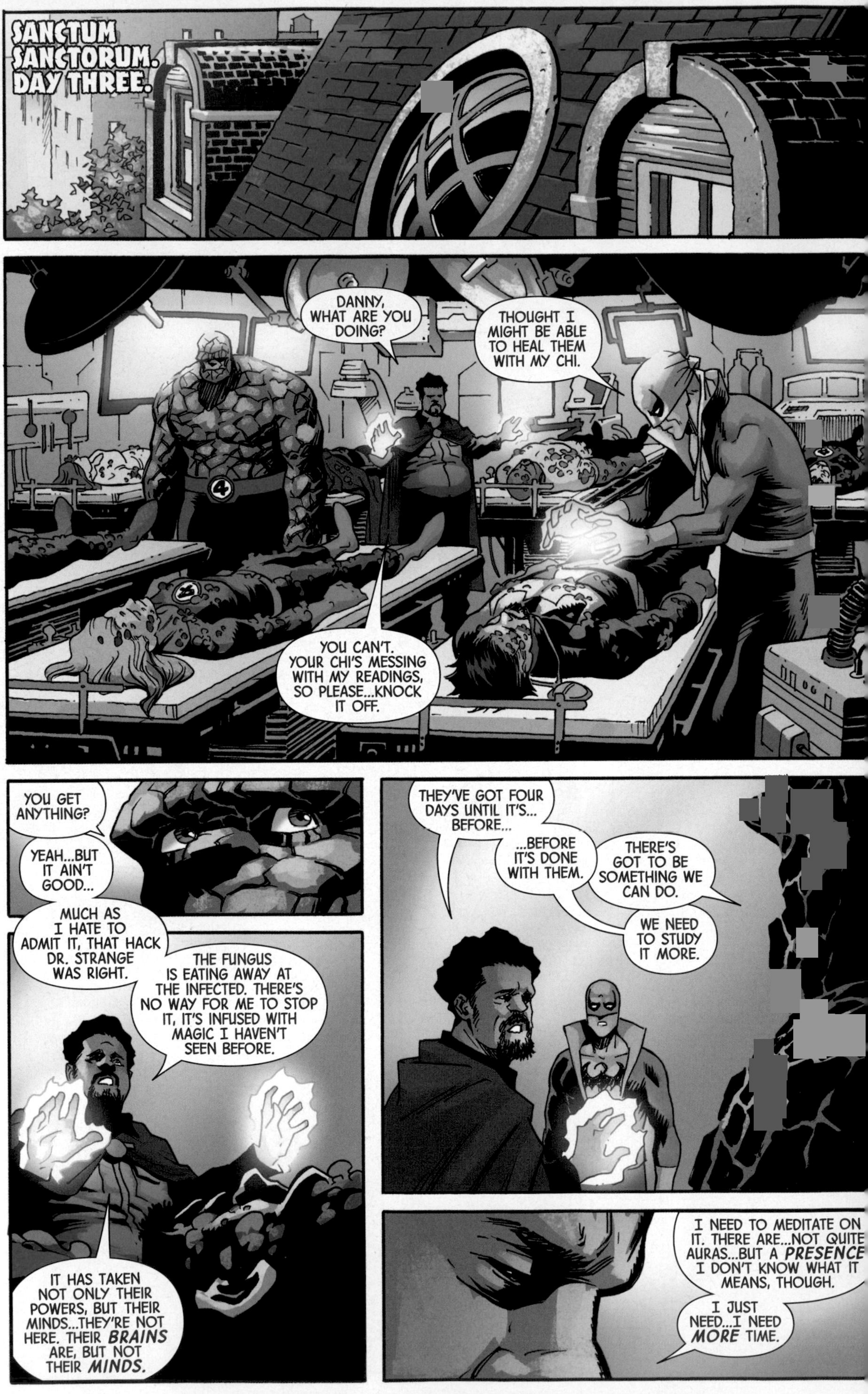
SANCTUM SANCTORUM. DAY THREE.
DANNY, WHAT ARE YOU DOING?
THOUGHT I MIGHT BE ABLE TO HEAL THEM WITH MY CHI.
YOU CAN'T. YOUR CHI'S MESSING WITH MY READINGS, SO PLEASE...KNOCK IT OFF.
YOU GET ANYTHING?
YEAH...BUT IT AIN'T GOOD...
MUCH AS I HATE TO ADMIT IT, THAT HACK DR. STRANGE WAS RIGHT.
THE FUNGUS IS EATING AWAY AT THE INFECTED. THERE'S NO WAY FOR ME TO STOP IT, IT'S INFUSED WITH MAGIC I HAVEN'T SEEN BEFORE.
IT HAS TAKEN NOT ONLY THEIR POWERS, BUT THEIR MINDS...THEY'RE NOT HERE. THEIR *BRAINS* ARE, BUT NOT THEIR *MINDS.*
THEY'VE GOT FOUR DAYS UNTIL IT'S... BEFORE...
...BEFORE IT'S DONE WITH THEM.
THERE'S GOT TO BE SOMETHING WE CAN DO.
WE NEED TO STUDY IT MORE.
I NEED TO MEDITATE ON IT. THERE ARE...NOT QUITE AURAS...BUT A *PRESENCE.* I DON'T KNOW WHAT IT MEANS, THOUGH.
I JUST NEED...I NEED *MORE* TIME.

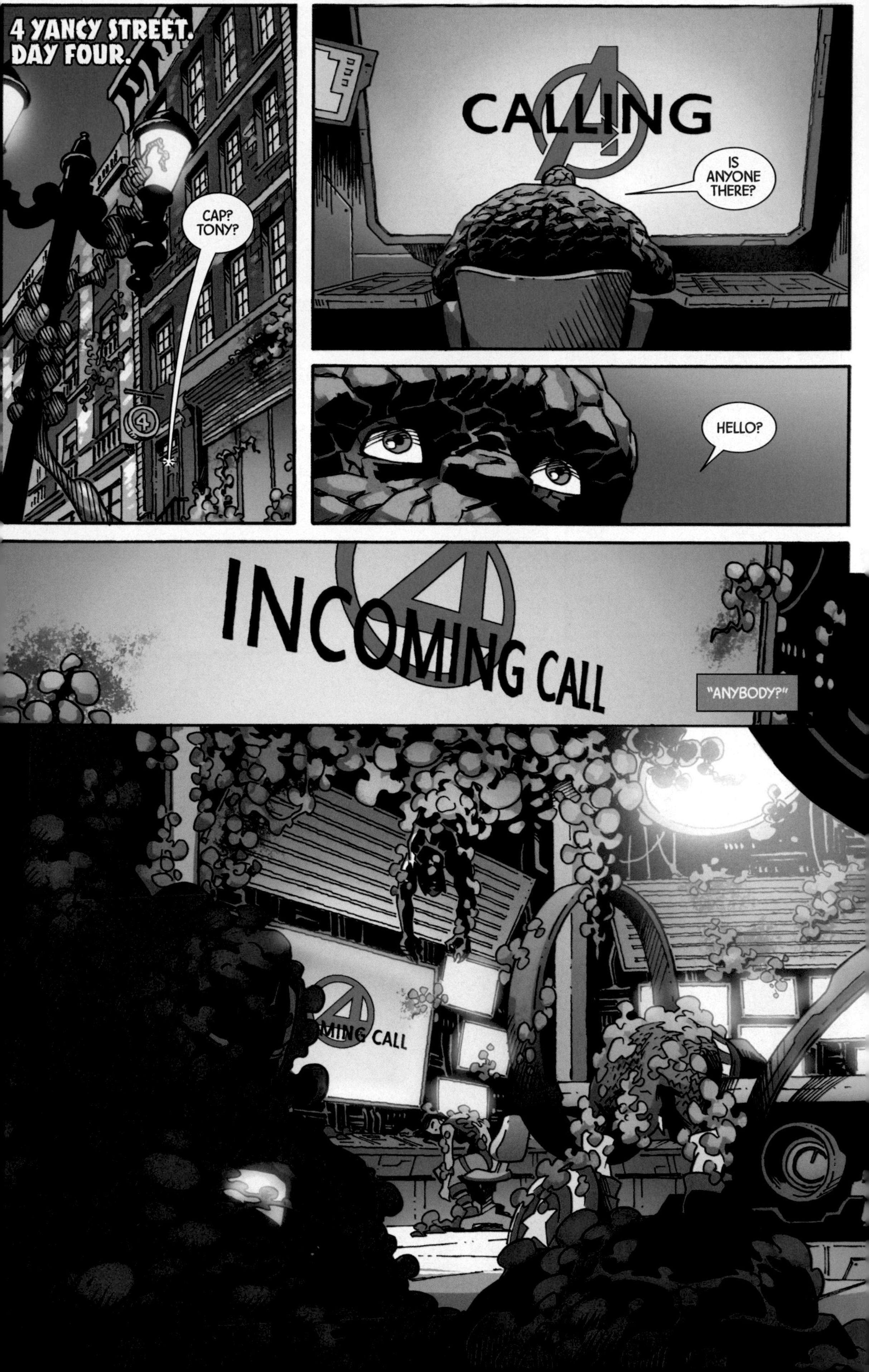
4 YANCY STREET.
DAY FOUR.
CAP? TONY?
CALLING
IS ANYONE THERE?
HELLO?
INCOMING CALL
"ANYBODY?"
MING CALL

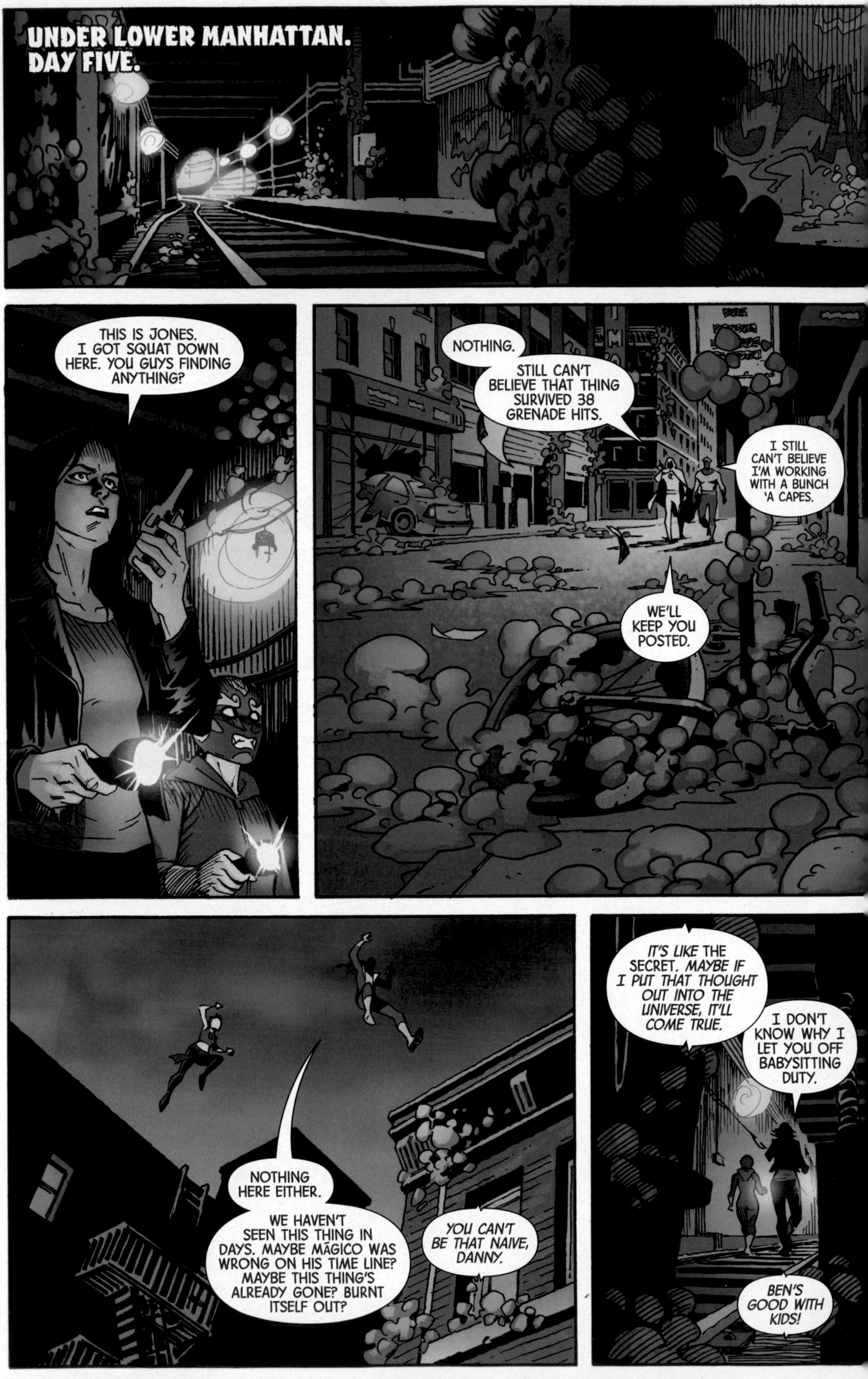
UNDER LOWER MANHATTAN.
DAY FIVE.
THIS IS JONES. I GOT SQUAT DOWN HERE. YOU GUYS FINDING ANYTHING?
NOTHING.
STILL CAN'T BELIEVE THAT THING SURVIVED 38 GRENADE HITS.
I STILL CAN'T BELIEVE I'M WORKING WITH A BUNCH 'A CAPES.
WE'LL KEEP YOU POSTED.
NOTHING HERE EITHER.
WE HAVEN'T SEEN THIS THING IN DAYS. MAYBE MÁGICO WAS WRONG ON HIS TIME LINE? MAYBE THIS THING'S ALREADY GONE? BURNT ITSELF OUT?
YOU CAN'T BE THAT NAIVE, DANNY.
IT'S LIKE THE SECRET. MAYBE IF I PUT THAT THOUGHT OUT INTO THE UNIVERSE, IT'LL COME TRUE.
I DON'T KNOW WHY I LET YOU OFF BABYSITTING DUTY.
BEN'S GOOD WITH KIDS!

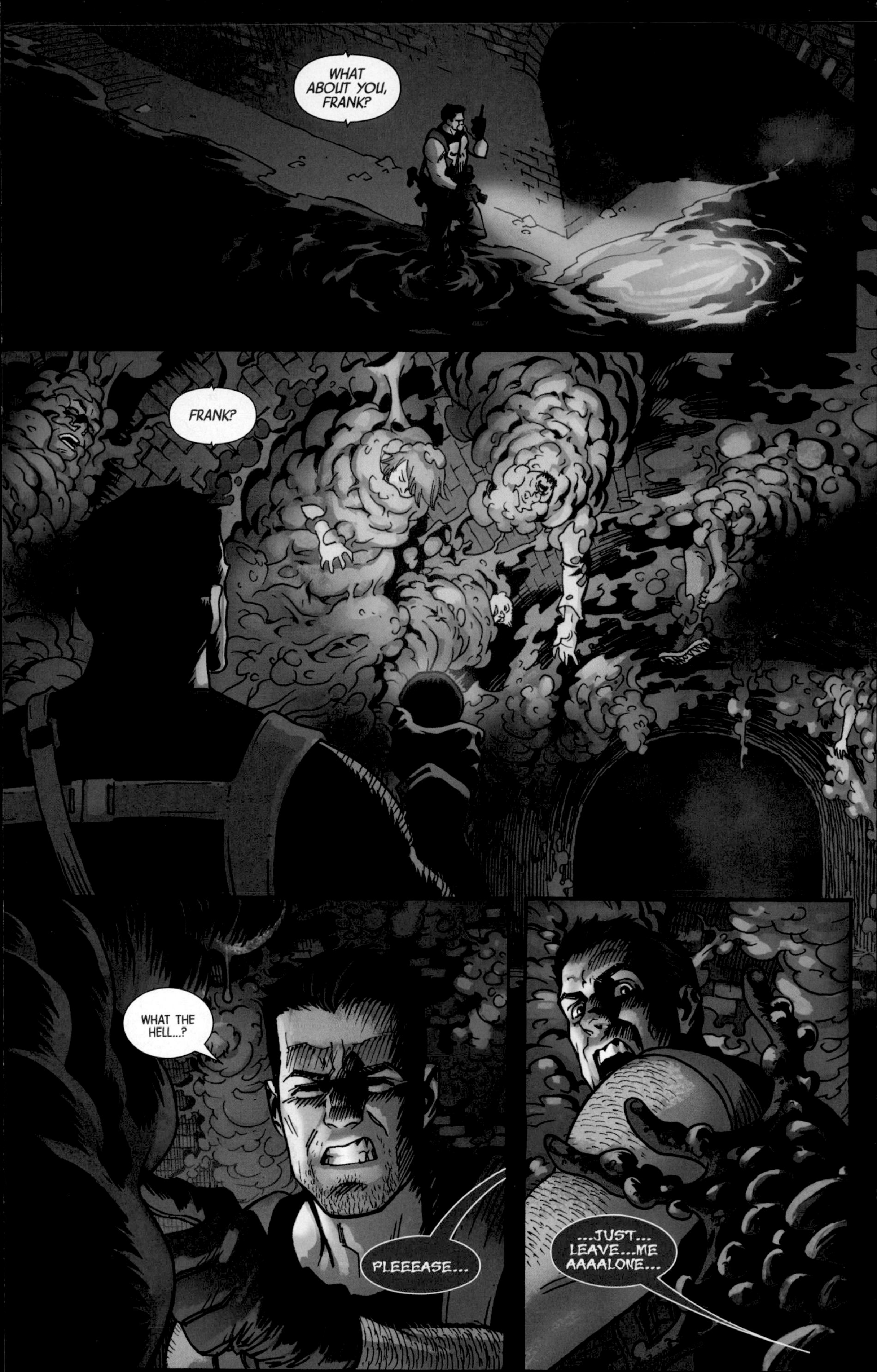
WHAT ABOUT YOU, FRANK?
FRANK?
WHAT THE HELL...?
PLEEEASE...
...JUST... LEAVE...ME AAAALONE...

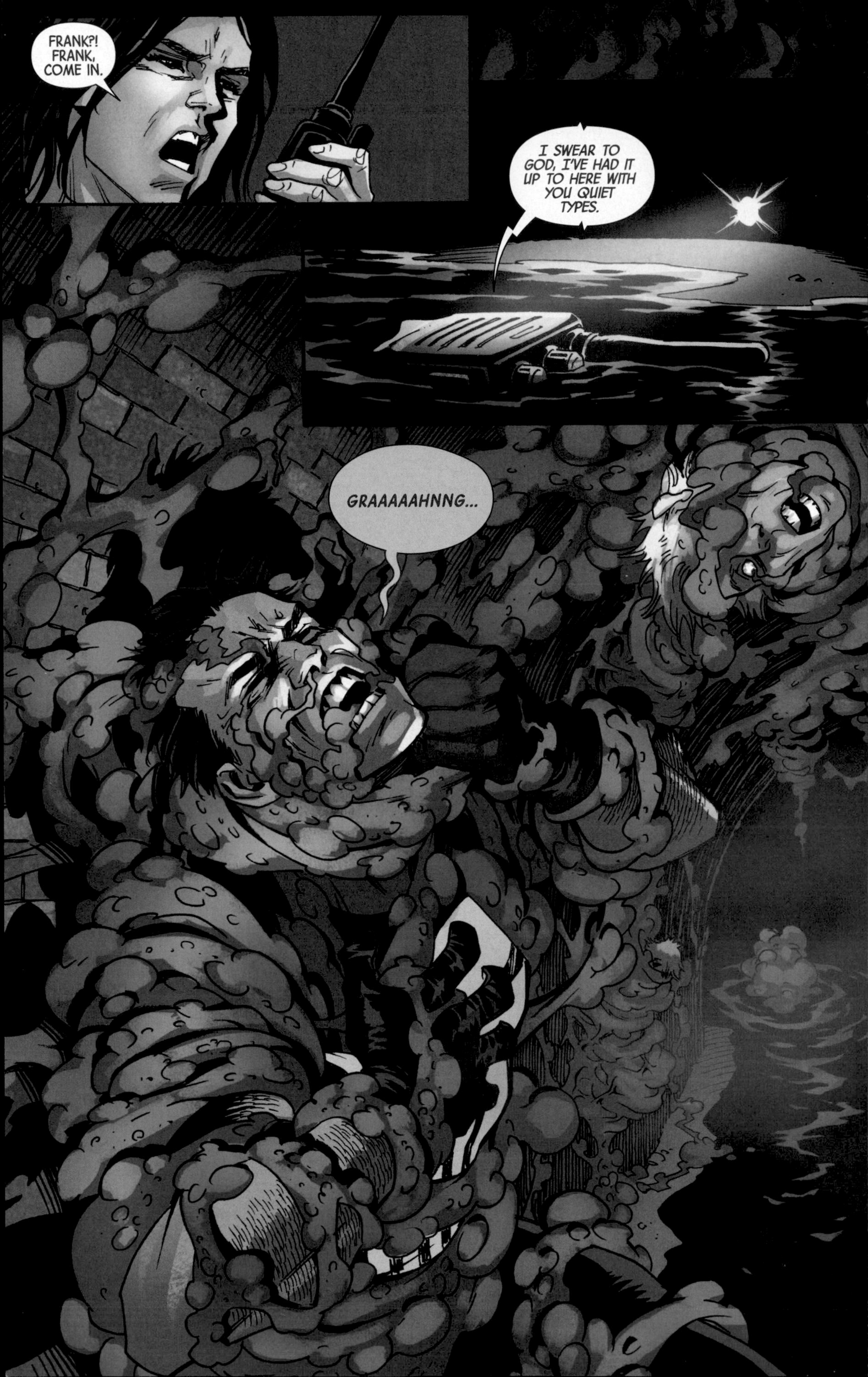
FRANK?! FRANK, COME IN.
I SWEAR TO GOD, I'VE HAD IT UP TO HERE WITH YOU QUIET TYPES.
GRAAAAAHNNG...

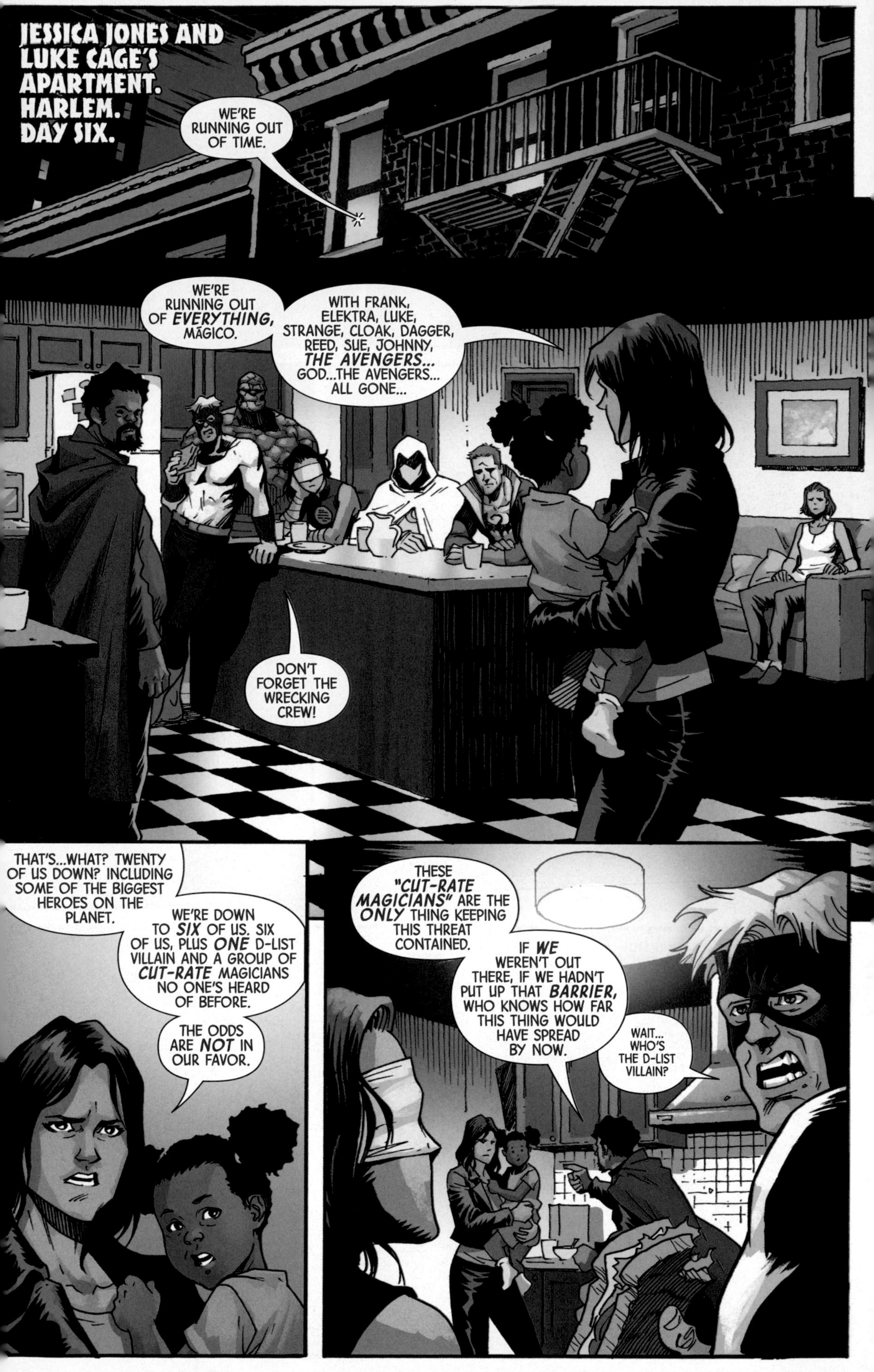

JESSICA JONES AND LUKE CAGE'S APARTMENT. HARLEM. DAY SIX.
WE'RE RUNNING OUT OF TIME.
WE'RE RUNNING OUT OF *EVERYTHING*, MÁGICO.
WITH FRANK, ELEKTRA, LUKE, STRANGE, CLOAK, DAGGER, REED, SUE, JOHNNY, *THE AVENGERS...* GOD...THE AVENGERS... ALL GONE...
DON'T FORGET THE WRECKING CREW!
THAT'S...WHAT? TWENTY OF US DOWN? INCLUDING SOME OF THE BIGGEST HEROES ON THE PLANET.
WE'RE DOWN TO *SIX* OF US. SIX OF US, PLUS *ONE* D-LIST VILLAIN AND A GROUP OF *CUT-RATE* MAGICIANS NO ONE'S HEARD OF BEFORE.
THE ODDS ARE *NOT* IN OUR FAVOR.
THESE *"CUT-RATE MAGICIANS"* ARE THE *ONLY* THING KEEPING THIS THREAT CONTAINED.
IF *WE* WEREN'T OUT THERE, IF WE HADN'T PUT UP THAT *BARRIER*, WHO KNOWS HOW FAR THIS THING WOULD HAVE SPREAD BY NOW.
WAIT... WHO'S THE D-LIST VILLAIN?

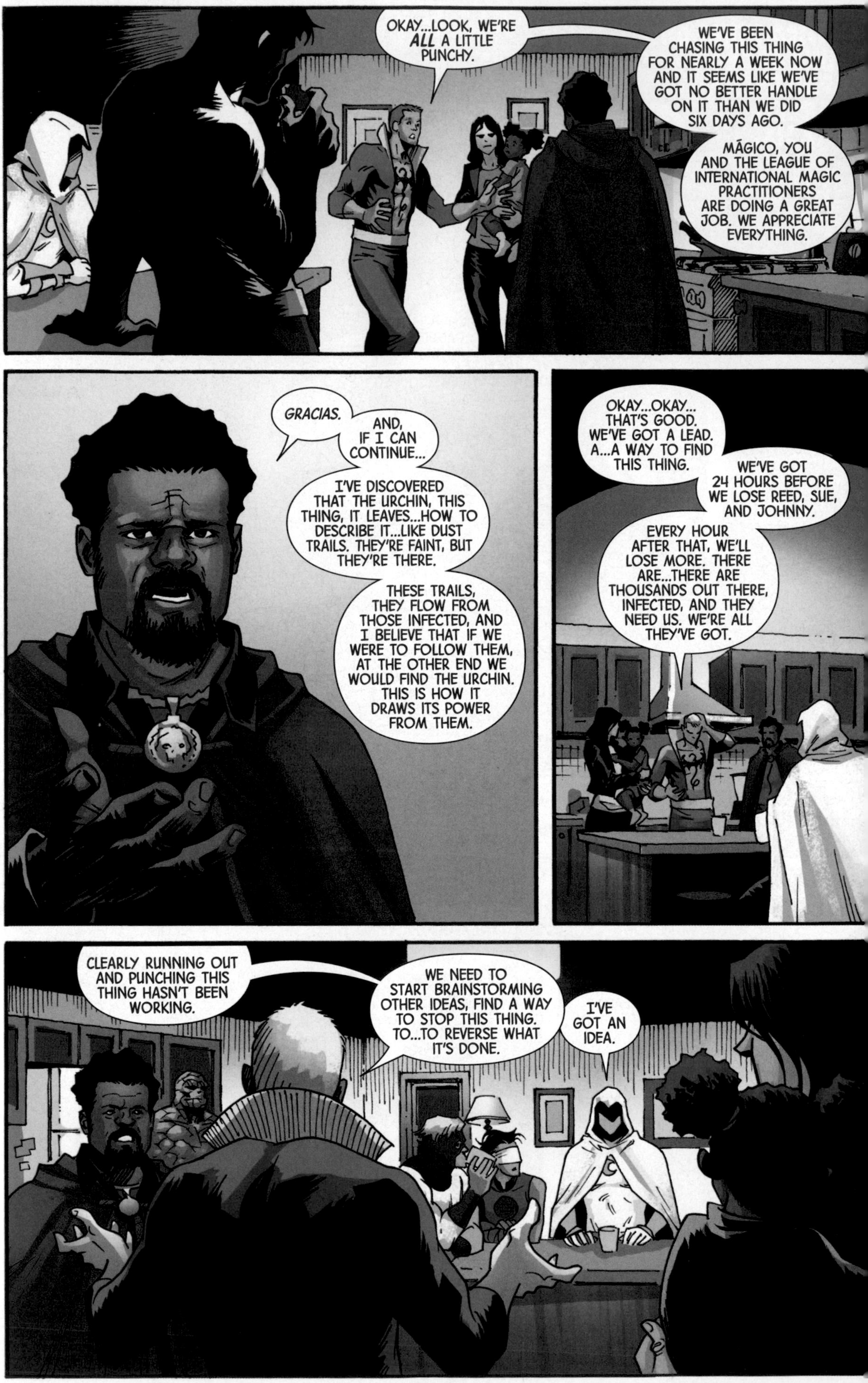
OKAY...LOOK, WE'RE ALL A LITTLE PUNCHY.
WE'VE BEEN CHASING THIS THING FOR NEARLY A WEEK NOW AND IT SEEMS LIKE WE'VE GOT NO BETTER HANDLE ON IT THAN WE DID SIX DAYS AGO.
MÁGICO, YOU AND THE LEAGUE OF INTERNATIONAL MAGIC PRACTITIONERS ARE DOING A GREAT JOB. WE APPRECIATE EVERYTHING.
GRACIAS.
AND, IF I CAN CONTINUE...
I'VE DISCOVERED THAT THE URCHIN, THIS THING, IT LEAVES...HOW TO DESCRIBE IT...LIKE DUST TRAILS. THEY'RE FAINT, BUT THEY'RE THERE.
THESE TRAILS, THEY FLOW FROM THOSE INFECTED, AND I BELIEVE THAT IF WE WERE TO FOLLOW THEM, AT THE OTHER END WE WOULD FIND THE URCHIN. THIS IS HOW IT DRAWS ITS POWER FROM THEM.
OKAY...OKAY... THAT'S GOOD. WE'VE GOT A LEAD. A...A WAY TO FIND THIS THING.
WE'VE GOT 24 HOURS BEFORE WE LOSE REED, SUE, AND JOHNNY.
EVERY HOUR AFTER THAT, WE'LL LOSE MORE. THERE ARE...THERE ARE THOUSANDS OUT THERE, INFECTED, AND THEY NEED US. WE'RE ALL THEY'VE GOT.
CLEARLY RUNNING OUT AND PUNCHING THIS THING HASN'T BEEN WORKING.
WE NEED TO START BRAINSTORMING OTHER IDEAS, FIND A WAY TO STOP THIS THING. TO...TO REVERSE WHAT IT'S DONE.
I'VE GOT AN IDEA.

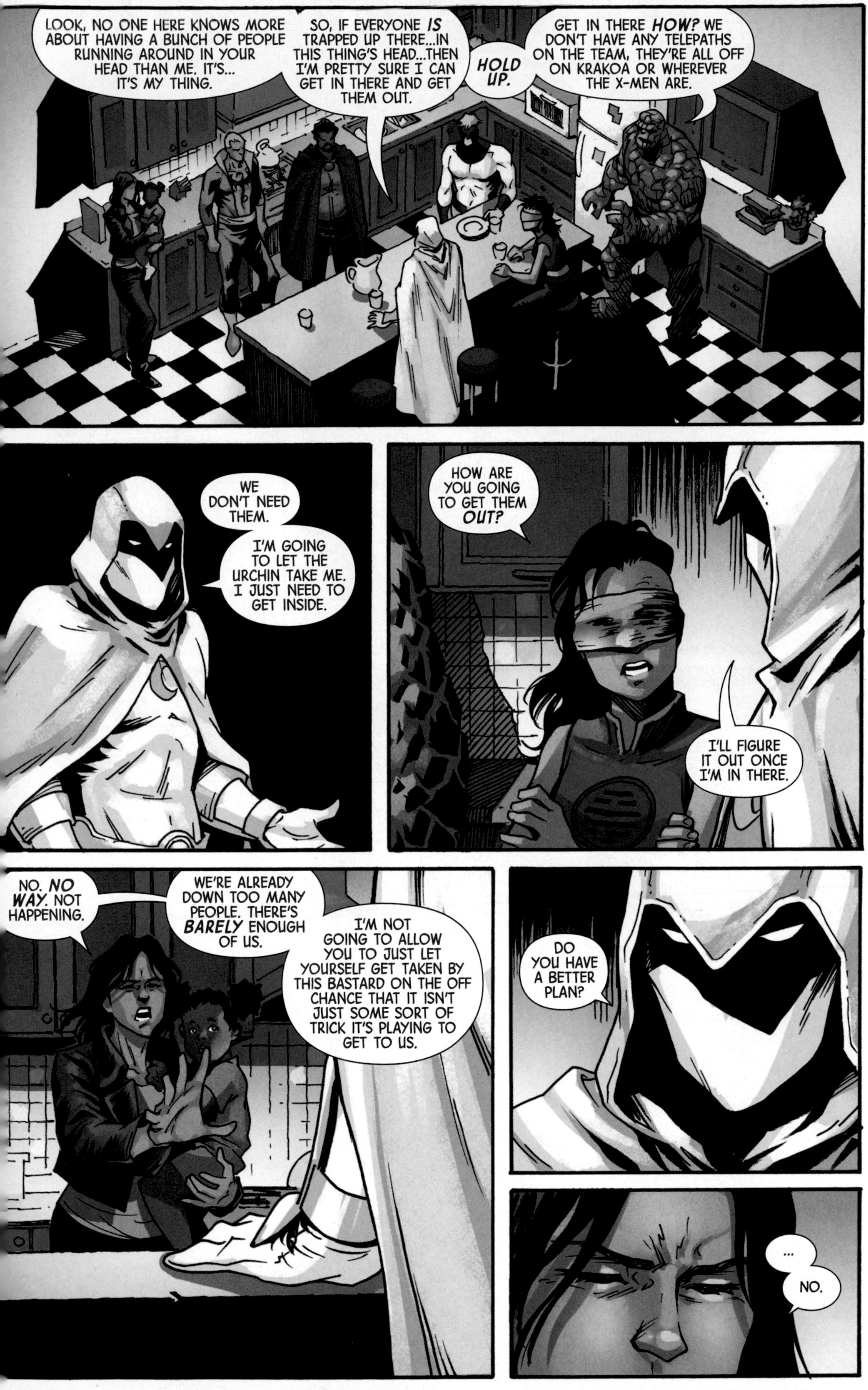
LOOK, NO ONE HERE KNOWS MORE ABOUT HAVING A BUNCH OF PEOPLE RUNNING AROUND IN YOUR HEAD THAN ME. IT'S... IT'S MY THING.
SO, IF EVERYONE *IS* TRAPPED UP THERE...IN THIS THING'S HEAD...THEN I'M PRETTY SURE I CAN GET IN THERE AND GET THEM OUT.
HOLD UP.
GET IN THERE *HOW?* WE DON'T HAVE ANY TELEPATHS ON THE TEAM, THEY'RE ALL OFF ON KRAKOA OR WHEREVER THE X-MEN ARE.
WE DON'T NEED THEM.
I'M GOING TO LET THE URCHIN TAKE ME. I JUST NEED TO GET INSIDE.
HOW ARE YOU GOING TO GET THEM *OUT?*
I'LL FIGURE IT OUT ONCE I'M IN THERE.
NO. *NO WAY*. NOT HAPPENING.
WE'RE ALREADY DOWN TOO MANY PEOPLE. THERE'S *BARELY* ENOUGH OF US.
I'M NOT GOING TO ALLOW YOU TO JUST LET YOURSELF GET TAKEN BY THIS BASTARD ON THE OFF CHANCE THAT IT ISN'T JUST SOME SORT OF TRICK IT'S PLAYING TO GET TO US.
DO YOU HAVE A BETTER PLAN?
...
NO.

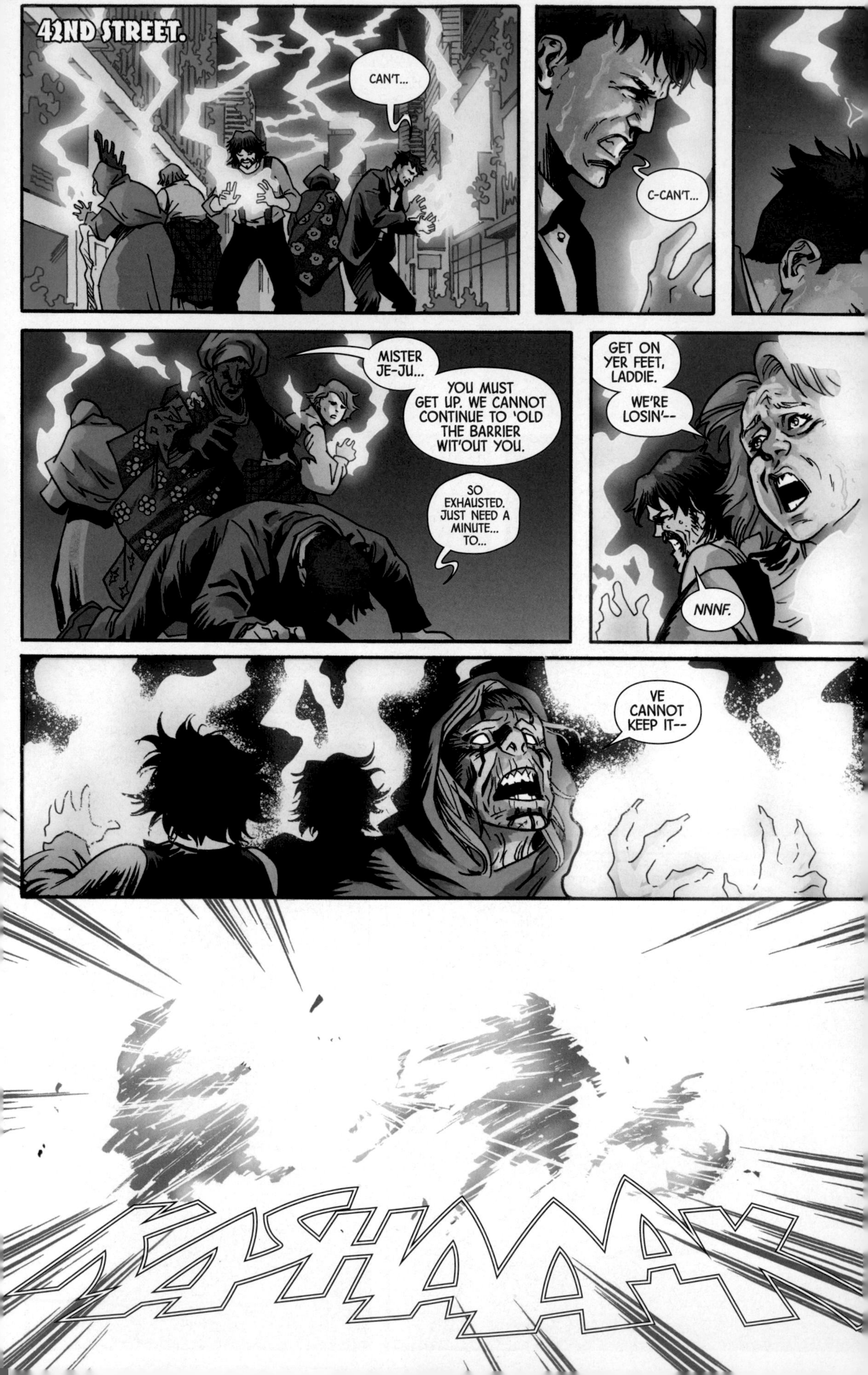
42ND STREET.
CAN'T...
C-CAN'T...
MISTER JE-JU...
YOU MUST GET UP. WE CANNOT CONTINUE TO 'OLD THE BARRIER WIT'OUT YOU.
SO EXHAUSTED. JUST NEED A MINUTE... TO...
GET ON YER FEET, LADDIE.
WE'RE LOSIN'--
NNNF.
VE CANNOT KEEP IT--
KASHAAAM

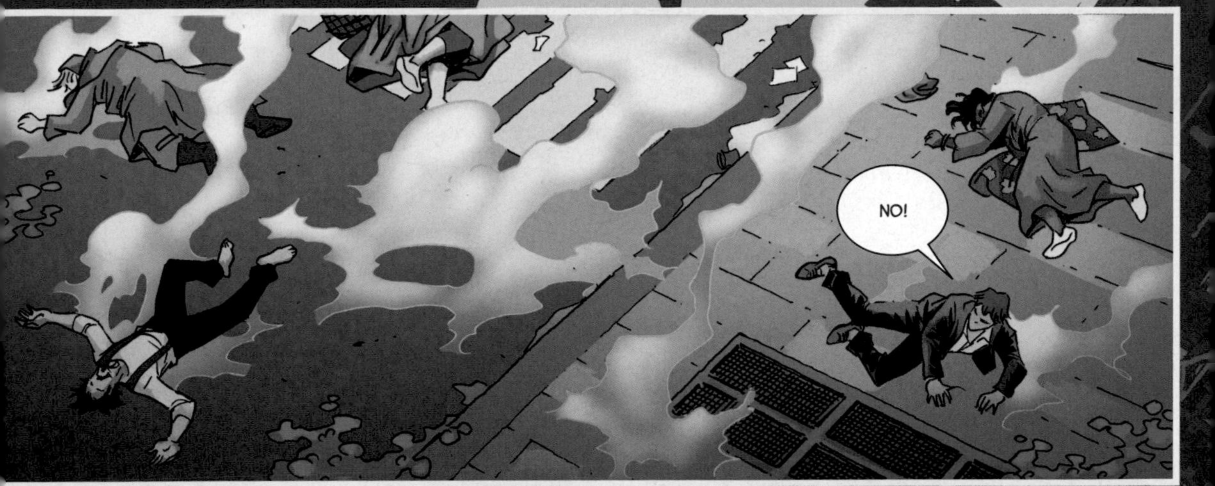
NO!

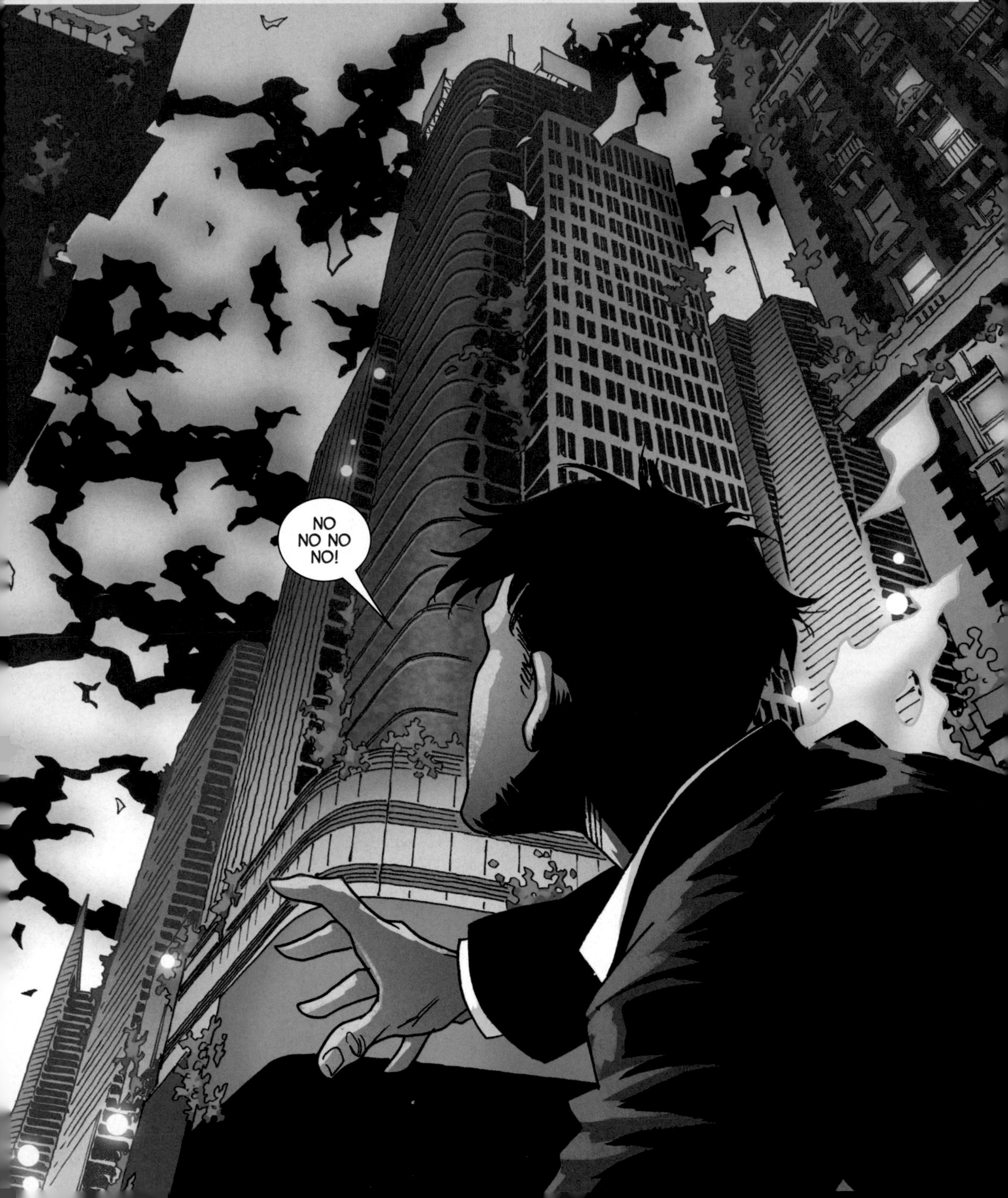
NO
NO NO
NO!

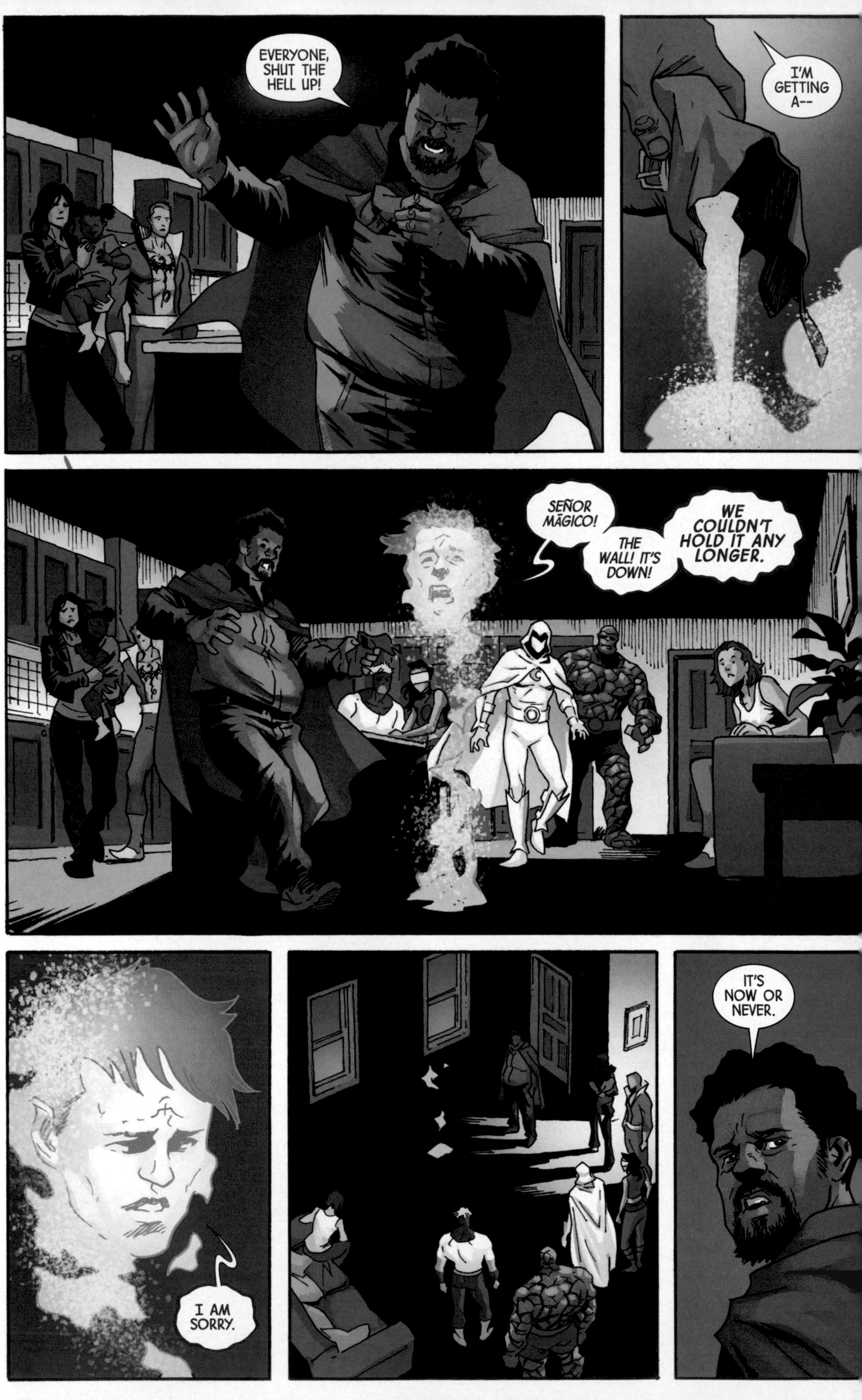
EVERYONE, SHUT THE HELL UP!
I'M GETTING A--
SEÑOR MÁGICO!
THE WALL! IT'S DOWN!
WE COULDN'T HOLD IT ANY LONGER.
I AM SORRY.
IT'S NOW OR NEVER.

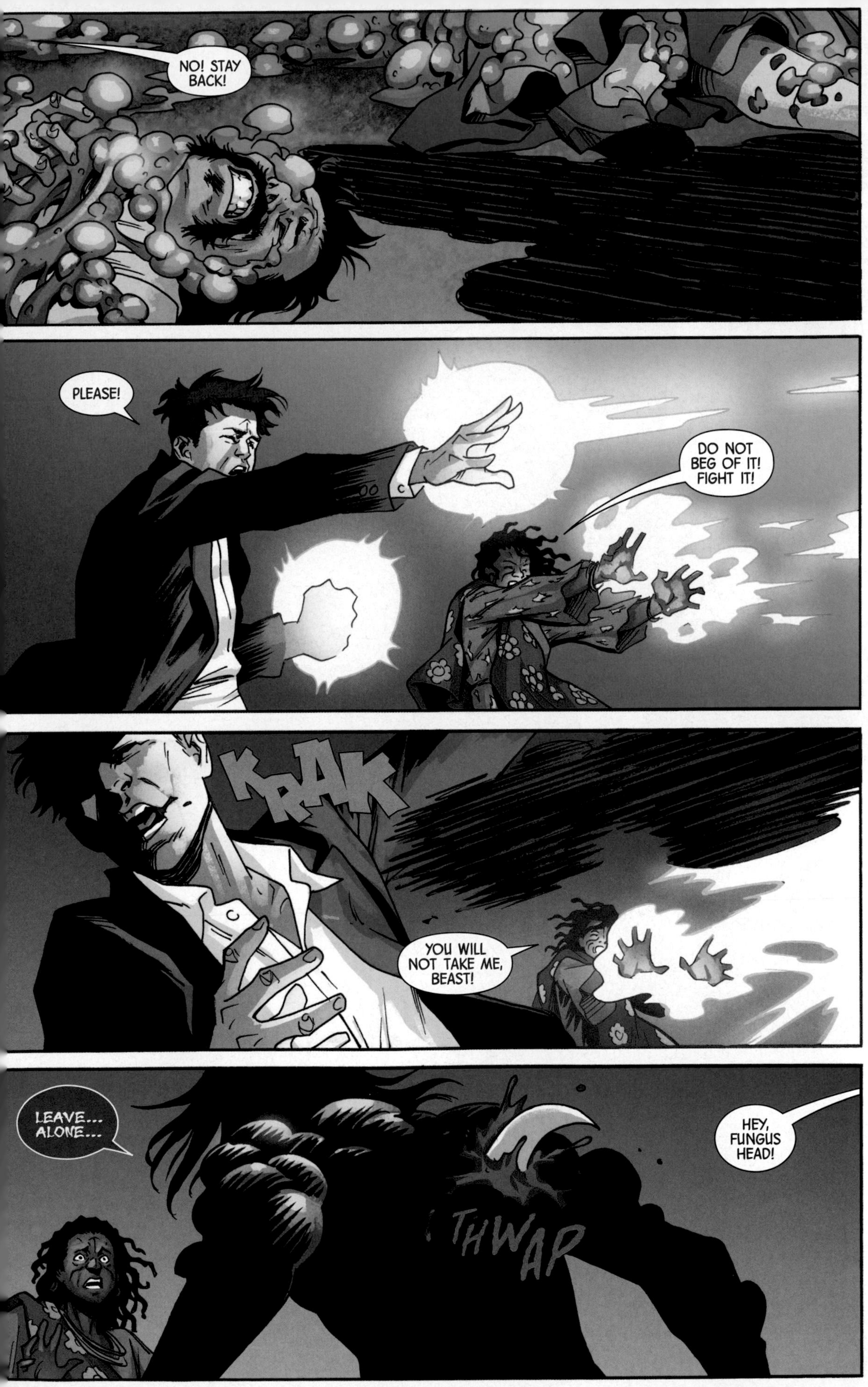
NO! STAY BACK!
PLEASE!
DO NOT BEG OF IT! FIGHT IT!
KRAK
YOU WILL NOT TAKE ME, BEAST!
LEAVE... ALONE...
HEY, FUNGUS HEAD!
THWAP

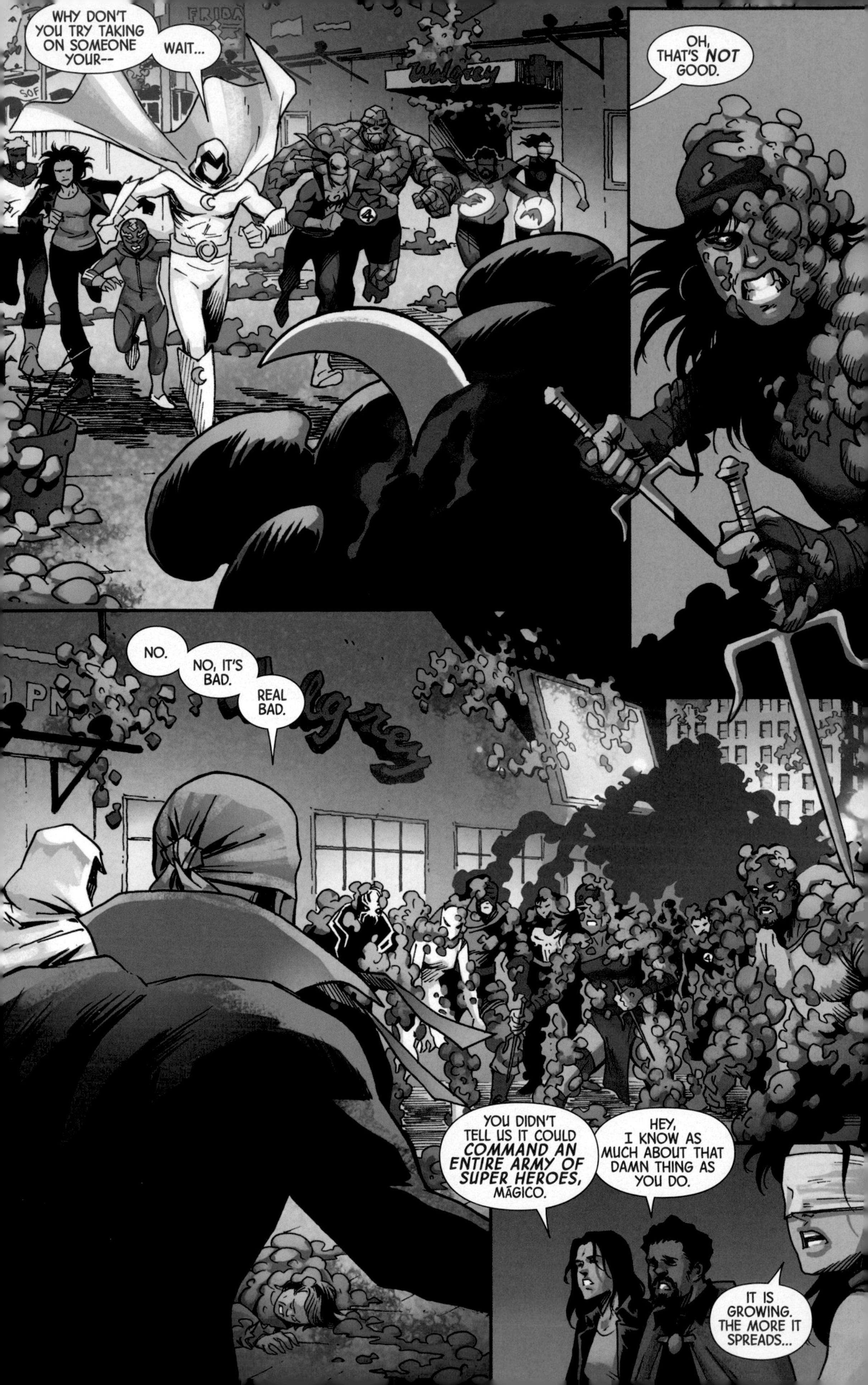
WHY DON'T YOU TRY TAKING ON SOMEONE YOUR--
WAIT...
OH, THAT'S *NOT* GOOD.
NO.
NO, IT'S BAD.
REAL BAD.
YOU DIDN'T TELL US IT COULD *COMMAND AN ENTIRE ARMY OF SUPER HEROES,* MÁGICO.
HEY, I KNOW AS MUCH ABOUT THAT DAMN THING AS YOU DO.
IT IS GROWING. THE MORE IT SPREADS...

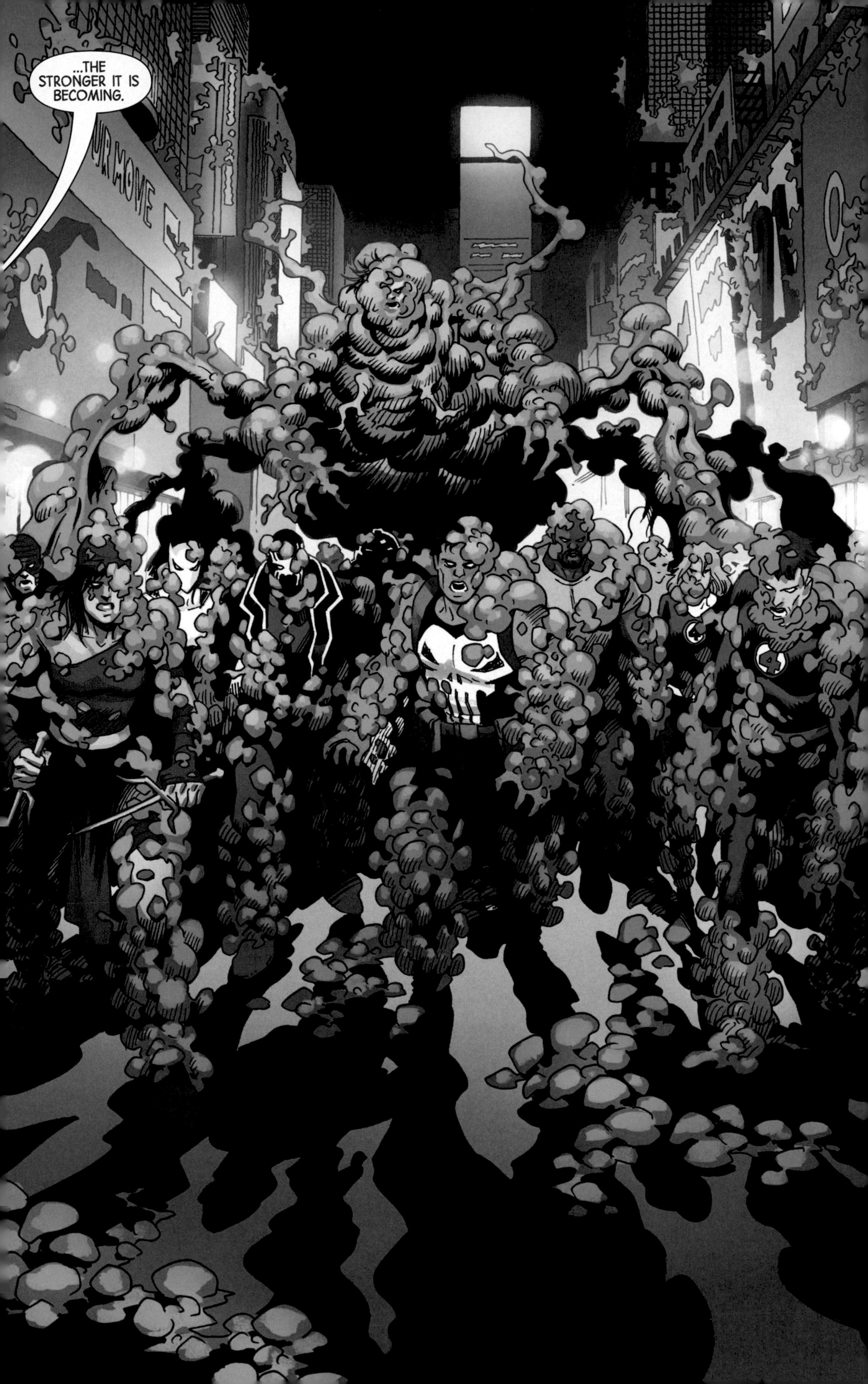
...THE STRONGER IT IS BECOMING.

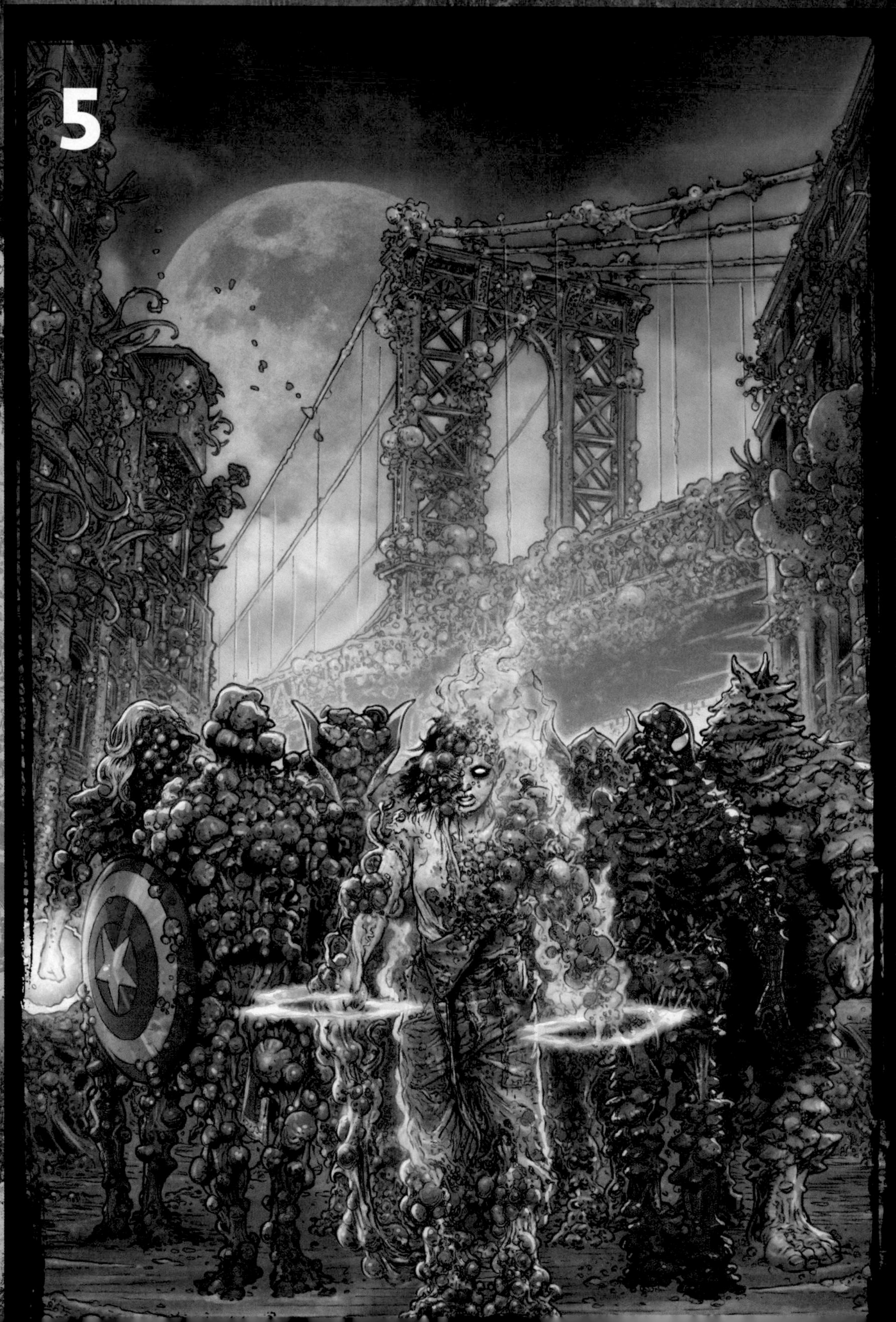
5

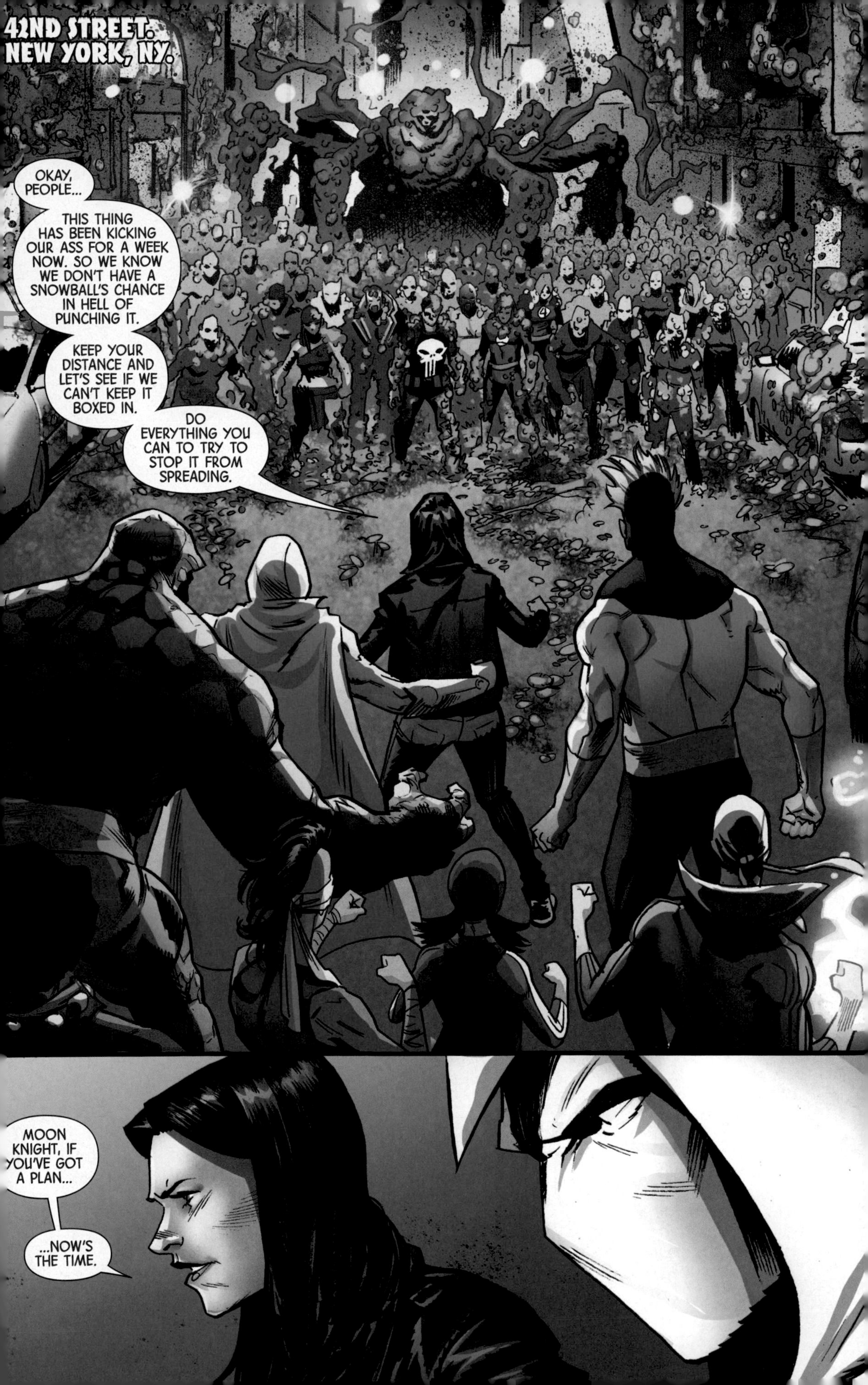
42ND STREET. NEW YORK, NY.
OKAY, PEOPLE...
THIS THING HAS BEEN KICKING OUR ASS FOR A WEEK NOW. SO WE KNOW WE DON'T HAVE A SNOWBALL'S CHANCE IN HELL OF PUNCHING IT.
KEEP YOUR DISTANCE AND LET'S SEE IF WE CAN'T KEEP IT BOXED IN.
DO EVERYTHING YOU CAN TO TRY TO STOP IT FROM SPREADING.
MOON KNIGHT, IF YOU'VE GOT A PLAN...
...NOW'S THE TIME.

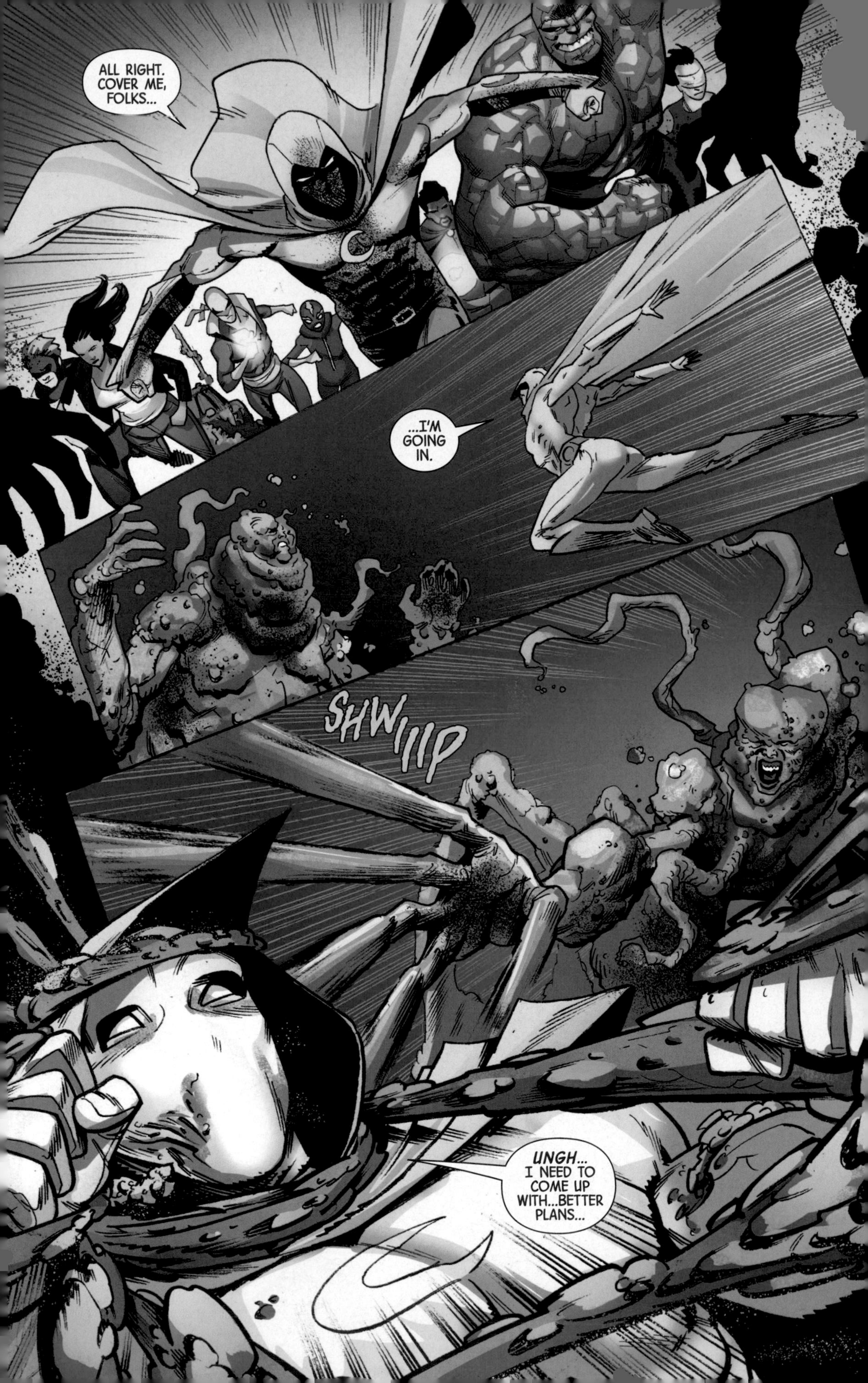
ALL RIGHT. COVER ME, FOLKS...
...I'M GOING IN.
SHWIIIP
UNGH... I NEED TO COME UP WITH...BETTER PLANS...

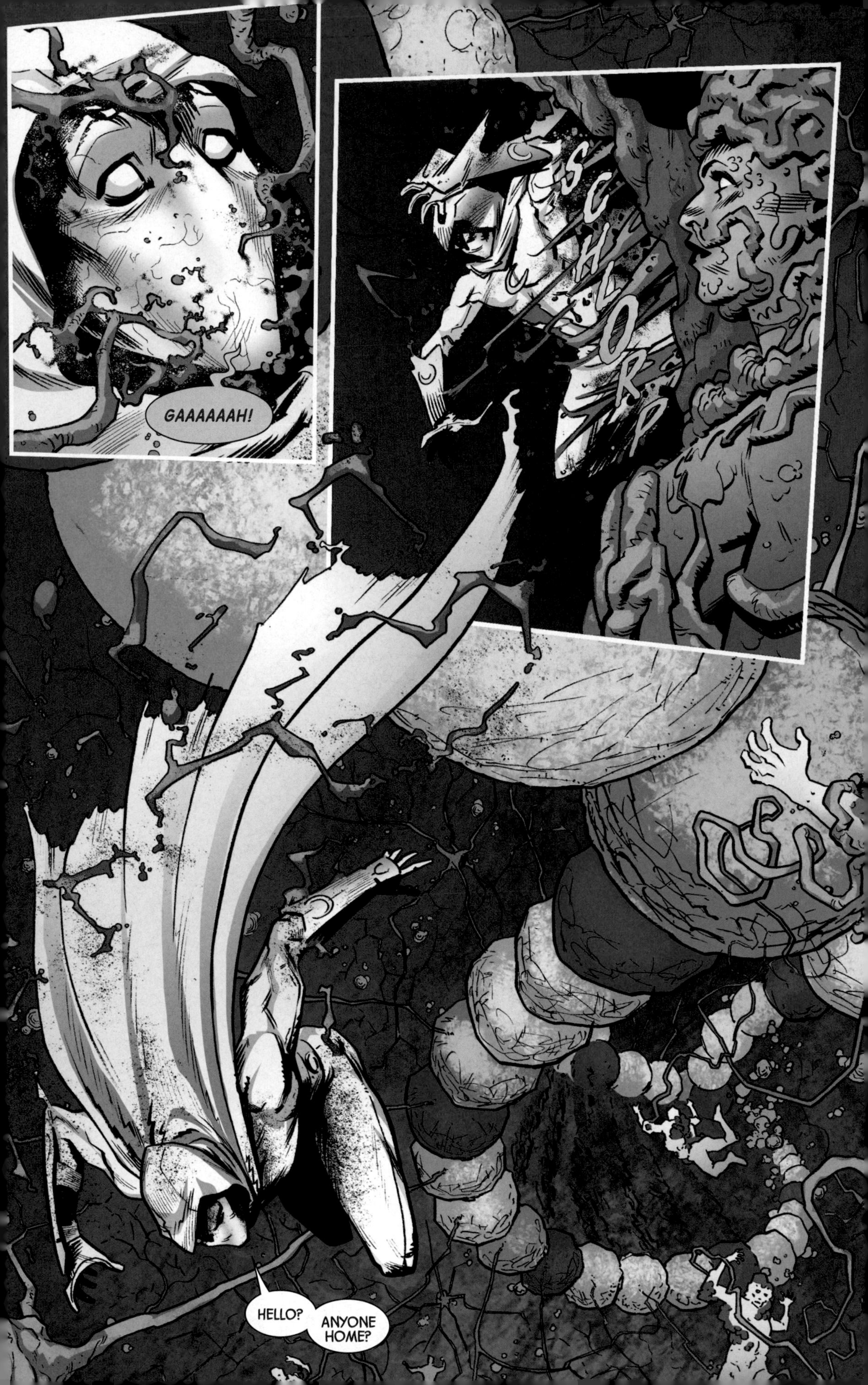
GAAAAAAH!
SCHLORP
HELLO?
ANYONE HOME?

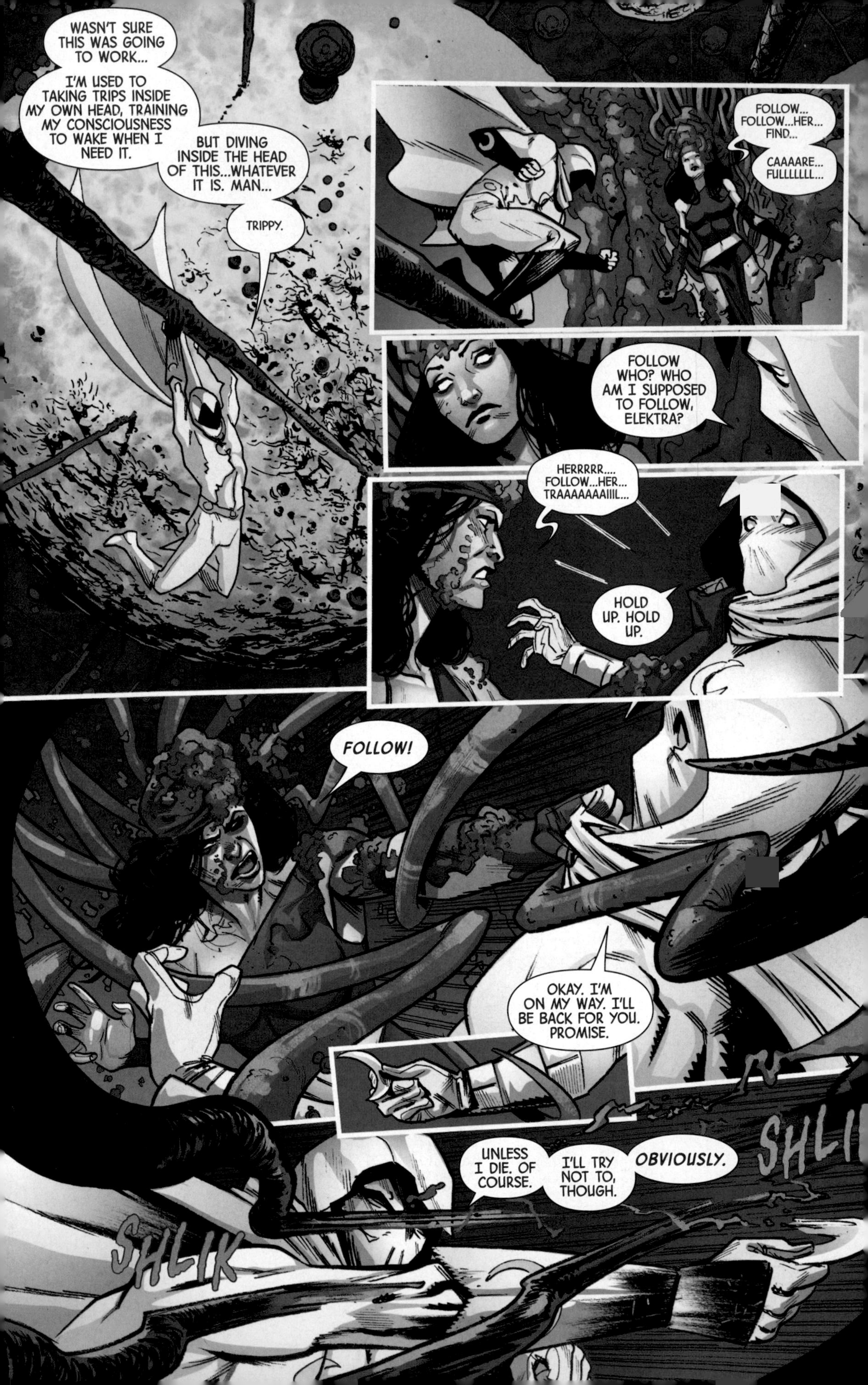

WASN'T SURE THIS WAS GOING TO WORK...
I'M USED TO TAKING TRIPS INSIDE MY OWN HEAD, TRAINING MY CONSCIOUSNESS TO WAKE WHEN I NEED IT.
BUT DIVING INSIDE THE HEAD OF THIS...WHATEVER IT IS. MAN...
TRIPPY.
FOLLOW... FOLLOW...HER... FIND...
CAAAARE... FULLLLLLL...
FOLLOW WHO? WHO AM I SUPPOSED TO FOLLOW, ELEKTRA?
HERRRRR.... FOLLOW...HER... TRAAAAAAAIIIL...
HOLD UP. HOLD UP.
FOLLOW!
OKAY. I'M ON MY WAY. I'LL BE BACK FOR YOU. PROMISE.
UNLESS I DIE. OF COURSE.
I'LL TRY NOT TO, THOUGH.
OBVIOUSLY.
SHLIK
SHLI

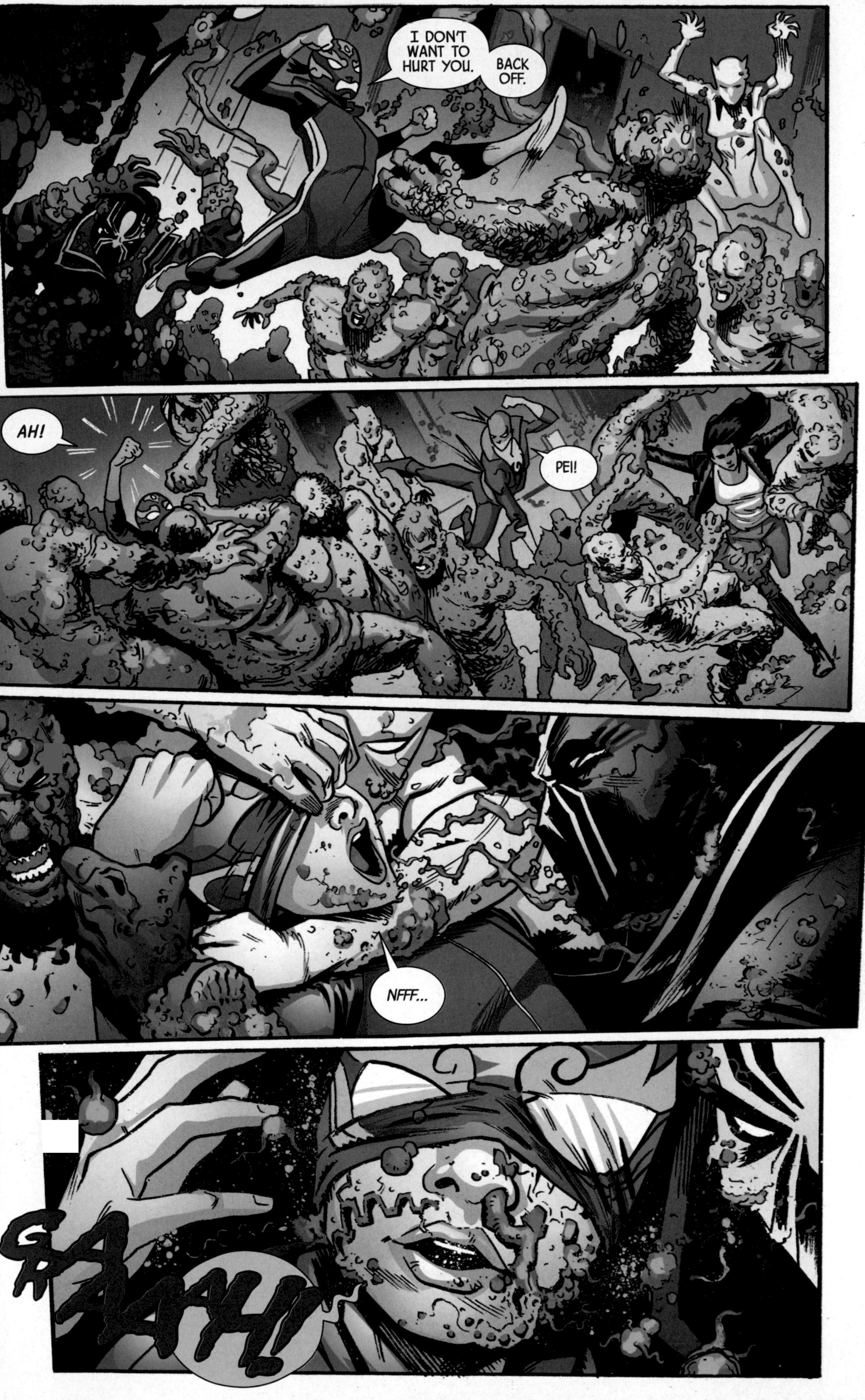
I DON'T WANT TO HURT YOU.
BACK OFF.
AH!
PEI!
NFFF...
GRAAH!!

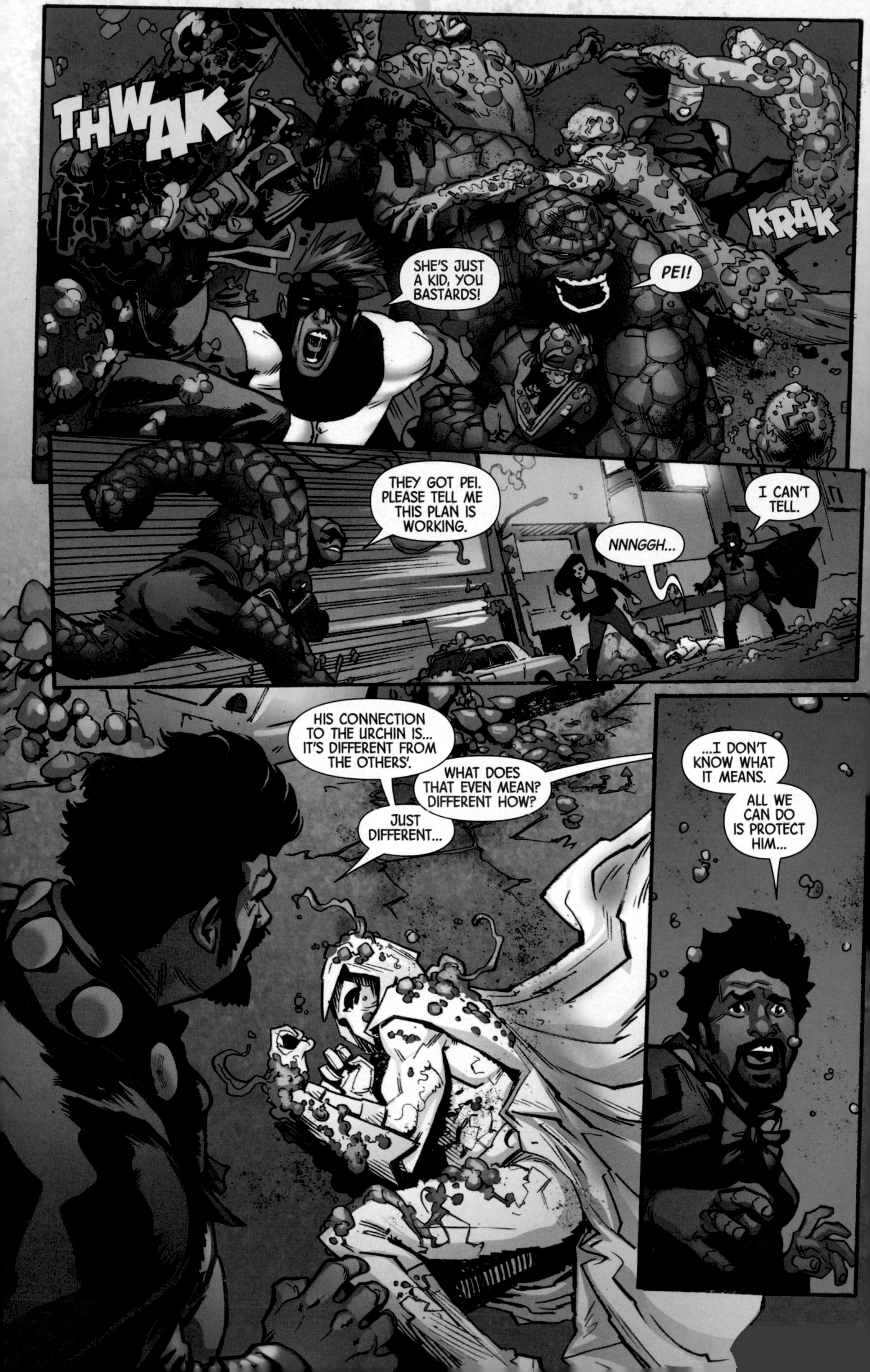
THWAK
KRAK
SHE'S JUST A KID, YOU BASTARDS!
PEI!
THEY GOT PEI. PLEASE TELL ME THIS PLAN IS WORKING.
I CAN'T TELL.
NNNGGH...
HIS CONNECTION TO THE URCHIN IS... IT'S DIFFERENT FROM THE OTHERS'.
WHAT DOES THAT EVEN MEAN? DIFFERENT HOW?
JUST DIFFERENT...
...I DON'T KNOW WHAT IT MEANS.
ALL WE CAN DO IS PROTECT HIM...

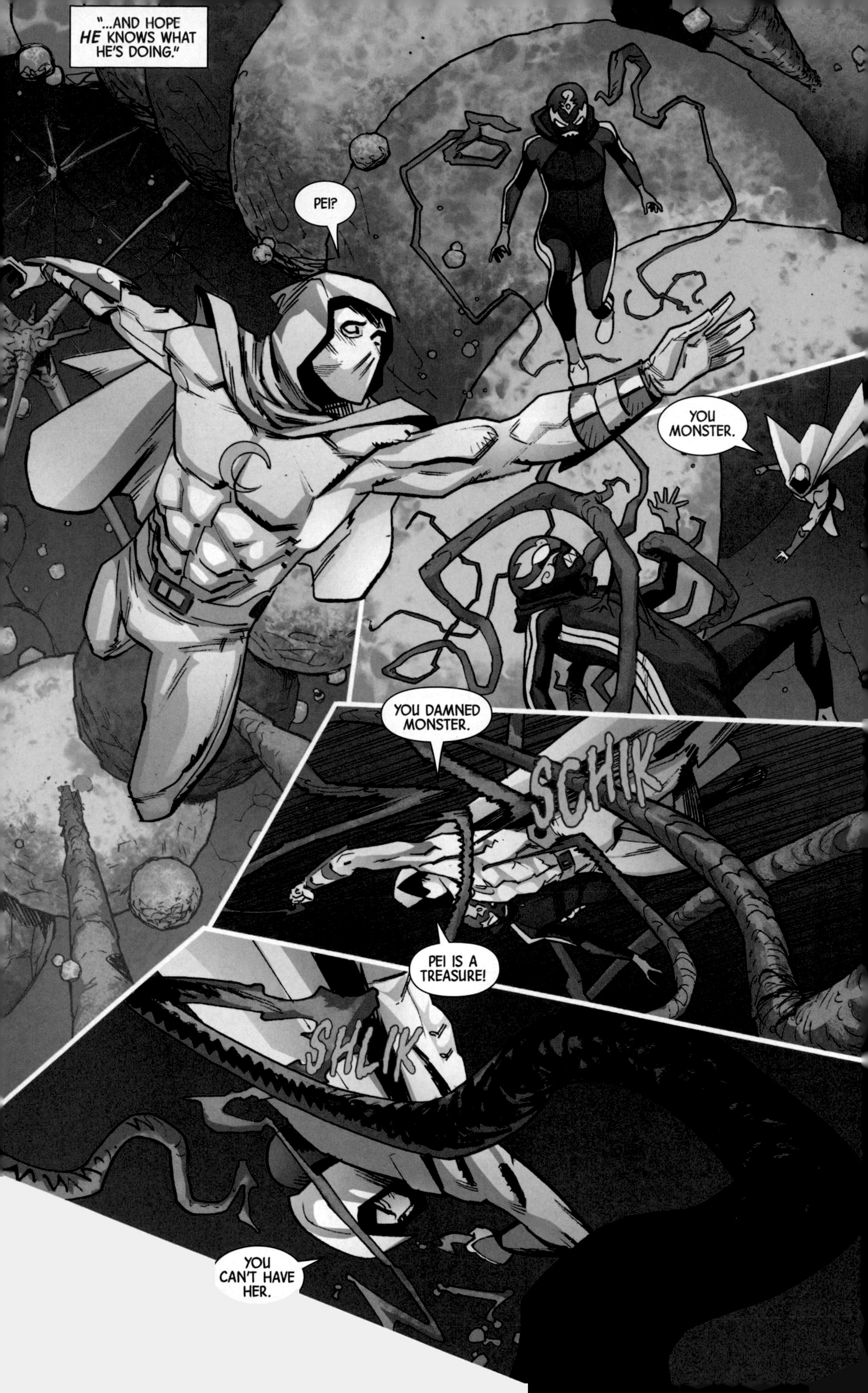
"...AND HOPE *HE* KNOWS WHAT HE'S DOING."
PEI?
YOU MONSTER.
YOU DAMNED MONSTER.
SCHIK
PEI IS A TREASURE!
SHLIK
YOU CAN'T HAVE HER.

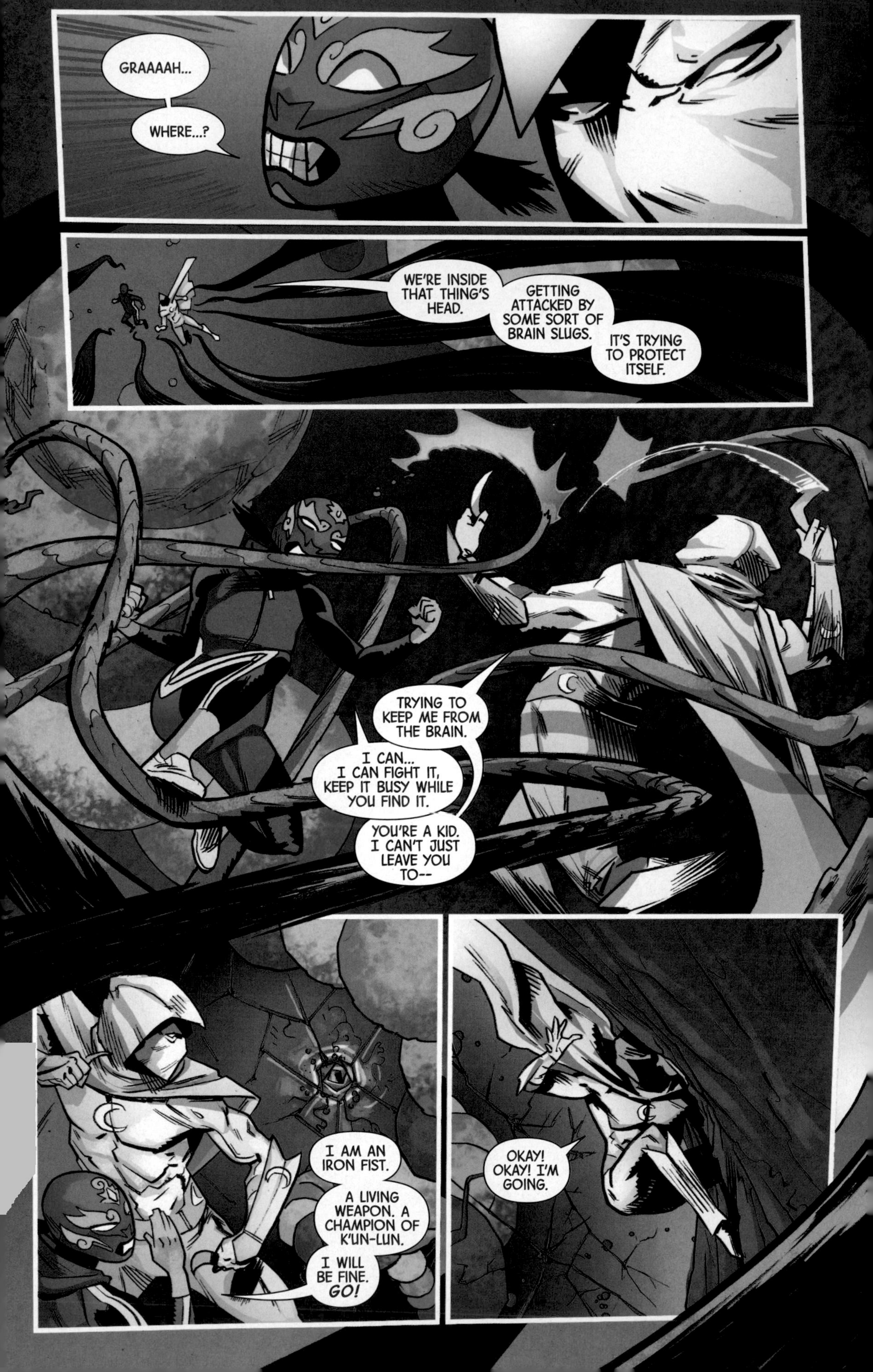
GRAAAAH...
WHERE...?
WE'RE INSIDE THAT THING'S HEAD.
GETTING ATTACKED BY SOME SORT OF BRAIN SLUGS.
IT'S TRYING TO PROTECT ITSELF.
TRYING TO KEEP ME FROM THE BRAIN.
I CAN... I CAN FIGHT IT, KEEP IT BUSY WHILE YOU FIND IT.
YOU'RE A KID. I CAN'T JUST LEAVE YOU TO--
I AM AN IRON FIST.
A LIVING WEAPON. A CHAMPION OF K'UN-LUN.
I WILL BE FINE. GO!
OKAY! OKAY! I'M GOING.

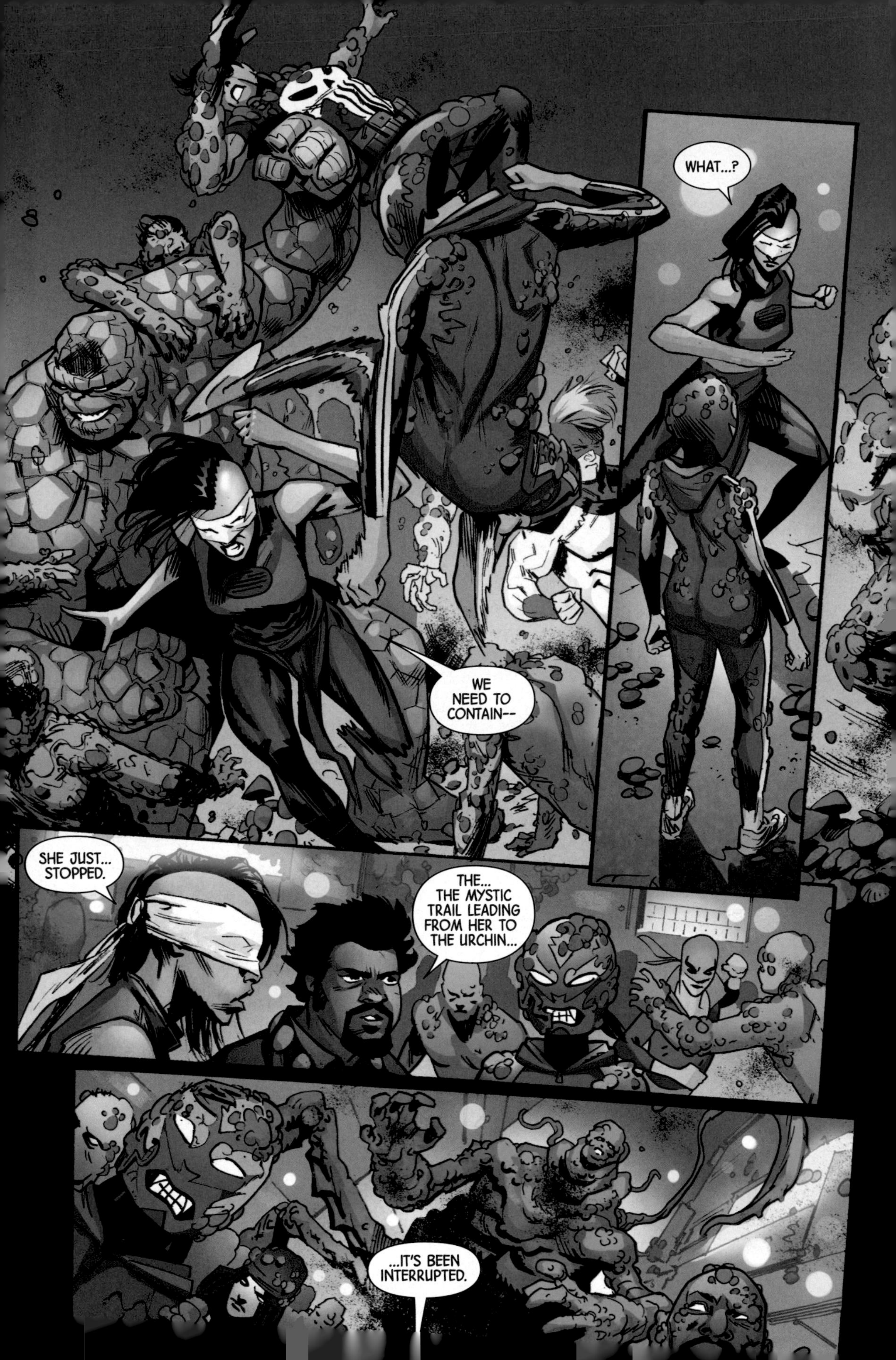
WHAT...?
WE NEED TO CONTAIN--
SHE JUST... STOPPED.
THE... THE MYSTIC TRAIL LEADING FROM HER TO THE URCHIN...
...IT'S BEEN INTERRUPTED.

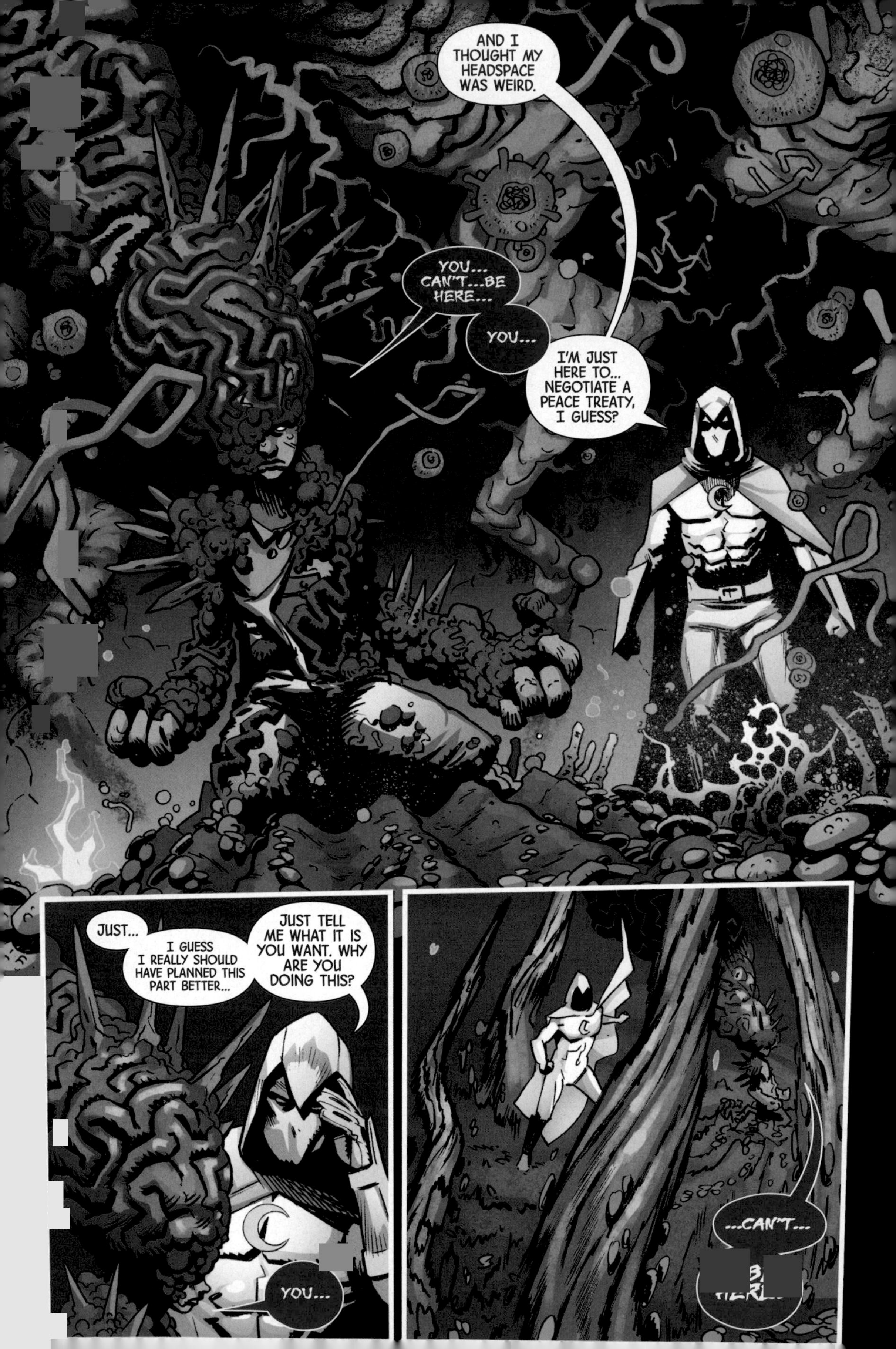
AND I THOUGHT MY HEADSPACE WAS WEIRD.
YOU... CAN'T...BE HERE...
YOU...
I'M JUST HERE TO... NEGOTIATE A PEACE TREATY, I GUESS?
JUST...
I GUESS I REALLY SHOULD HAVE PLANNED THIS PART BETTER...
JUST TELL ME WHAT IT IS YOU WANT. WHY ARE YOU DOING THIS?
YOU...
...CAN'T...

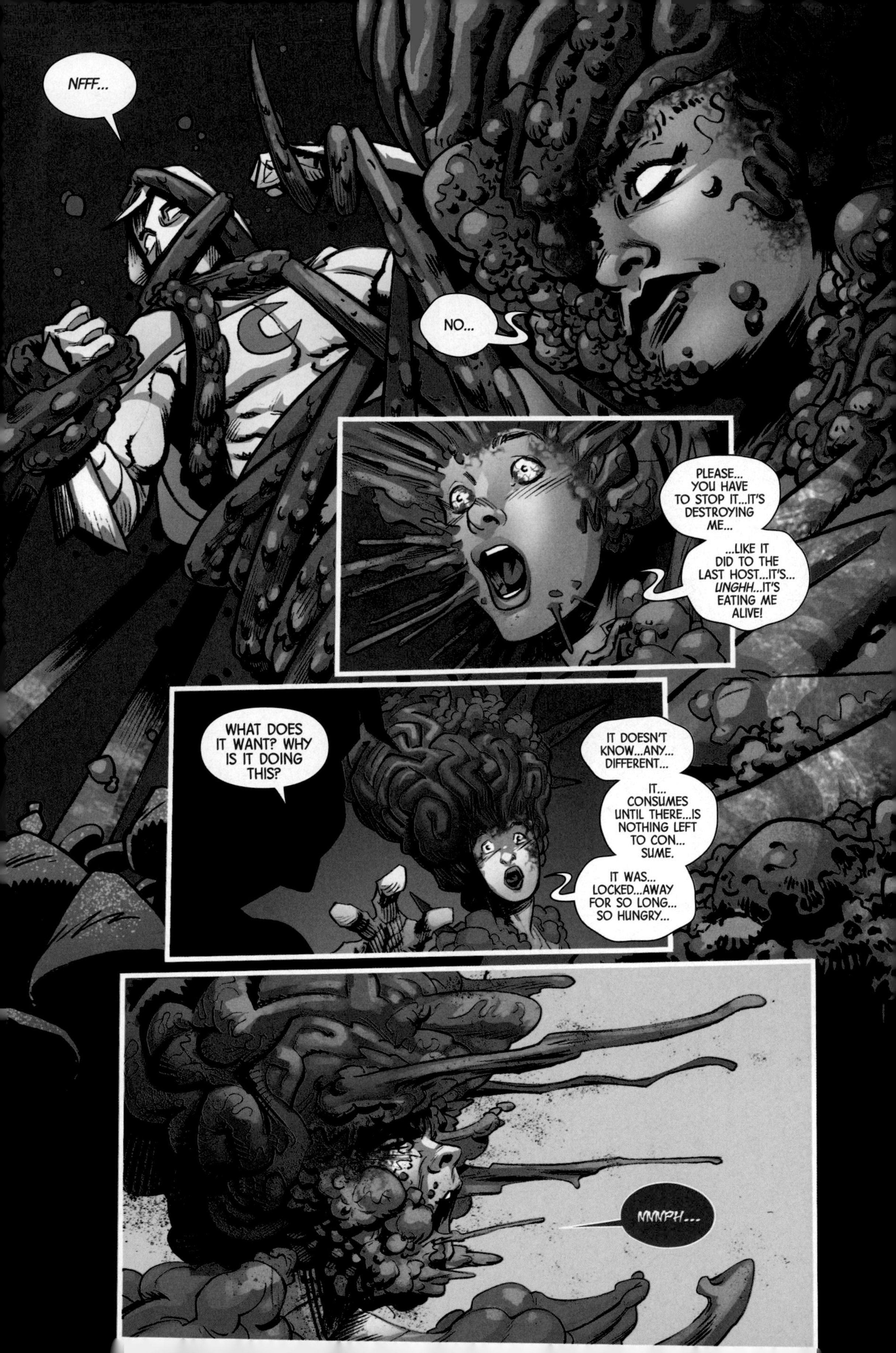
NFFF...
NO...
PLEASE... YOU HAVE TO STOP IT...IT'S DESTROYING ME...
...LIKE IT DID TO THE LAST HOST...IT'S... UNGHH...IT'S EATING ME ALIVE!
WHAT DOES IT WANT? WHY IS IT DOING THIS?
IT DOESN'T KNOW...ANY... DIFFERENT...
IT... CONSUMES UNTIL THERE...IS NOTHING LEFT TO CON... SUME.
IT WAS... LOCKED...AWAY FOR SO LONG... SO HUNGRY...
NNNPH...

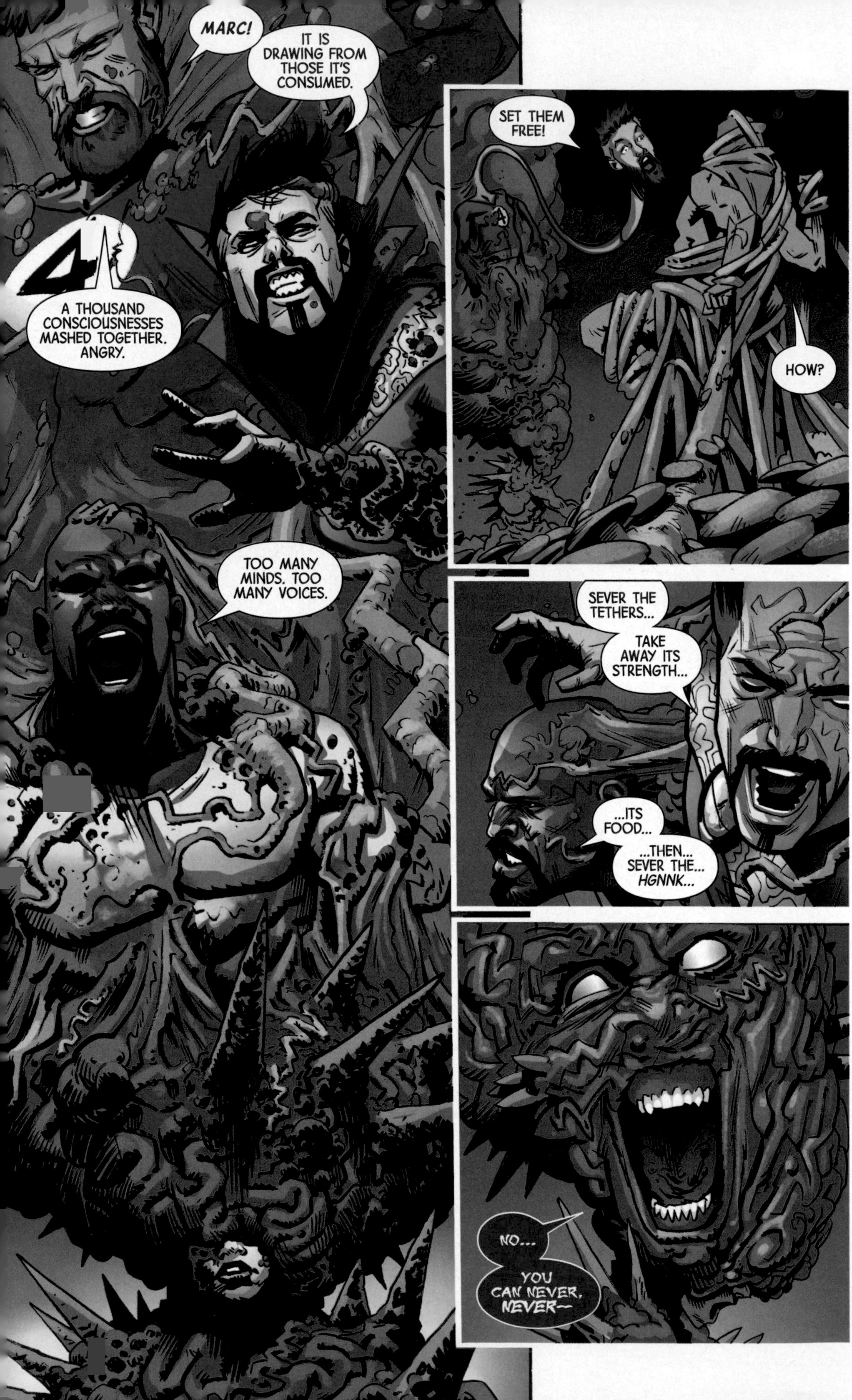
MARC!
IT IS DRAWING FROM THOSE IT'S CONSUMED.
A THOUSAND CONSCIOUSNESSES MASHED TOGETHER. ANGRY.
TOO MANY MINDS. TOO MANY VOICES.
SET THEM FREE!
HOW?
SEVER THE TETHERS...
TAKE AWAY ITS STRENGTH...
...ITS FOOD...
...THEN... SEVER THE... HGNNK...
NO...
YOU CAN NEVER, NEVER--

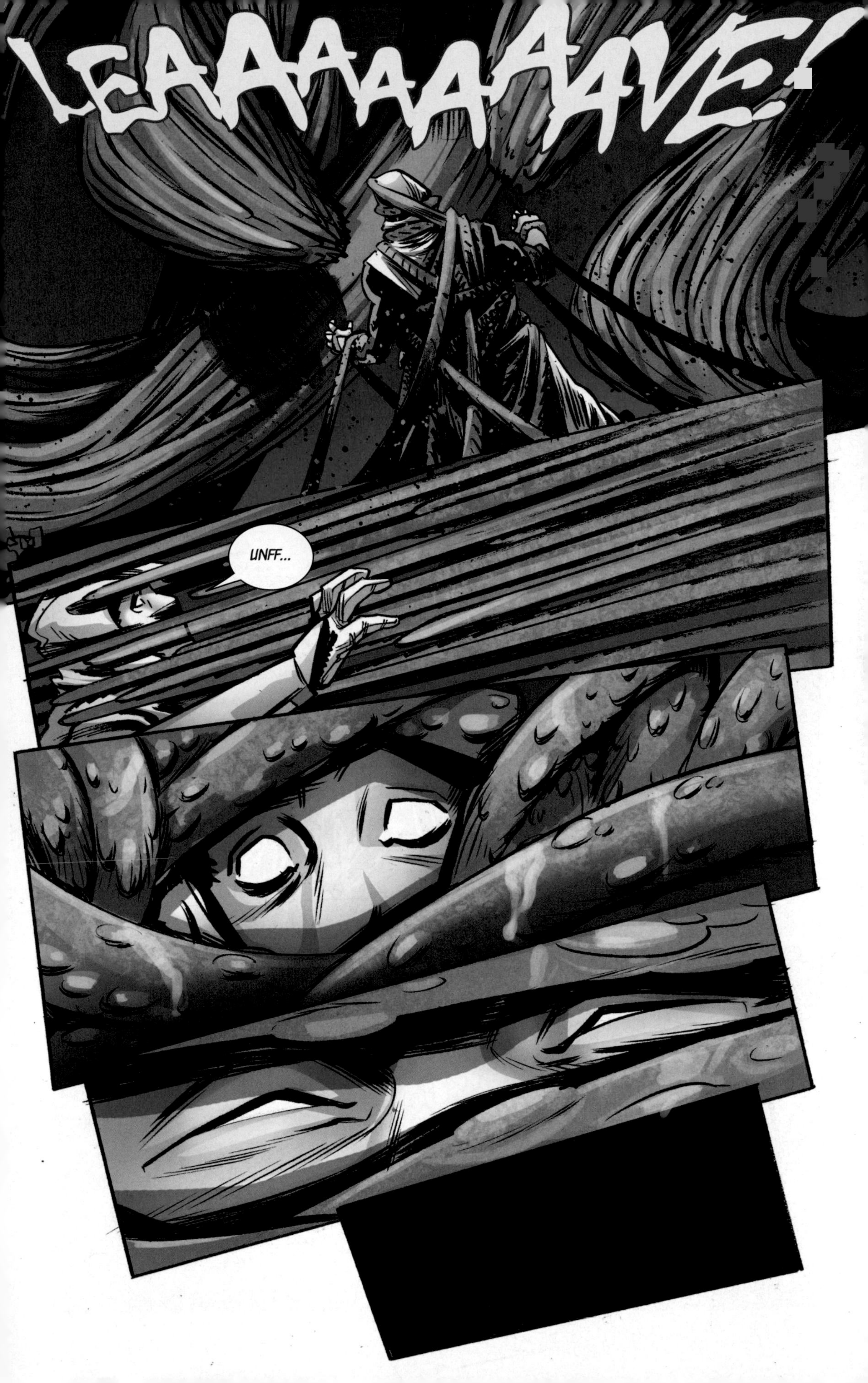
LEAAAAAAAVE!
UNFF...

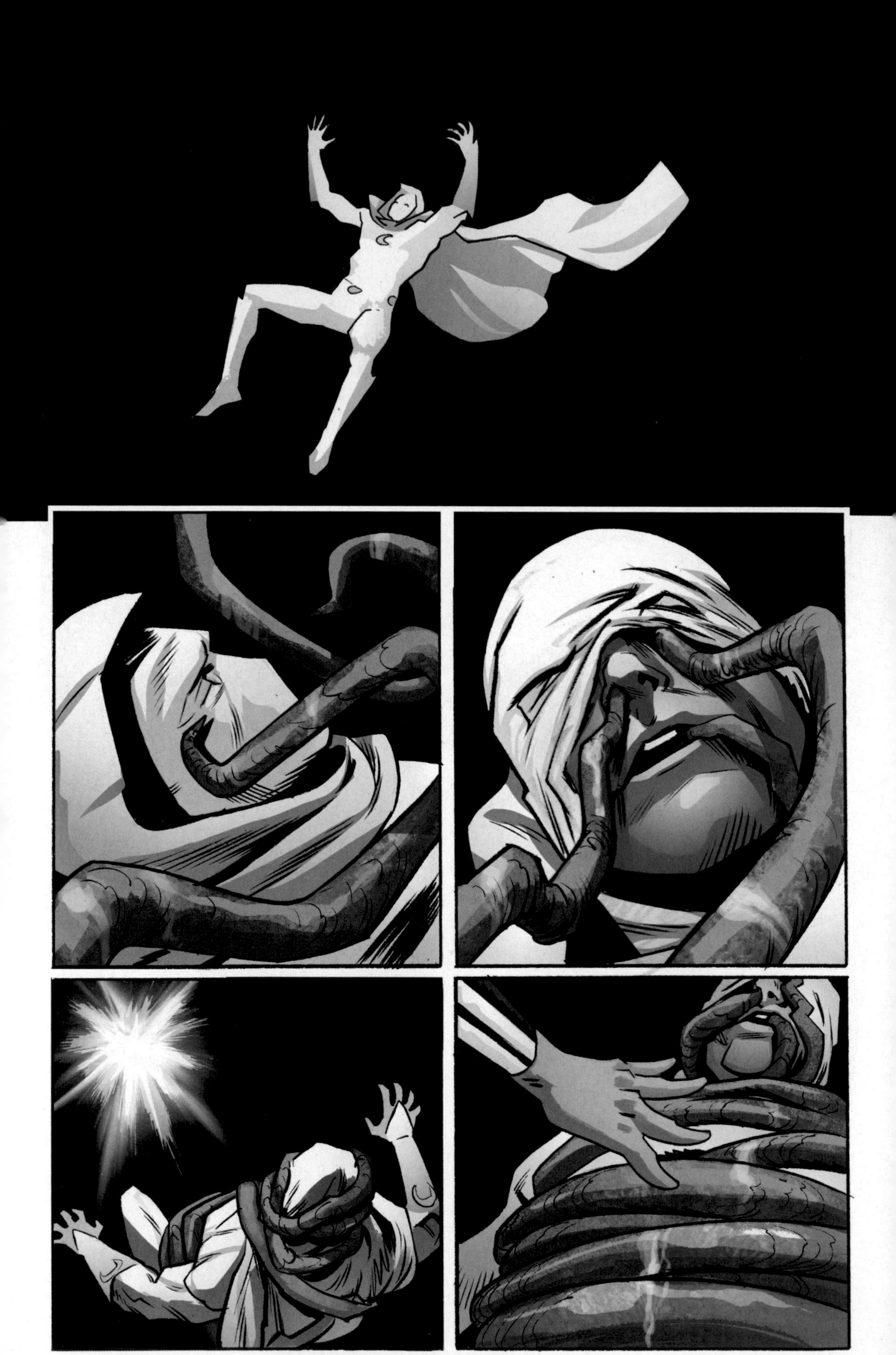

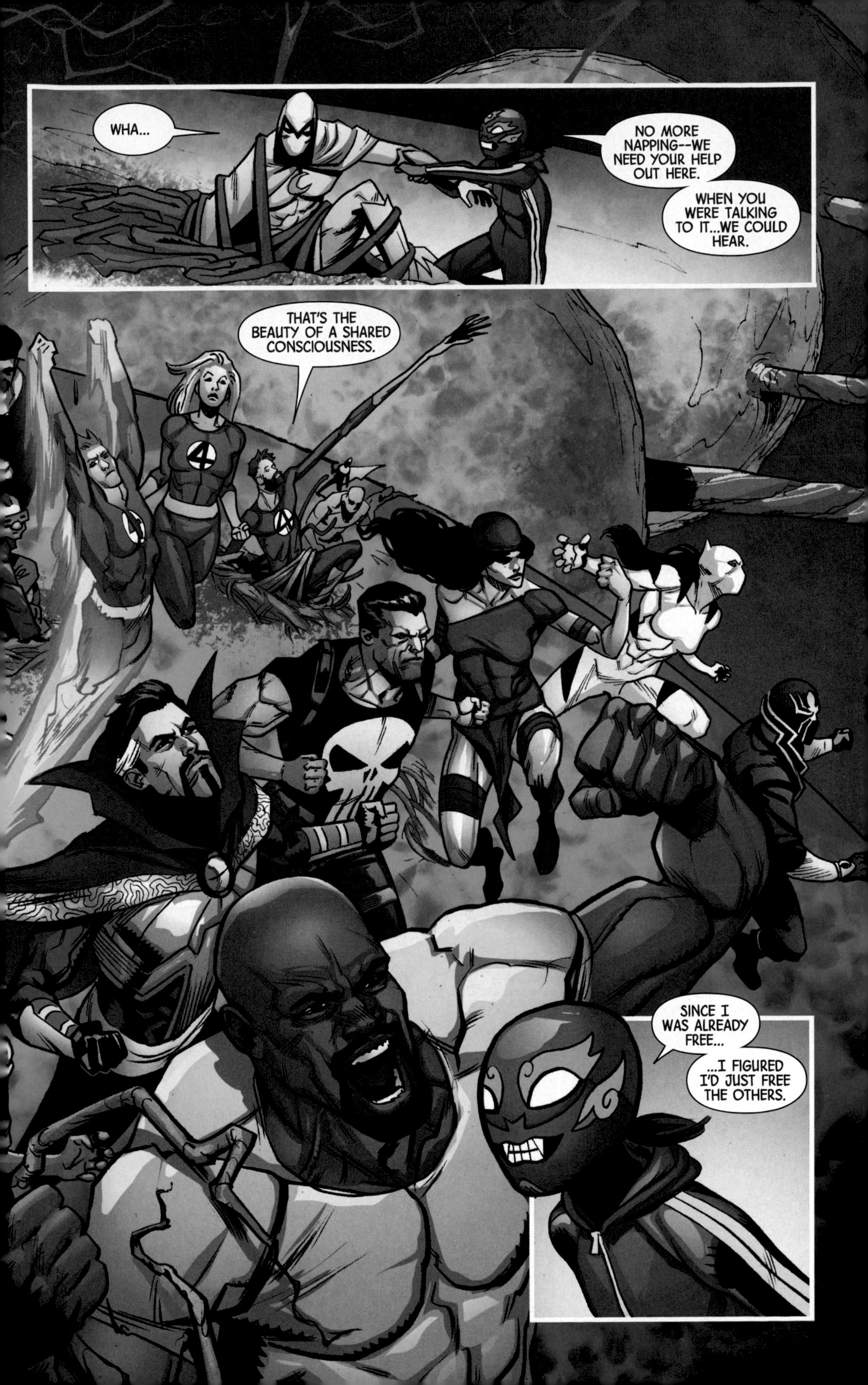
WHA...
NO MORE NAPPING--WE NEED YOUR HELP OUT HERE.
WHEN YOU WERE TALKING TO IT...WE COULD HEAR.
THAT'S THE BEAUTY OF A SHARED CONSCIOUSNESS.
SINCE I WAS ALREADY FREE...
...I FIGURED I'D JUST FREE THE OTHERS.

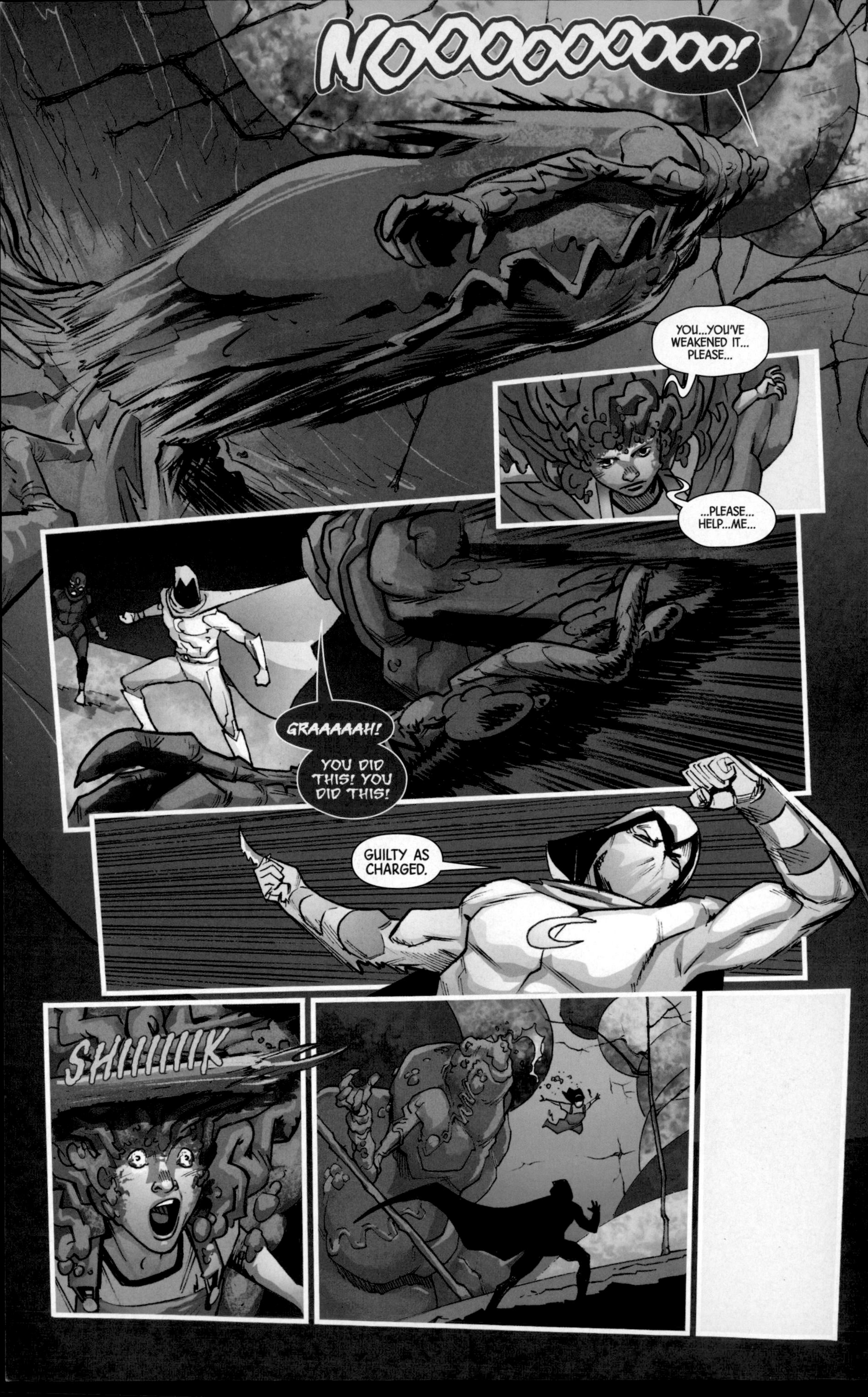
NOOOOOOOOO!
YOU...YOU'VE WEAKENED IT... PLEASE...
...PLEASE... HELP...ME...
GRAAAAAH!
YOU DID THIS! YOU DID THIS!
GUILTY AS CHARGED.
SHIIIIIK

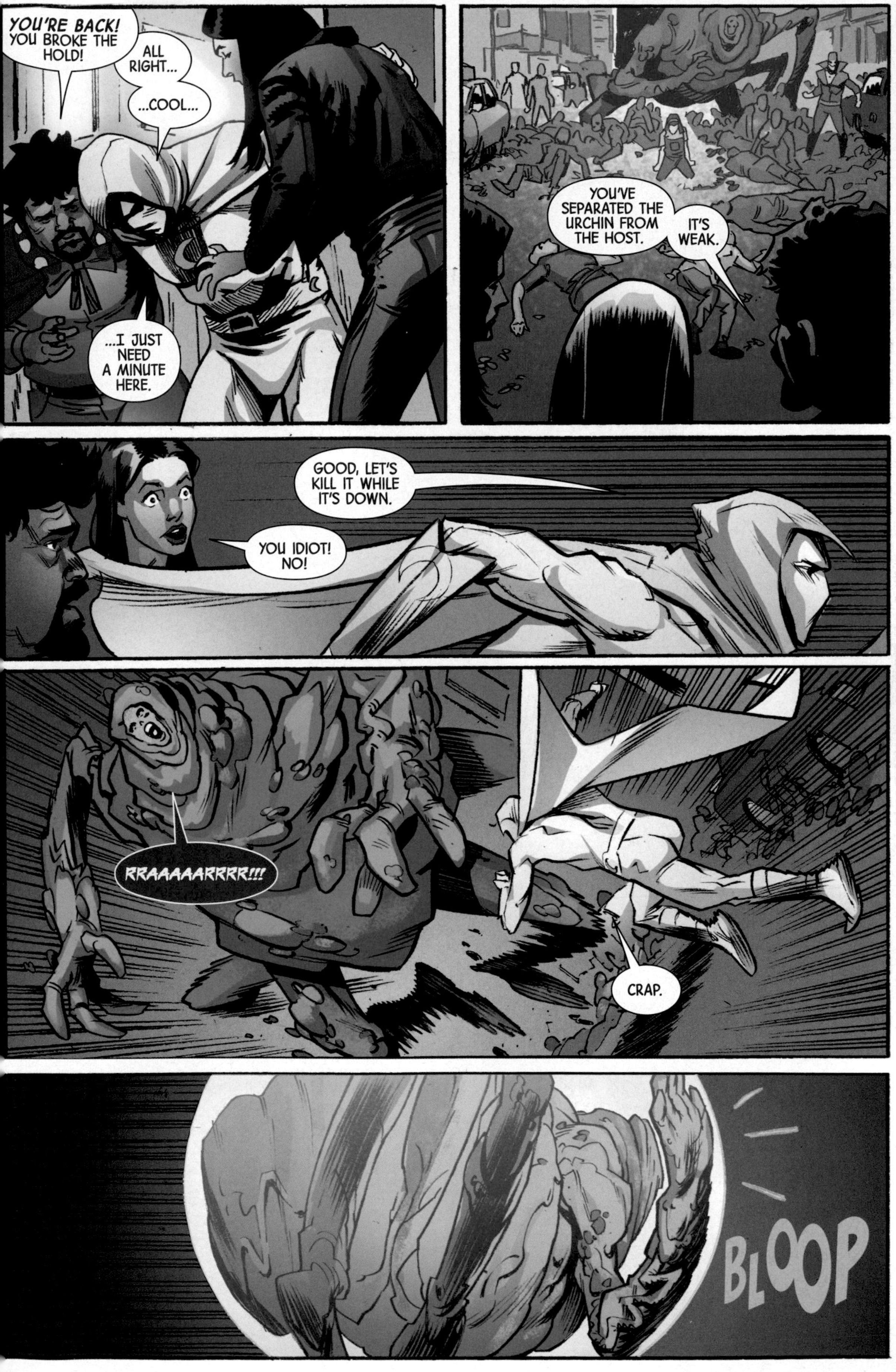
YOU'RE BACK! YOU BROKE THE HOLD!
ALL RIGHT...
...COOL...
...I JUST NEED A MINUTE HERE.
YOU'VE SEPARATED THE URCHIN FROM THE HOST.
IT'S WEAK.
GOOD, LET'S KILL IT WHILE IT'S DOWN.
YOU IDIOT! NO!
RRAAAAARRRR!!!
CRAP.
BLOOP

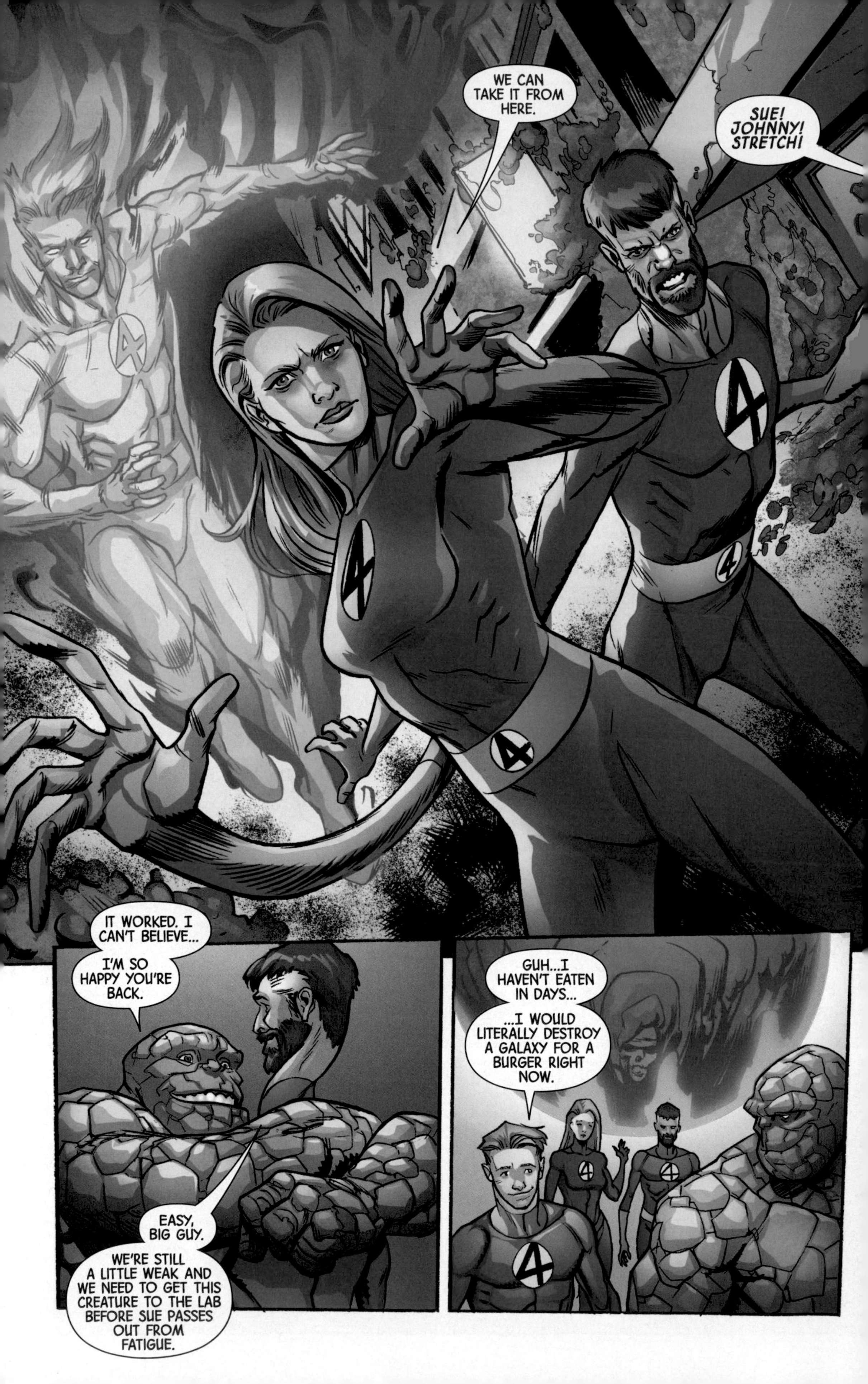
WE CAN TAKE IT FROM HERE.
SUE! JOHNNY! STRETCH!
IT WORKED. I CAN'T BELIEVE...
I'M SO HAPPY YOU'RE BACK.
EASY, BIG GUY.
WE'RE STILL A LITTLE WEAK AND WE NEED TO GET THIS CREATURE TO THE LAB BEFORE SUE PASSES OUT FROM FATIGUE.
GUH...I HAVEN'T EATEN IN DAYS...
...I WOULD LITERALLY DESTROY A GALAXY FOR A BURGER RIGHT NOW.

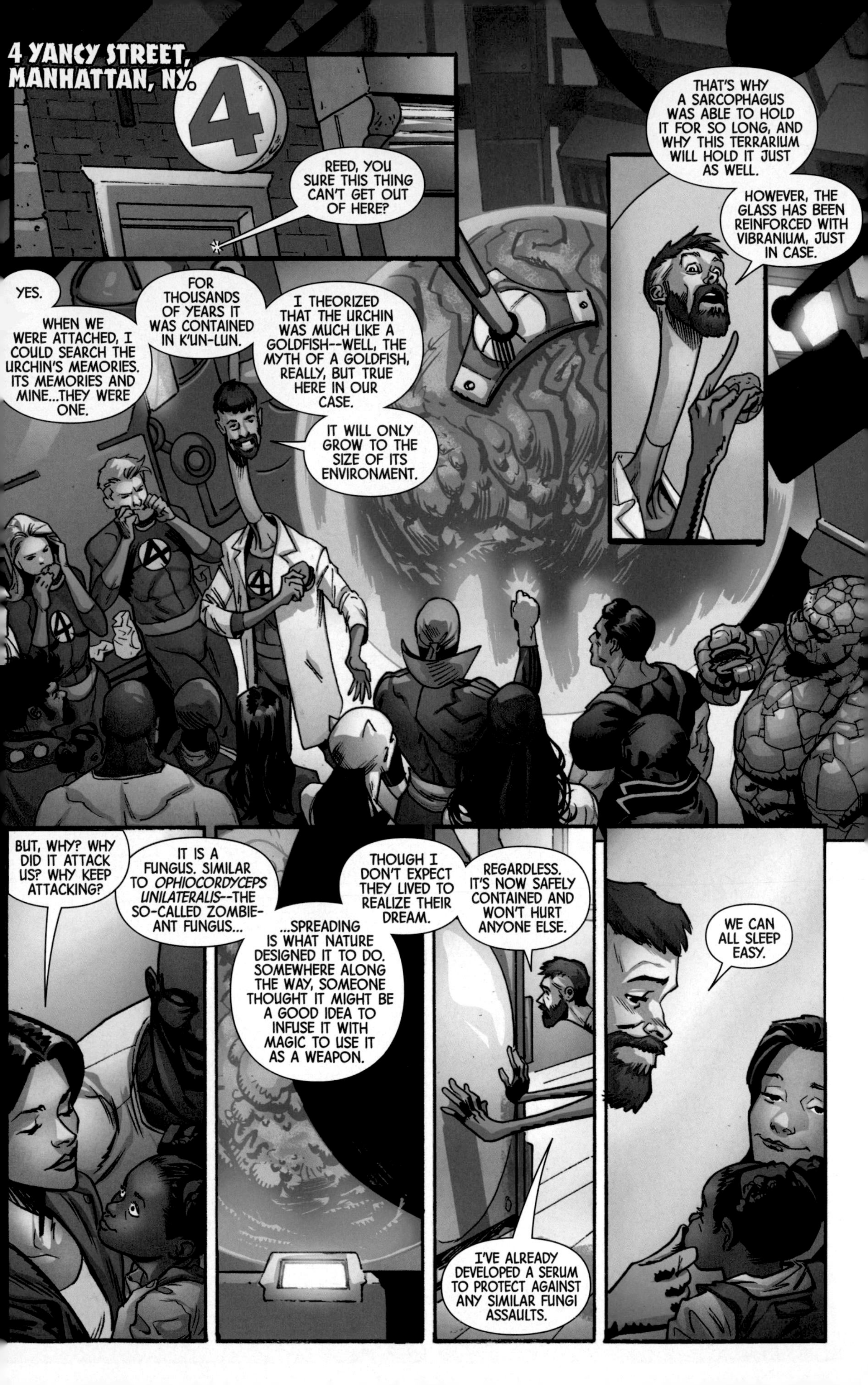
4 YANCY STREET, MANHATTAN, NY.
4
REED, YOU SURE THIS THING CAN'T GET OUT OF HERE?
YES.
WHEN WE WERE ATTACHED, I COULD SEARCH THE URCHIN'S MEMORIES. ITS MEMORIES AND MINE...THEY WERE ONE.
FOR THOUSANDS OF YEARS IT WAS CONTAINED IN K'UN-LUN.
I THEORIZED THAT THE URCHIN WAS MUCH LIKE A GOLDFISH--WELL, THE MYTH OF A GOLDFISH, REALLY, BUT TRUE HERE IN OUR CASE.
IT WILL ONLY GROW TO THE SIZE OF ITS ENVIRONMENT.
THAT'S WHY A SARCOPHAGUS WAS ABLE TO HOLD IT FOR SO LONG, AND WHY THIS TERRARIUM WILL HOLD IT JUST AS WELL.
HOWEVER, THE GLASS HAS BEEN REINFORCED WITH VIBRANIUM, JUST IN CASE.
BUT, WHY? WHY DID IT ATTACK US? WHY KEEP ATTACKING?
IT IS A FUNGUS. SIMILAR TO *OPHIOCORDYCEPS UNILATERALIS*--THE SO-CALLED ZOMBIE-ANT FUNGUS...
...SPREADING IS WHAT NATURE DESIGNED IT TO DO. SOMEWHERE ALONG THE WAY, SOMEONE THOUGHT IT MIGHT BE A GOOD IDEA TO INFUSE IT WITH MAGIC TO USE IT AS A WEAPON.
THOUGH I DON'T EXPECT THEY LIVED TO REALIZE THEIR DREAM.
REGARDLESS. IT'S NOW SAFELY CONTAINED AND WON'T HURT ANYONE ELSE.
I'VE ALREADY DEVELOPED A SERUM TO PROTECT AGAINST ANY SIMILAR FUNGI ASSAULTS.
WE CAN ALL SLEEP EASY.

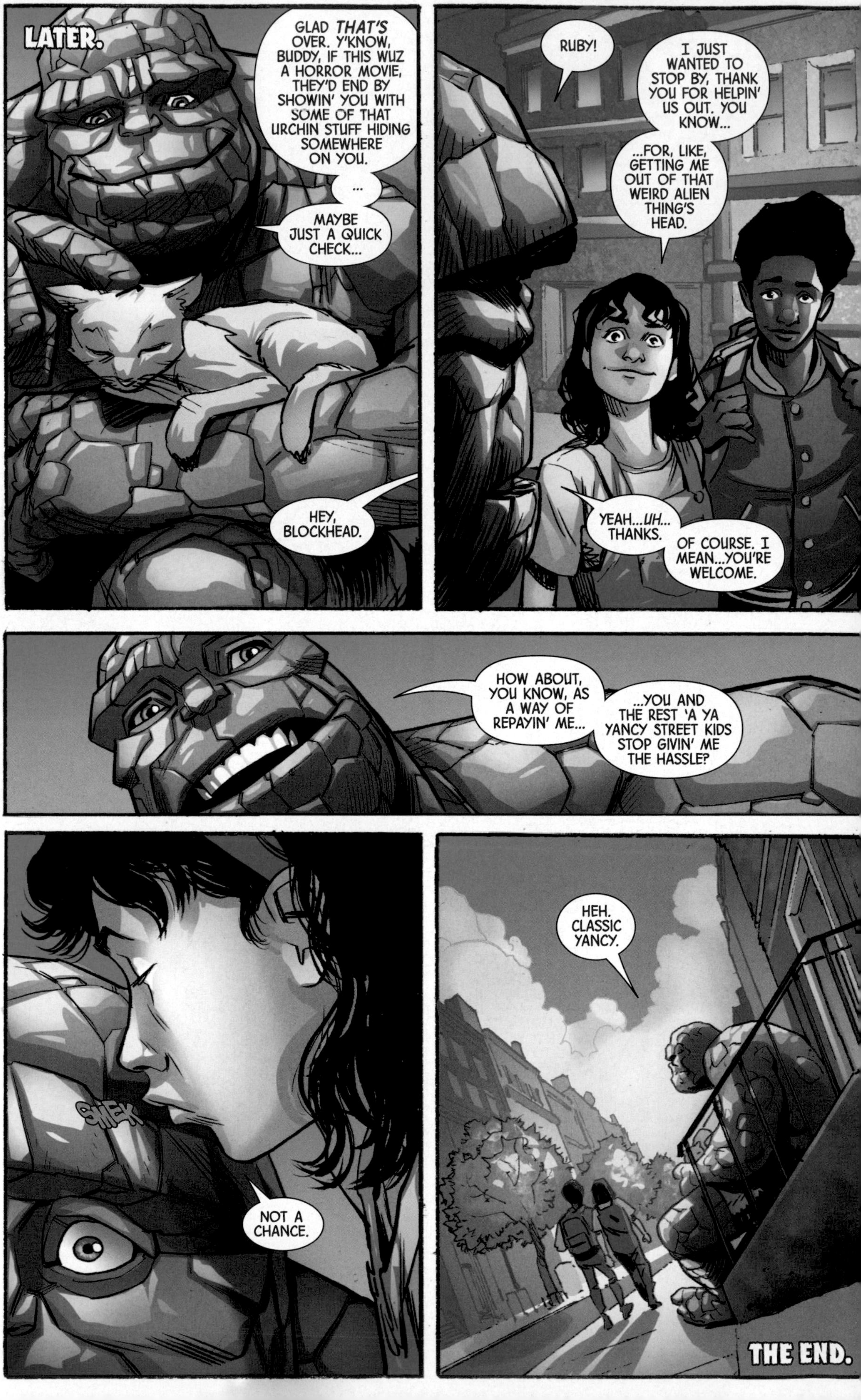
LATER.
GLAD THAT'S OVER. Y'KNOW, BUDDY, IF THIS WUZ A HORROR MOVIE, THEY'D END BY SHOWIN' YOU WITH SOME OF THAT URCHIN STUFF HIDING SOMEWHERE ON YOU.
...
MAYBE JUST A QUICK CHECK...
HEY, BLOCKHEAD.
RUBY!
I JUST WANTED TO STOP BY, THANK YOU FOR HELPIN' US OUT. YOU KNOW...
...FOR, LIKE, GETTING ME OUT OF THAT WEIRD ALIEN THING'S HEAD.
YEAH...UH... THANKS.
OF COURSE. I MEAN...YOU'RE WELCOME.
HOW ABOUT, YOU KNOW, AS A WAY OF REPAYIN' ME...
...YOU AND THE REST 'A YA YANCY STREET KIDS STOP GIVIN' ME THE HASSLE?
SNEK
NOT A CHANCE.
HEH. CLASSIC YANCY.
THE END.

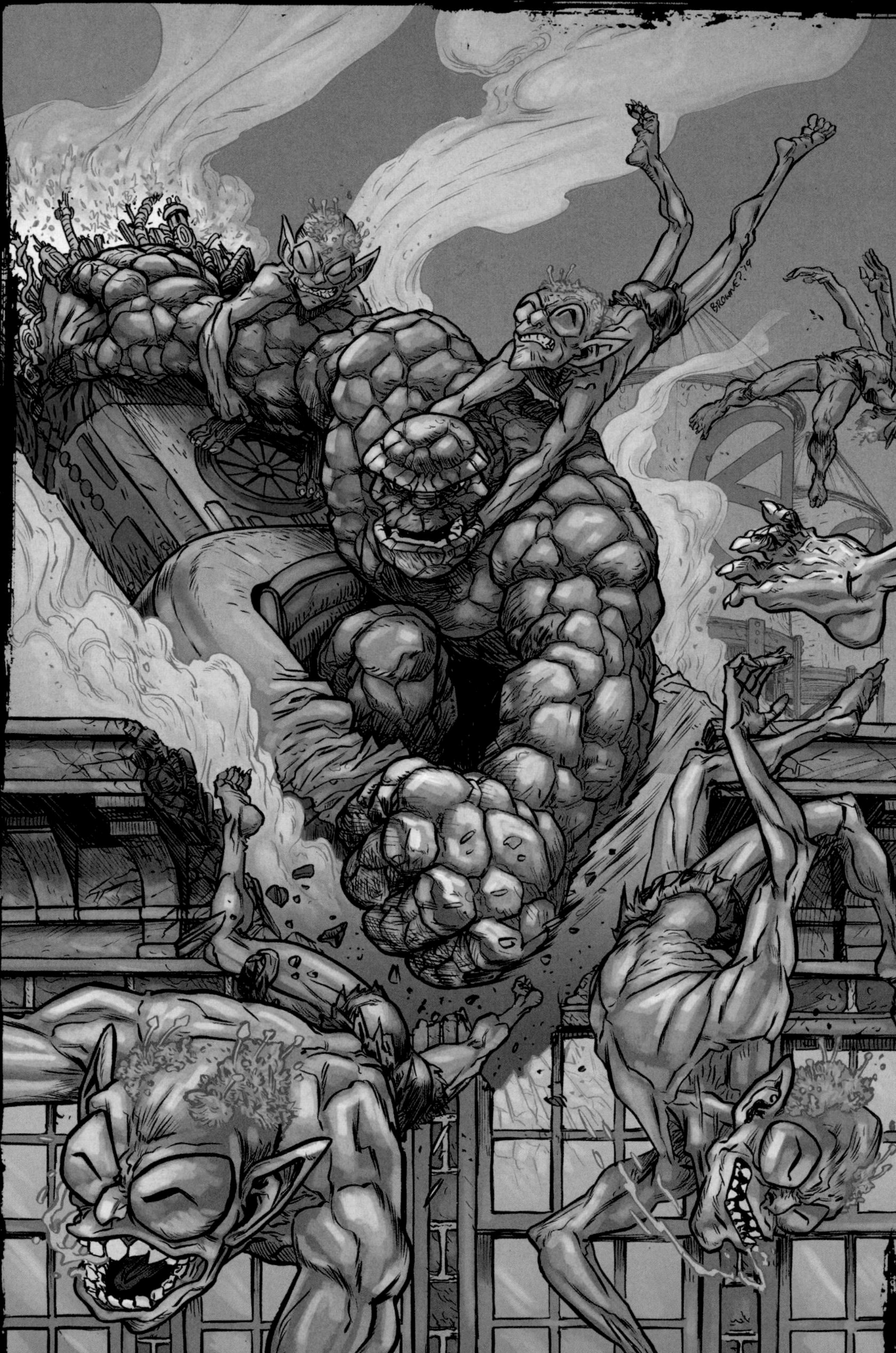
BROWNE?'19

#1 VARIANT BY **RYAN BROWNE**

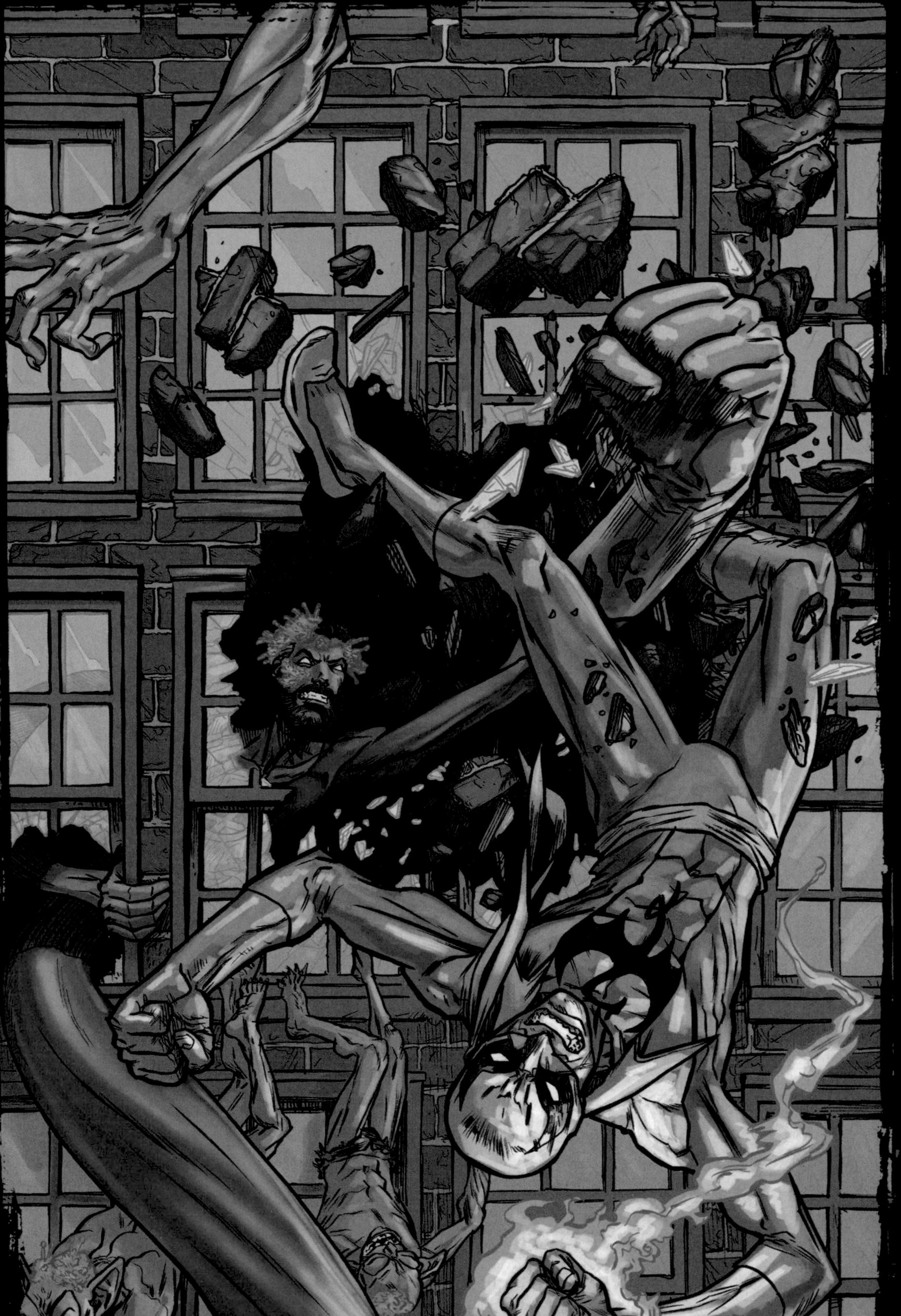

#2 VARIANT BY **RYAN BROWNE**

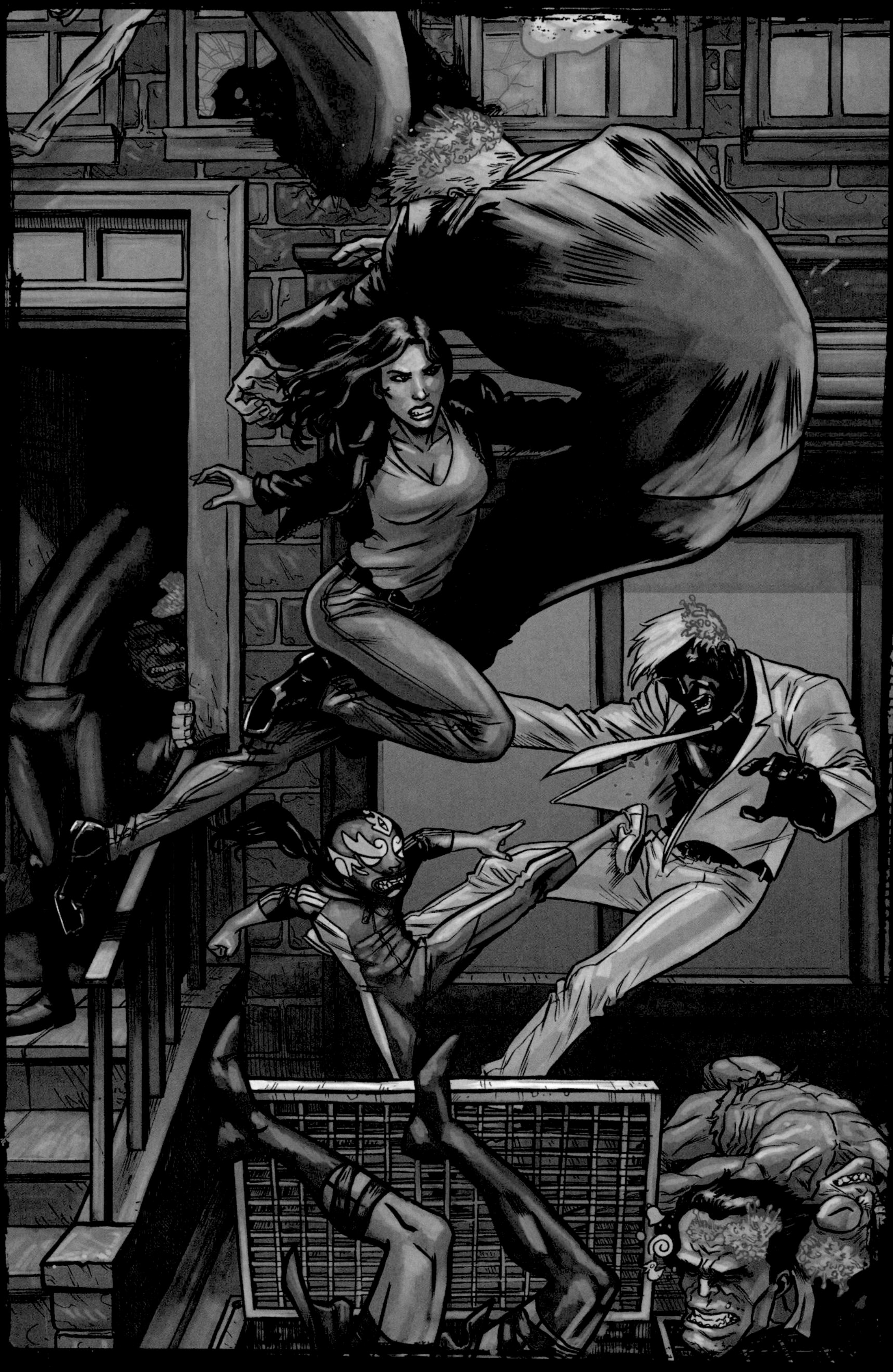

#3 VARIANT BY **RYAN BROWNE**

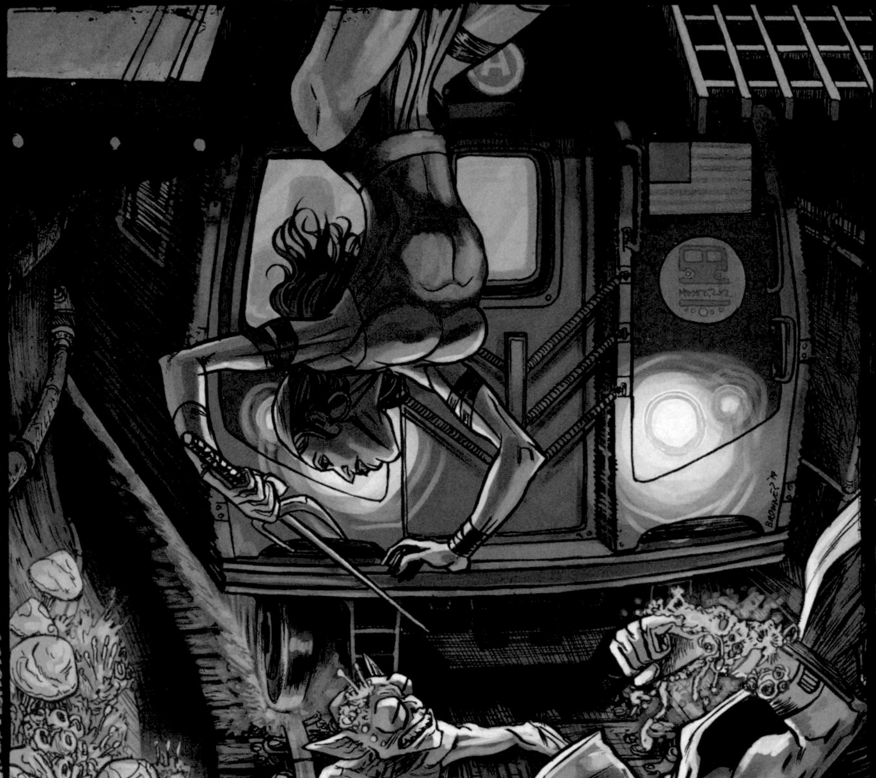

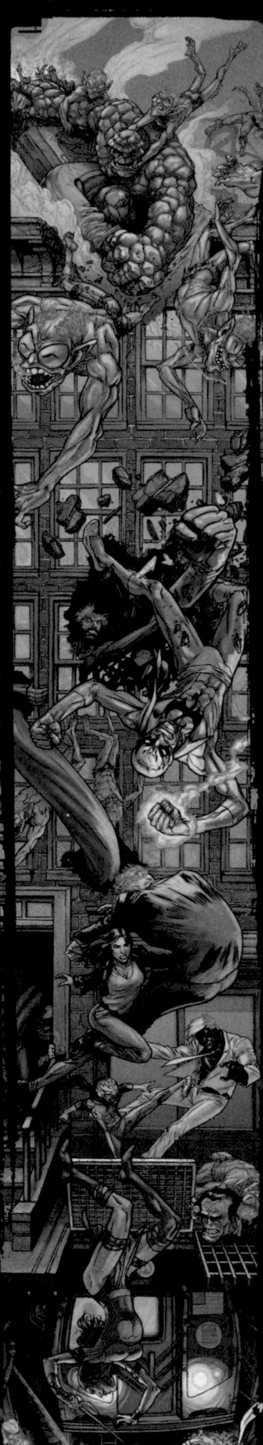

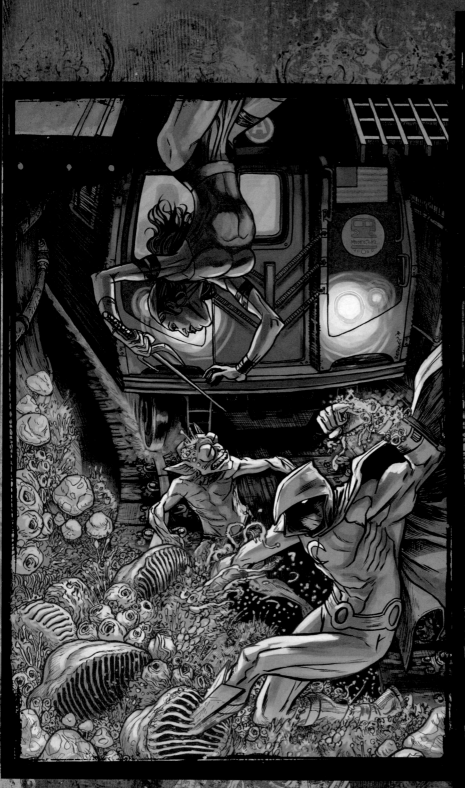

#4 VARIANT BY **RYAN BROWNE**